AF270332

Spiny Succulents: Euphorbias, cacti, and other sculptural succulents
and (mostly) spiny xerophytic plants

Text and photographs by Jeff Moore unless credited otherwise.

Photo on previous page and last page: Vanessa Shastine

Jeff Moore, Solana Succulents
solanasucculents@gmail.com
www.solanasucculents.com

ISBN 978-0-9915846-4-2
ISBN 978-0-9915846-5-9

Book Design: Russel Ray

Printed and bound in Malaysia by TWP Sdn Bhd

Spiny Succulents

Euphorbias, cacti, and other sculptural succulents and (mostly) spiny xerophytic plants

Fifty years of old growth, old world succulents living happily in the new world at Grigsby Cactus Gardens in Vista, California.

Photo: Earth Wind & Cactus

Table of Contents

This book is dedicated to my dad, Richard Moore, and my late mom, Lillian Moore. They provided me with a great life, growing up a short walk from the beach in a wonderful part of the world. They also were encouraging—well, they at least bit their lips—when I decided to open a small succulent nursery.

Preface

This is my fourth book about succulents. My first, *Under the Spell of Succulents*, was an overview of succulents in cultivation. The second was dedicated to aloes and agaves, and the third to the many genera that I grouped into a loose category called "soft succulents"—aeoniums, echeverias, crassulas, and the like. I tried with the second and third books to group plants from different genera together based more on feel or appearance than by botanical or alphabetical groupings. That also is what I have done here with *Spiny Succulents*.

The primary and largest groups examined here are euphorbias and cacti, plants that are mostly from different continents with almost no genetic relationship. They often have evolved very similar body shapes in response to similar environments, enough so that there are many cacti that often are confused with euphorbias, and vice versa. We'll talk more about what separates them, but for the plant enthusiast, at times it can be irrelevant where it belongs in the nomenclature tree as long as it works for you and your garden. I'm trying to help with inspiration first, then with identification and culture issues.

These plants, unlike smaller, softer, or more shrubby succulents, have an architecture, a solidness, that makes them stand out and command attention. Their spinescence, at least with the larger ones, can be secondary to their overall structure. You can build your garden around these larger specimens.

In my effort to eventually cover the entirety of the cultivated succulent realm in three or four volumes, I have grouped genera together in this book based on a somewhat similar look and landscape feel, and then at the end cast a bit wider net to include a few other groups that are near and dear to us succulent enthusiasts. In addition to the aforementioned primary genera, we'll also take a look at the pachypodiums, didieraceae (alluaudias), and cyphostemmas, the latter of which, along with some of the succulent trees, is the only major genus herein with no spiny members, but to my mind still belongs with its pokey allies in this book. Finally, there will be a section on the "succulent adjacent" plants which, while technically not meeting the definition of a succulent (juice-filled) plant, still belong in the conversation as they meet the "if you like those, you'll like these" test. We'll take a quick look at cycads, bromeliads, and even some xerophytic (dry-climate) trees, orchids, and plumerias.

I'm shooting at a mark between informational and inspirational with this book. As a nurseryman, I'll do the best I can on the former. The images of the plants themselves should take care of the latter. Hopefully, the images will also position it as worthy of a place on your coffee table. I have tried to populate this book with plants that are available (at least occasionally) and will grow in the Southwest USA, with images to prove it. Excepting some habitat sections, nearly all of the photos are taken of plants growing in California (and some in Arizona). After thirty years of playing with succulents, I've learned that there are some remarkable succulents that I know only from habitat images, or perhaps growing pampered in a greenhouse as they have not yet successfully made it into cultivation. I don't want to tease and tempt you with plants you either can't find or will likely kill. The plants on the following pages are, for the most part (exceptions will be explained), succulents you should be able to find and grow.

This book is primarily about plants we can acquire and grow in cultivation, but we'll have a look at a few habitat images just to show you some examples of succulents becoming all they can be. You can acquire young starts of the càrdon cactus or boojum tree—shown above in their native Cataviña desert habitat—but unless you are very young, you'll never grow them this big in your lifetime. Best to drive down to see them in their Baja home, or at some of the botanical gardens in California or Arizona. *Photo: Viggo Gram*

Above: This book isn't just about the spiny guys, and not just about succulents, either. The final section will show you some of the "succulent adjacent" xerophytic plants that we love, including xeric bromeliads (above), cycads, orchids, and semi-woody succulent trees.

We will be looking at succulent specimens from macro to micro. The thirty-foot tall columnar monstrosity above is a tangle of *Euphorbia ammak* variegata (yellow), *Cereus peruvianus* (green), and *Pilosocereus azureus* (blue). I wasn't privy to the original planting maybe forty years ago, but I bet there were three or four little waist-high columnars planted in an organized proximity. I doubt anything like this was anticipated as a result.

Right: *Echinofossulocactus (Stenocactus) crispatus*, an unusual form of an already unusual little globular cactus. Usually a solitary little baseball sized plant, this is the result of an overgrown seed flat. These little beauties remain diminutive throughout their long lives, hiding among the rocks of their Mexican habitat, not lording over the landscape like the monsters above.

Alluaudia procera

Introduction

For most readers, the phrase "spiny succulent" will immediately be synonymous with "cactus." Cacti, indeed, are the embodiment of that description. But there are so many more sharpies in the world of dry-climate plants. Even though most succulents have a "Hey, look at me!" appeal, the plants herein are mostly on the higher end of the "Wow, what the heck is that?" scale. Many are larger landscape specimens, others more modest in scale yet equally attention-grabbing. Most are suitable as landscape specimens in California, but we'll also look at many that are better suited to container culture, owing to either size or cultural requirements.

All of the plants on the following pages are low-water (xerophytic), although despite the book's title, a few groups are not technically succulent in nature (more on that later). Most importantly, they are all water-wise, sun-loving, and low-maintenance. But I always look at those characteristics as just bonus points. Most of us love these plants because they are so dang cool—they just make you happy when you look at them (although some are not so fun to trim or weed around).

Many of these groups are famous for their spines. In fact, you can't even say the word "cactus" without thinking of spines. I've realized over the years at my nursery that I can't convince an anti-spinite to consider a cactus or sharp euphorbia or pachypodium. If you tend to lean that way, I hope you'll reconsider after seeing some of these images and getting a feel for the beauty of these beasts. And some of the non-cactus spines (most euphorbias) can look a lot worse than they really are. Plant them off the beaten path so you won't run into them. I've learned to appreciate some cacti *for* their spines, a position I came to gradually.

If there is an overriding visual kinship among the plants in this book, it is that these are solid and chunky, sculptural succulent plants, most (but not all) carrying some of sort of spiny armament. There are a few leafy subgroups and relatives included, but in the main these are not your fluffy cottage-garden plants. These are the desert sentinels, striking and often spiny statement succulents.

If you've ever been to a show put on by your local cactus and succulent club, you might be aware of the fascinating, often miniature container specimen/show plants that are part of the categories in this book. Some of those will be shown, but we're mostly looking at the big stuff here. I'm hoping for a future volume on the smaller succulent show plants.

In the following pages, we'll examine some of the cultural issues regarding light, soil, water, climate, pests, and a few of the other considerations that are important for the succulent enthusiast. But the thrust of this book is more encyclopedic than it is a "how-to" manual. I hope you'll come away with an appreciation of just how incredible and varied these living art pieces can be. Whether you are already a succulent hobbiest, new to the addiction, or are happy to appreciate them from afar (especially if you are afraid of spines), I hope you will get out there into your neighborhood or local botanical gardens or nurseries and see some of these beauties in person. They make you happy.

Agave franzosinii

Echeveria agavoides 'Ebony'

Haworthia limifolia variegated

Not included in this book....

You will notice that this book excludes some types of succulents that certainly qualify as statement plants that often do have spiny members. Aloes and agaves are not included here, many of which are the type of succulents that really command attention as spiny sculptural icons in a landscape. The reason for this is that those groups are so broad that I have already devoted a book to them and their botanical kin: *Aloes and Agaves in Cultivation*. I am an aloe guy, and that book is close to my heart. I hope you can track it down if you like those plants and their relatives. Also not included are the "soft" succulents—aeoniums, crassulas, echeverias, kalanchoes, sedums, etc. Those genera are united by their complete lack of spines. Have I mentioned I wrote a book about those as well? A book I haven't done yet, but hope to do in the future, is about some of the bonsai/caudiciform/collector container plants, such as the *Adenium obesum* below left.

Adenium obesum

Aloe 'Hercules'

Beaucarnea recurvata

It is amazing how compatible succulents from different continents—even different hemispheres—can be, both in a visual and cultural sense. The Golden Barrel cactus (*Echinocactus grusonii*) above is from Central Mexico, while the "Moroccan Mound" (*Euphorbia resinifera*) that frames it is from Northern Africa. Both are extremophiles that are happy to grow in any benign Mediterranean climate. Lots of sun, occasional water with some nice drying-out time, preferably little to no snow or hard freezes, and you've got yourself an intercontinental happy menagerie.

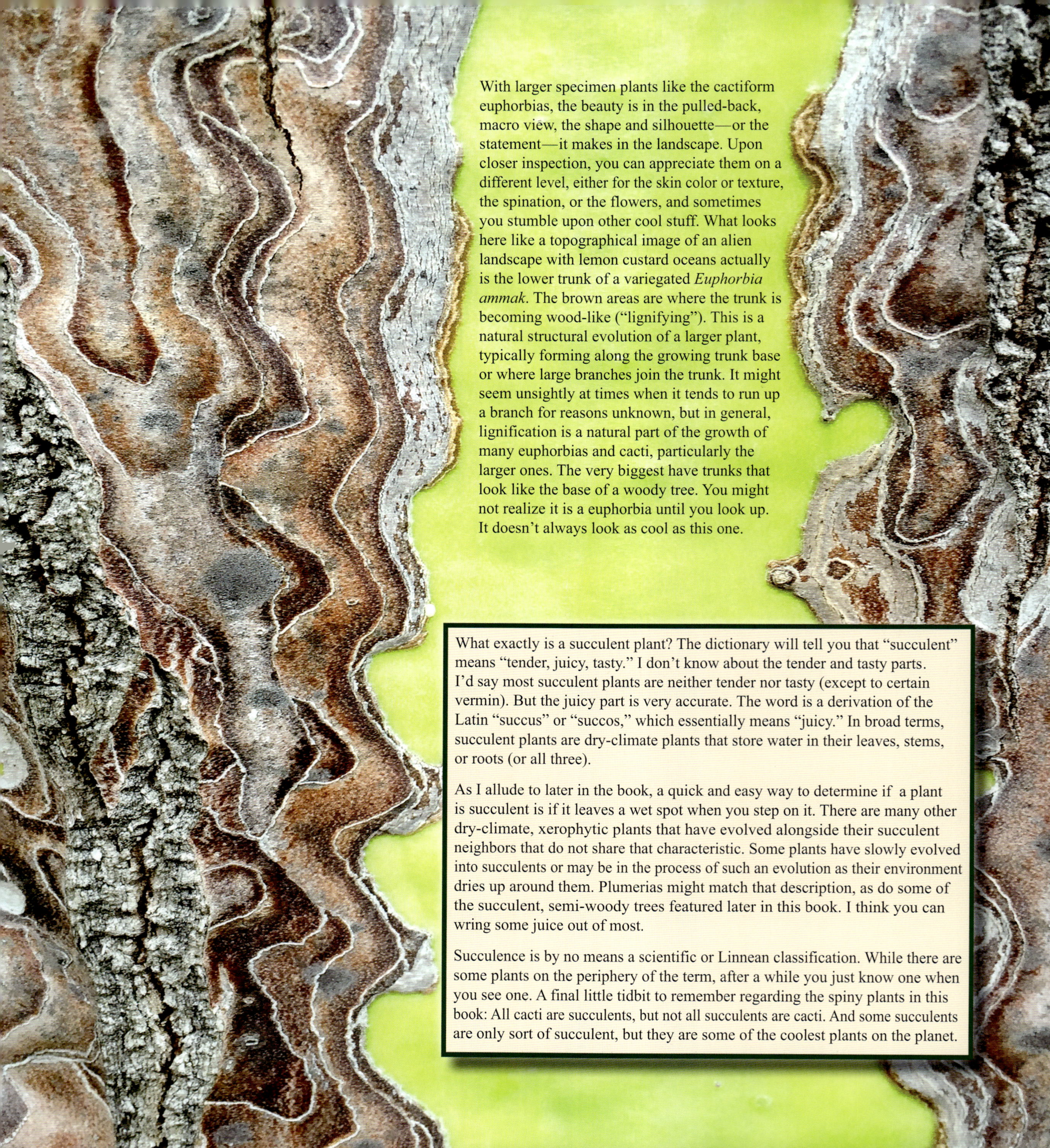

With larger specimen plants like the cactiform euphorbias, the beauty is in the pulled-back, macro view, the shape and silhouette—or the statement—it makes in the landscape. Upon closer inspection, you can appreciate them on a different level, either for the skin color or texture, the spination, or the flowers, and sometimes you stumble upon other cool stuff. What looks here like a topographical image of an alien landscape with lemon custard oceans actually is the lower trunk of a variegated *Euphorbia ammak*. The brown areas are where the trunk is becoming wood-like ("lignifying"). This is a natural structural evolution of a larger plant, typically forming along the growing trunk base or where large branches join the trunk. It might seem unsightly at times when it tends to run up a branch for reasons unknown, but in general, lignification is a natural part of the growth of many euphorbias and cacti, particularly the larger ones. The very biggest have trunks that look like the base of a woody tree. You might not realize it is a euphorbia until you look up. It doesn't always look as cool as this one.

What exactly is a succulent plant? The dictionary will tell you that "succulent" means "tender, juicy, tasty." I don't know about the tender and tasty parts. I'd say most succulent plants are neither tender nor tasty (except to certain vermin). But the juicy part is very accurate. The word is a derivation of the Latin "succus" or "succos," which essentially means "juicy." In broad terms, succulent plants are dry-climate plants that store water in their leaves, stems, or roots (or all three).

As I allude to later in the book, a quick and easy way to determine if a plant is succulent is if it leaves a wet spot when you step on it. There are many other dry-climate, xerophytic plants that have evolved alongside their succulent neighbors that do not share that characteristic. Some plants have slowly evolved into succulents or may be in the process of such an evolution as their environment dries up around them. Plumerias might match that description, as do some of the succulent, semi-woody trees featured later in this book. I think you can wring some juice out of most.

Succulence is by no means a scientific or Linnean classification. While there are some plants on the periphery of the term, after a while you just know one when you see one. A final little tidbit to remember regarding the spiny plants in this book: All cacti are succulents, but not all succulents are cacti. And some succulents are only sort of succulent, but they are some of the coolest plants on the planet.

Above left: A very confused saguaro working its way in and out of crested growth. We'll explore cresting later in the book.
Above right: Spines!! How do you not like spines? Just because your skin lost a few battles? Get over it. Behold the dangerous beauty of *Stetsonia coryne*'s spiny throne. Okay, enough waxing poetic.
Below left: *Echinocereus reichenbachii* offers a much softer and finer form of spinescence, more forgiving but it still bites.

That's a pretty amazing plant in the image below middle, huh? It truly is, but I'll admit to cheating just a bit here, although for a purpose. This same *Astrophytum ornatum* cultivar is shown at true color below right, and still looks really cool. But I goofed around a bit with color saturation on the middle image, and decided to run it here to make a point. A lot of the succulent images you see online have been over-saturated or otherwise tinkered with as I've done here. So please adjust your expectations if you have seen an incredible iridescent turquoise cactus and are desperate to find one. It probably doesn't exist, at least not as presented. With the exception of the image here, all of the photos in this book are fairly true to life. At times I've slightly adjusted brightness or color, but only enough to make it look like it really should. A brief note about the image at right: The plant in the background is a mounding *Euphorbia polygona*, which shares a basic body form with many cacti, an example of convergent evolution, as discussed later in this section.

Assuming you live in a temperate, Mediterranean climate like California, you should think of most cacti and succulents as outdoor plants. They evolved to live and grow in full sun. Having said that, many will grow well enough indoors if they are close to a window or skylight so as to get at least a few hours of preferably direct sun. The farther away from direct sun exposure they sit, the less happy they will be. In lower light situations, they start to slowly stretch towards the light, and get extra skinny and green. This might fool you into thinking they are healthy and happy, but it is actually an attempt to increase surface area to absorb more light.

If you have a situation calling for a taller "pot-on-the-floor" succulent, euphorbias seem to handle lower light better than cacti. The *Euphorbia ingens* at right would be happier a few feet away in front of the window, but the owner thought the plant would look better in this corner, and it really does look great there. If it decides the reflected ambient light of the light-colored walls is enough, it might be happy there for many years and eventually reach the high ceiling, at which point it can be cut back. Another option would be to move it into the yard and plant it in the ground. A word of caution there: After many years of no direct sun, it will certainly fry upon first exposure. It should spend perhaps a few months in filtered tree shade before transitioning to full sun exposure.

These wonderful plants make us happy for a purely aesthetic reason, but there are a myriad of little creatures that are just delighted in what we've provided for them. Not that we're playing God, but the bees in the image above are getting drunk on the pollen of a tricholobivia hybrid that wouldn't even exist if it weren't for us obsessed botanical romantics making something new out of something old, and growing it in a place far from its ancestral roots.

Above: Succulents of all types can be happily combined in the landscape. Here, a purple-padded *Opuntia santa-rita* snuggles up with a crested form of *Astrocylindropuntia subulata*. At first glance, these plants don't look very closely related, at least not enough to belong to the same genus. In fact, the crested *A. subulata* looks quite a bit like a crested euphorbia.

Left: Cresting, in this case a mammillaria, is a happy aberration and is something we'll look at quite a bit on the following pages.

Far left: *Stenocereus gummosus v. spiralis*. Such abnormalities are mutations that might occur in rare instances in habitat, likely not appreciated by the native fauna, unless that fauna is human with an eye for aesthetics. That would apply to all of us involved with ornamental plants, and we'll do all we can to turn it into more plants.

The Spiny Landscape

A well-executed succulent garden can be a fantastic collection of living sculptures. A softer succulent garden that features primarily aeoniums, crassulas, and various shrubby succulents can be a thing of colorful beauty. But if you are bold, a dynamic and more spartan desert garden of cacti, euphorbias, and some of the other plants included in this book, along with perhaps some of the aforementioned softies, as well as aloes and agaves, will provide you with low-maintenance joy for years to come. The garden above in Del Mar, California, occupies a narrow bed on the east-facing side of the house. It is hand-watered as needed, and the decomposed granite top dressing cuts back on—but doesn't totally prevent—weeds. There are some basic landscaping principles that you can see used here—rocks, repetition, varied sizes—that are important to consider. These plants make a statement that the owner of this garden is bold, has excellent taste in plants, has done the research, isn't afraid of a few spines, and is mindful of creating a low-water yet high aesthetic contribution to the neighborhood.

Above: A grower's field stand of càrdon cacti (*Pachycereus pringlei*). You will notice there is some variability in the density of the spines. There are, indeed, varying degrees of spination between individual seed-grown plants that are apparent even in a young plant, but some cacti—including the càrdon—eventually can begin to shed spines on the upper growing tips as they age, becoming almost spineless, with the exception of the older base of the plant. That might make sense as a defense against ground-based grazers. There are forms of large South American browningias that have extremely dense and long spines at the base, yet are completely smooth higher up on the majority of the plant.

Cactus Wrangling

You might find it surprising that many of us in the cactus business rarely wear gloves. This primarily is because many spines will easily penetrate most gloves. Heavy duty welding gloves might work, but they give you almost no tactical feel when handling smaller plants. More typical gardening gloves give you a false sense of security, and not wearing gloves just forces you to be more careful about what you're doing.

So absent gloves, how do you handle golden barrels or columnars such as the càrdons at left? Try wrapping the plant with a towel, old carpet or burlap. You can form a sling for the spiny portion of the plant and use your hand (glove optional) to hold the non-spiny lower portion. The guys below opted for both gloves and a towel—nothing wrong with being cautious.

Left: Russel Ray has found a good use for his old volleyball kneepads once his athletic career ended. Soft on the inside, hard on the outside, they are ideal for handling small cacti or other spiny plants. Use whatever you can find that allows you to handle them that keeps the spines out of your hands without damaging the plant.

Below: These cactus slingers are wearing gloves to be extra cautious, but you should transport spiny plants by using towels like they are, or blankets or burlap whenever possible. Wadded up paper or towels also can serve as replacement "gloves" to provide some distance between you and the spines.

While most of the plants in this book have spines, the cactus family by far has the most wicked. They can detach easily and lodge themselves into your skin. Most euphorbias, pachypodiums, alluaudias, and fouquierias do have sharp spines, but they generally are more rigid, and you can handle them gently without the risk of taking part of them home with you under your skin. However, if you do get a piece of certain pachypodiums and euphorbias in you, there is, at times, a mild form of toxin that can be quite irritating and make it seem a little more painful than a little thing like that should be.

Most opuntias have a yellowish "fuzz" on the pad edges and inside the little polka dots on the pads themselves. These are glochids, tiny hair-like spines that can be quite irritating. Other cacti have large, nasty needle spines, up to six inches long. Most opuntias have both glochids and large spines. Nastiest of all are the members of the opuntia tribe known as chollas that have barbed tips that grab hold at the slightest touch and really don't want to let go.

If you've had a bad encounter with cactus spines, it may have set you up for a lifetime aversion to cacti, and that isn't something I've found I can talk a person out of. But if you're reading this book, hopefully that means you're not hostile to succulents that have built up such an effective defense. Or maybe you just prefer to look at them at a distance or as photos rather than get close to them in person.

As the owner of a cactus and succulent nursery, I have had so many encounters with spines—primarily cacti, but also euphorbias, pachypodiums, and agaves—that I don't really get that mad at myself for each new piece of broken spine under my skin. I can steer you here through the stages of what to do once you've been stabbed. First, try not to let it happen. Move slowly around cacti. I usually don't wear gloves as they can give you a false sense of security—many spines will penetrate most gloves. Use wadded up towels or paper as a cradle, when you can. One thing I've learned over and over (which means I'm not learning it properly, I suppose) is that it rarely is the plant you are being careful with that gets you—it's the sneaky little spiny dude next to it. I think I've taken as many spines in the back of my hand as the front for that reason.

If you do get stuck, hopefully it was just an "in and out" that might hurt and cause a little bleeding, but that passes soon. Often, however, a little tip will break off under your skin, and you're not sure about it until a day or two later when it still bothers you and might start to itch. If you can see a little black spot under the skin, you need to take a needle and start working at it, maybe breaking a little skin to get the needle in. If you can feel the slight "click" of contact with the hard little invader, you need to just slowly scrape back and forth, and eventually it might start to slide out. It usually is so small you can't believe it bothered you as much as it did. It might come out easier a few days later after a bit of pus (sorry, it's just biology) begins to form around it. Glochid spines sometimes can be removed with sticky tape or even by letting some Elmer's glue dry over the skin. Some spines you just never find, and after a few weeks you forget about them. After thirty years of working with spiny critters, I think my body has absorbed so many spines that I might make good grafting stock. Just part of the job.

You might think that the spines of cacti and other succulents are primarily a defensive adaptation, as I always have, but we both might be wrong. Ernesto Sandoval is the curator of the UC Davis Botanical Conservancy and makes quite a convincing argument that one of the primary functions of spines is to radiate heat away from the plant body. They also provide a bit of shade, or at least break up the direct sun somewhat. A dense covering of spines also can provide a slight bit of a buffer against hot and dry air circulating above, preserving any moisture closer to the flesh beneath. Ernesto has cited studies of cacti that had their spines removed, comparing interior temperatures to those without the procedure, and the latter group often were five to ten degrees cooler inside. I love a good science project with no apparent economic benefit other than pure knowledge— i.e., "basic science"—and perhaps a bit of fun trivia. I guess I learned not to cut the spines off of my cacti.

As this book is geared towards hobbyists, I tend to steer away from too much science. Having said that, another chestnut of botany you should be aware of is Crassulacean Acid Metabolism (CAM) which many plants, including most succulents, have evolved in arid climates. In simple terms, CAM plants close down their stomata (pores) during the heat of the day to preserve moisture, and open at night to collect carbon dioxide. It gets more complicated and you don't need to know all the science to keep succulents happy, but knowledge is good and you can impress your friends and relatives.

About the spines....

While assembling images from my photo library for this book, I pulled the one at right for my bromeliad section. Then I took a longer look and I think it might be an aloe hybrid, perhaps *Aloe* 'Fire Ranch' with some seasonal stress. Some aloes will form imprinting on the leaves, as shown on this plant. The plant at left for sure is a hechtia. One way you could tell the difference would be to drag your fingers along the edge. The rigid hechtia has a serious bite, the aloe much less so. You also could snap off an aloe leaf with your fingers, but the hechtia needs clippers.

Middle left: The African *Euphorbia echinus*. The mounding cactus below it is *Copiapoa cinerea* from Chile. Both of these long-lived plants have spines, but there is quite a difference in the skin texture and especially in the blooms. The euphorbia will have hundreds of small yellow flowers on the stem edges and tips, while the cactus will have larger, softer, and more papery creamy yellow flowers more typical of cacti. Cacti flowers are more spectacular, but also much more short-lived.

Middle right: A photo from Paul Lawler's Instagram page. My first thought was that it was a euphorbia with a bit of a spiral twist. But if you look at the background plants, those are all cacti. Then I thought it could be a type of gymnocalycium, or some weird astrophytum hybrid. So I emailed Paul and he confirmed my initial guess. He said it was just identified as a euphorbia hybrid; he'd bought it years ago from Harvey Welton of Mexican Hat Cactus Nursery (now shuttered) in Riverside, California. I wish there was more of this one on the market.

The cute little bonsai at right certainly has the profile of a cactus or euphorbia, but is neither. It is *Hoodia gordonii*, an African stapeliad.

Cactus/Not a Cactus—Convergent Evolution in Succulents

The euphorbia and cactus families are not even remotely related, but despite being primarily from different continents and hemispheres, members of these families have evolved similar shapes as they adjusted their body types in response to hot and dry climates to maximize water storage and minimize sun exposure. An example, above far left, shows an African *Euphorbia symmetrica* (likely hybrid) contrasted with a *Copicpoa cinerea* cactus from South America, above center left. Aside from the globoid and eventually clustering body, each plant has defenses against predation. The euphorbia lacks spines, but its sap is caustic and off-putting enough to keep diners at bay. The copiapoa has spines as a defense, a technique also found at times in the euphorbia family, but not as prevalent as with cacti. Above center right is another cactus, *Astrophytum asterias*, compared to a *Euphorbia obesa,* above far right. A major difference between cacti and the cactiform euphorbias will be apparent when they flower—euphorbias will have clusters of tiny, mostly yellow flowers, while cacti offer large, thinner or more papery, short-lived, and colorful blooms.

Far left: A crested specimen of *Trichocereus pachanoi* is reverting to regular form with a columnar appeal somewhat like the cactiform look of *Euphorbia royleana*, near left. Both of these types are only nominally spined.

Near right is the true ocotillo, *Fouquieria splendens*, of the New World, contrasted with *Alluaudia procera* from Madagascar, which often is called the "Madagascar" or "False" ocotillo.

The names....
the damn names....

If you have read any of my other books, you will have noticed that I can be a bit insecure and defensive about getting the plant names right. As a nursery owner and author, it is kind of important that I do that. Even with a genus that I'm slightly more "expert" in, such as aloes, there are those I know for sure on sight, and then a whole bunch more that might be hybrids or those that might be seed-variable cultivars or look different due to growing conditions. I'm always relieved when someone who knows a group better than I do is also flumoxed and has to throw out guesses. I was also happy to see this passage by Daryl Koutnik in Volume Ten of *The Euphorbia Journal* that helps explain things:

> Nature is not organized in such a way that natural objects (organisms) can always be placed into distinct, clearly-defined categories. It is we humans that want organization and we classify organisms into distinct (sometimes arbitrary or artificial) categories. The classification or organization of a plant group (in our case the succulent euphorbs) should reflect the natural evolutionary relationships between individuals of the group—this is the goal of the taxonomist (one who classifies). A taxonomist tries to reflect genetic (evolutionary) relationships into a classification. This human-made classification of a taxonomist will not always be consistent with nature because the natural world is a continuum of variation. This is one reason why one person's *Euphorbia valida* is another person's *E. meloformis*. It is a matter of whether a classification emphasizes similarities or differences between organisms.

That last line relates to the issues between the "lumpers" and the "splitters." I've always had a foot in both of those camps. I get why the splitters want to keep dividing plants into increasingly numerous categories, but they go overboard at times. All of a sudden we have to start calling a plant we've known forever by a new name. But it works both ways. Sometimes the lumpers win and a distinct plant or group gets lumped back into a larger category, and then we have to unlearn a name. This has happened (or is still happening) with the trichocereus cacti being lumped into the echinopsis group for genetic reasons. But there are certain echinopsis that just visually stand apart (the ones that used to "own" the title). So maybe now they are the "echinopsis" tribe of trichocereus. I still just call them echinopsis as a sort of protest, or maybe just laziness. Recently I've learned that they may be soon split back out. Advancement in genetics is slowly putting some debates to rest. As I've said elsewhere, love the plant and figure out the name later. A final thought on the subject: A paraphrase I ran into when researching the changing names is that *Nomenclature is fluid*. Yes it is. The plants don't change much (well, I guess every living thing is slowly evolving), but our opinions and ideas do.

Euphorbia kibwezensis, primarily cristate, with normal sections at right.

Turbinocarpus pseudopectinatus

Pelecyphora aselliformis

Identification

Right: The comically adorable tubercule-topping spines of *Pelecyphora aselliformis* make a nice geometric piece of natural art. Also see the image of this plant on page 235. The species name "aselliformis" draws a parallel to *Oniscus asellus*, the woodlouse bug (a.k.a. "pill bug" or "rolly polly") that the spines resemble, if the bugs were upside down.

Learning to identify succulents on sight is a skill you develop over time and with exposure to the plants. As previously mentioned, I have been an aloe enthusiast for many years and have gotten pretty adept at identifying most of those in cultivation on sight; the job is made much easier if you have a flower to help out. Even some that are superficially very similar in appearance just tend to differentiate themselves in very subtle ways over time. Of course, hybrids will always throw you a curve, but I find it fun to hazard an educated parentage guess when I do see a nice cross. You can kinda tell sometimes.

Cacti and many euphorbias have always presented a greater challenge for me. A case in point is two very similar (at first) looking plants at left. You might think they are different species but at least in the same genus. You would be wrong. They look so similar, at least at a distance, that the fact that I kept seeing different genus and species names attached to them caused me to believe it was another case of taxonomists making us learn and unlearn different names for the same cactus. I knew one of them had an ungainly Latin name like "polysefilawhatchamacallit." Multisyllabic binomial nomenclature takes a while to learn. Quite often I'd see it labeled "turpinocarpus" as well.

The internet was of little help as many sites indicated that the names were synonyms for the same plant. I did notice a difference in flowers. So I contacted cactus expert Elton Roberts who provided me with a thorough answer, as well as these images. *Pelecyphora aselliformis* is, indeed, its own plant in its own genus while *Turbinicarpus pseudopectinatus* is a visually distinct species in an entirely different and more diverse genus.

Both plants appear to have evenly spaced colonies of cottony "mealybugs" or white "woodlice" marching towards the apex. But if you look closely, the turbinocarpus has little "hairs" that cover the tubercules (the small nodular protuberances from the body that hold the spines), whereas the "woodlouse spines" of the pelecyphora are neatly aligned with the oval edges of the tubercules, has minor white hair growing at some of the tubercule bases, and will have a fuschia-type flower similar to that shown. The turbinocarpus will have more of a white or white/pink striped flower. Finally, the turbinocarpus can reach five inches in height, and the pelecyphora is more squat. There are also differences in how the seed pods form.

After all that, I don't know how I could confuse them. Well, actually I still totally see how this little example of almost convergent evolution will stump a lot of folks. You will find a few other naming/identification discussions in other parts of this book, such as the cactus conundrum on page 208. According to Elton, the turbinocarpus has been labeled variously as *Pelecyphora pseudopectinata*, *Mammillaria pseudopectinata*, *Normanbokea pseudopectinata*, and *Neolloydia pseudopectinata* over the years. At least the species name remained consistent. To complicate things, *Mammillaria bertholdii* also resembles these woodlouse plants.

All images this page by Elton Roberts.

I've been fortunate to have visited many of the premier succulent collectors' and growers' "not for sale" greenhouses. Every time I walk into one of these museums of living treasures, it's hard to keep my brain from exploding. I don't even ask if any of the plants are for sale, as they rarely are. I'm just happy to take some photos of these magnificent creatures that nature has produced, and which humans have sometimes mutated into things even more wondrous.

Above left: A grower's offering of *Mammillaria parkinsonii* 'Owl Eyes' recently dug from the field and potted up for sale.
Above middle: One of several iterations of the legendary Peyote cactus, *Lophophora williamsii*.
Above right: A prized cultivar of *Astrophytum asterias* that has fantastic fuzzy rib decorations.
Below left: This one really threw me. It looked like a "spiralis" section of *Eulychnia castanea* has emerged from a crested portion of the parent plant.
But I've never seen *E. castanea* crest in that way. It turns out that Mark "Dr. Frankenstein" Fryer was just playing around with grafting opportunities.
Here the eulychnia is grafted onto a crested section of *Trichocereus pachanoi*, which has a remarkably similar skin color and texture. Fun with plants.
Below middle: One of my favorite collector's crowded greenhouses. They fill up so fast.
Below right: Variegation in any plant always stands out, but sometimes spectacularly so with cacti.

Here is a garden of happy immigrants enjoying life at the beach in Southern California. The cactiform euphorbias are primarily of African origin; the colorful sedum and echeveria are cultivars of Mexican plants. Their ancestors were brought here many generations ago so field collection is no longer necessary. A note about these non-natives: Virtually none of the plants in this book can be considered invasive species, at least in California or the desert Southwest. Most need at least some token summer irrigation to survive (or at least to reproduce) on their own outside of captivity since most are from locales with summer rainfall, which California almost never enjoys. Quite a few can become "vacant lot durable" once established. More importantly, volunteer seed germination without our help (irrigation again) is all but impossible. I do find the occasional seed volunteer around mature and flowering African plants at my nursery, but without my incidental dry-season watering, I'm sure they wouldn't germinate and spread. The "Mother of Millions" kalanchoes will also drop new little plants below them to the extent that I consider them to be succulent weeds, but they'll only colonize their little piece of real estate and don't spread via wind or birds (at least in nontropical climates—it apparently is becoming invasive in the tropics).

An exception would be some of the opuntia species which have become a nuisance after being introduced to other desert or Mediterranean parts of the world, such as Australia and Africa. The only non-native succulents that I consider invasive in California are a few of the "iceplants" from South Africa—*Carpobrotus edulis* and *Mesembryanthemum crystallinum* are the main offenders, and the genie is out of the bottle with both of those. The latter has colonized the most inhospitable parts of Northern Baja, as they spread via seed and wind, and are tolerant of our rain schedule. The sculptural plants herein won't do that. You usually have to spend money to acquire one. Have I mentioned I own a succulent nursery?

The Will to Live

Succulents can get impatient waiting for you to repot or plant them. At my nursery, I have several columnar euphorbias, 20 to 30 feet tall (and almost as wide), that decided they liked where I set them down in their plastic pots and would live out their lives right there. Roots will find their way out of drainage holes and into the ground, and eventually split the pot as they grow. Whenever I notice a potted euphorbia that looks a little too vigorous and happy next to its for-sale potted brethren, it's almost always the case that it is because the roots have gotten loose and it is growing in place. I have a huge *E. abyssinica* (x?) at the shop (page 56) that did just that, and now, after close to 25 years, is an absolute tree with a woody trunk. Until recently, you could still make out a few black plastic pot shards embedded in the base, but that pot has now been subsumed. That plant decided long ago it wasn't going anywhere, although I do spirit off an occasional cutting.

The *Euphorbia grandialata* in the photo at left has made a similar decision at Moorten Botanical Garden and Cactarium in Palm Springs. You can be sure that the root has taken a hard left turn and has split the pot, and now resides below ground.

Most succulents, including those in this book, don't go gently into that good night. If a growing tip is lopped off or damaged, a previously healthy plant will take some time (weeks to months in many cases) to reorganize an internal response, often sprouting many heads to replace the missing growing apex (known as a meristem). If I may mix metaphors, they respond like the mythical hydra, or maybe more like whack-a-mole. The *Parodia* (*Notocactus*) *schumanniana* at the University of California Botanical Garden at Berkeley, below left, decided to sprout as many new heads as it could after it sustained some tip damage. The *Neobuxbaumia polylopha*, below right, looks like it has had some time to recover from whatever took it out—it could have been physical damage or a hard frost, or insect related. The *Trichocereus terscheckii* above it appears to be in an earlier stage of recovery. One disadvantage in the long run is that such plants can get top heavy after sprouting multiple heads—this can be a particular issue with large euphorbias harvested for cutting stock. Sometimes that top-heavy, multi-head new growth topples to the ground and roots in place.

There are some typical steps taken on the ascension to savvy succulentophile. It usually begins with one plant, either a gift or an impulse buy. Then you get a few more. People start giving them to you after they see that you have a collection going. Then you start noticing more and more varieties. A little list begins to develop in your head. At this point, proper botanical names are still way off. You're looking for one of those fuzzy little cacti, or one of those "brainy" type plants. Unsatisfied with the limited offering of cacti and succulents at your local nursery, you start to cast a wider net. In the old days, we'd try to procure cactus and succulent catalogs, or visit succulent specialty nurseries if we could, which have always been few and far between. Now we've got the worldwide interweb, but I'd like to think there still are some fine books on the topic to provide information and inspiration. You might be reading one right now. Then you might join your local cactus and succulent club. I highly recommend going that route, and you can start by attending its annual show and sale. In the meantime, your couple of plants likely have morphed into many more and have taken over your balcony or windowsill. If you have ground available, you might have started an in-ground succulent garden.

So when have you crossed over from casual enthusiast to bona fide collector? It starts by learning the Latin names for the plants you have or seek. At my nursery, I've enabled quite a few folks through the process. Once they start speaking Latin, the transformation is complete. They might ask for *Euphorbia neriifolia* crested form, not that "green wavy cactusy thing." Now we're speaking the same language. You have become one of us—I'm sorry, and welcome to the club. Once you're in, its almost impossible to get out. Why would you want out?

Photo: EW&C

The nice thing about being a cactus and succulent enthusiast (or "collector," depending on how far down the rabbit hole you've gone) is that you can take a break from your menagerie of spiny specimens for a while and they mostly are still there waiting for you when you're ready to get back into it. That is something more traditional plant or bonsai enthusiasts can't really do—or almost any other hobby that involves living things. Take the little front porch tableau, top left, that I came upon in San Luis Obispo. This appears to be a collection patiently awaiting some love from an owner who may have moved on to other things, maybe even moved out of the house. The plants are big for the relatively small pots, meaning they're in need of repotting, and the color isn't great, nothing in bloom at the moment—just hunkered down, shriveling somewhat, as cacti have evolved to do in the desert. The dudes abide. Rain will certainly help when it arrives, or better yet, an owner willing to buy a new bag of cactus/succulent soil, an hour of repotting time, followed by water every few weeks. When you see a collection like this, you might understand why people think of cactus as ugly and nasty. But with a little kindness, you might end up with a collection like that of the serious hobbyists at middle left and upper right, or some beautiful flowers like those in the middle right image, and later in this book. It doesn't take much effort.

Top right: Paul Lawler subscribes to the one plant/one pot method of staging. I'm sure he can name every plant on sight, and where and when he acquired it. All of us can. It's our thing... What?

Middle left: A small part of Peter Walkowiak's stunning succulent collection of show plants.

Middle right: A lovely little cactus section of Earth Wind & Cactus's collection in bloom; this is part of the same shelf of plants on page 23.

Bottom left: A nicely potted and staged collection of cacti from a large grower, on display at a reasonable price at a retail nursery. It has an orientation, small in front to big in back, and some nice specimens. It is rather crowded, but they can handle that. This entire grouping eventually will need liberation from the small pot, and should either be separated into several pots, or replanted en masse into a much larger bowl.

Bottom right: A splendidly cristate and monstrose form of what probably is *Cereus forbesii*.

There are subcategories of succulent collectors. Every club will have several specialists with collections oriented towards cacti, or euphorbias, or crests, or variegates. And within a group, say cacti, they may concentrate on copiapoas, or astrophytums, or the blooming echinopsis group. Eventually you move on to another niche. You get to the point where you need something new to focus on. You can tell from collector Joe's greenhouse at left that he's not satisfied with the common stuff. If everybody's got it, it's time to find something new. And something new always comes along. You can order a little treasure from Romania or Singapore if you're willing to take the risk of transportation. Plants travel surprisingly well in a little box as long as it only takes a few days.

Most enthusiasts will take a stab at becoming propagators as well. While some of the plants in this book—particularly euphorbias, but also many cacti—can be grown from cuttings, others need to be grown from seed. This is particularly true for some of the globular cacti, such as the various mammillarias and ferocacti in the backyard grower's flat, bottom right. Many mammillarias will form clusters over time, but the pups aren't as easy to detach as it is with other clustering succulents such as aloes or aeoniums. And much of the beauty is in growing it on to an impressive clump as occurs in nature, without cuts or hack marks.

Seed collection and germination takes a bit of art and science, combined with finesse, patience, and attention to detail. I'm not a great seed grower as I lack a few of those qualities, but I'm happy others take the time, either for economic reasons or personal satisfaction. Seed-grown plants can and should be more expensive, due to the effort and time involved to grow them to a salable size. The plants at right might be three to four years old, and will be priced accordingly. We will get into more propagation issues on page 38.

Astrophytum myriostigma
by Ron Harris

Geohintonii mexicana
by Bill Munkacey

Tephrocactus bonnieae
by Karen Ostler

Matucana aurantiaca
ssp. currundayensis
by Peter Walkowiak

Euphorbia poissonii
by Rob Skillen

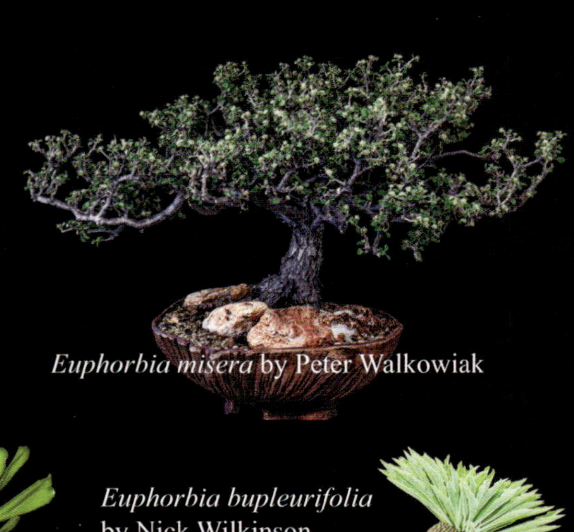

Euphorbia misera by Peter Walkowiak

Euphorbia bupleurifolia
by Nick Wilkinson

Tephrocactus alexanderi v. geometricus by Ron Harris

Uncarina roeoseliana
by Peter Walkowiak

Ariocarpus retusus
by Rob Skillen

Stenocereus hollianus
by Linda Drake

Astrophytum ornatum
by Markus Mumper
and Maggie Wagner

Fouquieria purpusii
by Nick Wilkinson

Rebutia collection by Snake

On the assumption that you already are fascinated with succulents, please try to check out your local cactus and succulent club's annual show. You will see some fantastic and expertly staged show plants. All the "museum pieces" on this page have been displayed and photographed at the Central Coast Cactus and Succulent Society's spring show in San Luis Obispo, California. Bear in mind the plants on this spread are only representative of the genera in this book. There will be many more varieties on display at these shows as well, including aloes, agaves, mesembs, and more obscure genera. All photos by Gene Schroeder and/or Loring Manley.

Euphorbia guillauminiana
by Brandon Taylor

Pachypodium horombense
by Rob Skillen

Euphorbia obesa
by Nick Wilkinson

Commercial Growers

Even the most dedicated succulent enthusiast wouldn't have a yard like this, which is a grower's field stock in Vista, California. With an ideal climate for growing cacti and succulents from around the world, there are a number of wholesale growers in San Diego's inland north county area. Plants that have reached the size of the plants above may be dug and sold as large landscape specimens, which would be the case with the large *Euphorbia resiniferas* (left center) and Golden Barrels (right center). But the columnar *Euphorbia acrurensis* (far left) and *Cereus peruvianus monstrose* (far right) will likely be chopped into more manageable sizes for sale. The remaining stumps will regenerate new growth for future cuts. They just keep giving.

Above: *Trichocereus pachanoi* is a columnar cactus that will infrequently form spectacular crested sections. A savvy propagator will chop one crest into many and field-grow them, as seen here. Notice the reversions to normal, which will be decapitated and grown separately.

Below: More field-grown specimens of crested *Myrtillocactus geometrizans* (blue), *Espostoa lanata* (white), and Golden Barrels (*Echinocactus grusonii*).

Botanical Destinations

The Huntington Botanical Gardens
San Marino, California

If you're new to the world of succulents, you should schedule a visit to see some of these plants as they were meant to be seen. In Southern California, The Huntington Botanical Gardens in San Marino offers the largest and most impressive succulent collection in the world (!). Close by is the Los Angeles County Arboretum and Botanic Garden, another amazing collection of otherworldly botany—check out their Madagascar garden. The San Diego Botanic Garden in Encinitas is also wonderful, as are the plantings at the San Diego Zoo, and the San Diego Zoo Safari Park in Escondido offers the best Baja California garden not in Baja California. Several colleges have outstanding xerophytic gardens as well, such as Cal State Fullerton, Pitzer College in Claremont (California), and several others.

The Desert Botanical Garden in Phoenix, Arizona, is outstanding—go in the cooler part of the year if you're a coastal wimp like me. The Boyce Thompson Arboretum in Superior, Arizona, is a hidden treasure. Tucson has some nice botanic gardens as well (Tohono Chul), but I mostly go for the nurseries—there are some excellent cactus nurseries in Tucson.

Desert Botanical Garden
Scottsdale, Arizona

Ruth Bancroft Garden
Walnut Creek, California

California has several world-class succulent botanic gardens—or at least botanic gardens with a serious succulent section. If you're in northern California, two must-visits are the University of California Botanical Garden at Berkeley and the Ruth Bancroft Garden in Walnut Creek. The Bancroft has evolved over the years into a spectacular garden of xerophytic wonders under the tutelage of Brian Kemble, among others. Owing to its inland location in the East Bay, it is more prone to extreme heat and, of more concern, the once-a-decade serious sub-freezing snap, but they have figured out how to deal with such events.

The University of California Botanical Garden at Berkeley is tucked into a west-facing canyon in the hills just above the campus and benefits from a more benign coastal-influenced climate. It offers regional gardens from around the world but also has many long-established succulents in its African and New World succulent sections. It has one of the tallest specimens of *Trichocereus terscheckii* I've ever seen.

Farther south, Lotusland in Santa Barbara almost defies superlative description—you just need to visit. Of particular note for those interested in the plants contained in this book is their columnar cactus collection and large euphorbias. I won't try to describe it further here. Just go—you need to schedule an appointment, and it is closed from mid-November to mid-February.

Climatically Challenged?

Visitors to my California nursery from the East Coast—or indeed almost anywhere else in the U.S.—are always a bit amazed and envious of how easily we can grow succulents in our Mediterranean climate. While we do have to scramble just a bit in late fall when we get our first wet and "cold" winter conditions to protect some equatorial plants, it is nothing like the process most folk have to go through earlier in the year. The little container cuties in the window display at left are part of the collection of Jean Butler in Westborough, Massachusetts. They were just moved inside in early October on their usual schedule. She is a member of a very enthusiastic cactus and succulent club in her state, and they grow some amazing plants. It just takes more work and lots of sunny windows or a heated greenhouse to get through the cold months if you are truly committed.

You can create an outdoor in-ground succulent garden that can survive long periods of snow, but the range of suitable plants is very limited. There are some cold-hardy cacti, such as some of the echinocereus native to colder parts of the U.S., and other succulents including some sempervivums and sedums and cold-weather euphorbias, but the vast majority of plants in this book will need to be overwintered in greenhouse conditions in areas other than most of California and the desert Southwest.

Left: There are some very impressive cacti and succulent collections at public gardens in cold-winter climate parts of the world. One of the best is the Princess of Wales Conservatory at Kew Gardens in London. Also on display in this temperate house are excellent beds of bromeliads, carniverous, and aquatic plants, as well as a host of Mediterranean plants that can't quite handle the London winters outdoors. Maybe in a few more years....

At the other end of the climate spectrum you will encounter quite different issues. Some people who make the move to a desert region are surprised to find that many of the cacti and succulents they thought would love the desert sometimes just can't take the intense heat. Most of the softer succulents, such as aeoniums, echeverias, crassulas, etc., as well as even some aloes, agaves, and euphorbias, cannot tolerate the dry, triple-digit desert summers. Filtered or dappled sun, along with extra hydration, might help a bit. It is often not the heat as much as the intensity of the sun and how quickly plants dry out that is the issue.

In broad terms, most cacti will happily grow in the desert Southwest. There are exceptions, and there is a difference between the lower deserts, including the Palm Springs area and Phoenix/Tucson, versus the higher desert, where winter cold becomes more of a factor. As I write this, some of my friends in those lower desert locales have told me about the past summer of three solid months of triple digit heat, and a few spells where nighttime lows stayed in the nineties. Apparently that last factor can be a killer, even for cacti—extremely high nighttime "lows." Even cacti need to cool off a little—some long-established Golden Barrels collapsed under those conditions. Extra water may help, but even that didn't save some of their cacti. Suburban "heat islands" created by miles of concrete exacerbate this issue. This may be a new reality we have to deal with unless we all can manage to get our act together.

Featured here is the "OuchHouse," a rather deluxe greenhouse in the Boston area. This private collector started with some window succulents, then made an add-on small glass porch adjacent to the house, and ultimately went all-out with a European style structure. It remains open and ventilated through the warm season, and is heated and uses thermal blankets and lights through the winter, as shown below. Heaters and/or fans are employed as needed. There is quite a bit of automation, but much of the adjustment is done manually. It sits on top of a four-foot deep enclosed "pool" of aggregate and succulent soil, enjoying excellent drainage regardless of how wet it is outside.

The owner has spent time procuring the larger plants in Arizona and California. When I visited in the fall months, the plants looked as fat and happy as any I've seen in the Southwest. His initial inspiration to go all-out was a drive through the Sonoran Desert and seeing some of the desert sentinels in habitat.

The saguaro is the crowning glory of the OuchHouse, but there are a host of other impressive cacti and succulents as well. The view at left is primarily of the New World section. Behind the photographer there are more of the Madagascan and African plants. The problem the owner quickly encountered is the "Damn, my greenhouse is full" dilemma. It is amazing how fast they fill up. I asked him if that meant he was done. He said at one point he was thinking about expanding, but moved off of that. Now he says it is a happy day when something dies, so he can plant something new. Yep, been there.

Succulent Soil Science 101

There are many disparate theories and formulas for the proper cactus/succulent soil. The one commonality is that it needs to be light and fast-draining. The components to get you there vary widely, and in some sense, nearly all of them work. What most of us want is the one mix that works for everything. In an ideal world, we would have different mixes for different plant groups, even for different seasons. A magic mix would be very light and fast-drying for the wet winter months, and then transmogrify to a richer/thicker mix for the hot and dry part of the year. Absent access to alchemy, let's take a look at some of the mixes that are used by seasoned growers.

Pure pumice

One way to make a mix light is to use granular/pebble-sized natural pumice or the artificial substitute known as Perlite. Both are light and keep the soil airy and also have micro pockets to temporarily hold water for new roots to seek out. Either combined or used individually, some form or other of "white stuff" components have been a staple of succulent mixes for as long as the hobby has existed. Some long-time growers like a mix that is almost entirely pumice with a minimum of organic components—"dirty pumice." This does make fertilizing a more regular necessity. I know of a few growers who have moved away from pumice and Perlite as they think that the pockets might harbor damaging pathogens as well as water, but at present I don't have the science to back that up. An alternative to pumice/Perlite can be a similar igneous component—dark lava scoria of various sizes.

A very light Perlite mix.

In addition to the non-organic pumice or lava, mixes should have an organic component. This varies widely by grower, but most traditional potting soils will have some mix of dark organics, which might be composed of leaf mold, fir bark, manure, mushroom compost, etc. In short, a thicker, darker, soft or friable potting mix. Many soil mixes are a 50/50 split of the organics and non-organics mentioned above. A smaller portion of the mix might be coarse sand or decomposed granite, but too much of either can lead to a heavy and wet mix. Some soil companies will also add a small percentage of time-release fertilizer, mycorrhiza, wetting agents, and other forms of special sauce. One thing I've noticed at my nursery is that there are some mixes—usually richer and heavy with peat or coir, that succulents seem to thrive on in the greenhouse conditions that they were started in, but have a tough time adjusting to the elements of the more neglected real world they will end up living in.

A fir bark-based mix.

I know of a few expert growers who are always tinkering with their mixes, and every couple of years they have hit on "the one final mix," only to change it later. Having more of a left-hemisphere, non-engineer type of brain, I'm just looking for one that works on most of my collection, so I can stick a plant in it and fuggitaboutit.

Fakies

What kind of cacti are best for indoors? Fake ones! The real things will grow in a sunny window (ideally with some direct sun through the window for a few hours minimum), but for most indoor tabletop or bookshelf situations, I recommend plastic, silk, or ceramic. My position on fake succulents has evolved over the years. I have been impressed at times by how realistic some of the knock-offs are, and I can even identify them by genus and species. The little globes at far left look like a fuzzy form of ferocactus; the opuntia at far right is likely a hybrid with very nice "spines," and the ceramic beauties (second from left) look like a neobuxbaumia with an inermis (non-spined) form of parodia. The middle image might be a cactus garden of knitted, or macrame, or.... I'm out of my depth here, but it involved yarn and she did a great job. Second from right is literally a "pincushion cactus" (creation of Susan Morse)—a common name that is given to quite a few varieties of mammillarias, pediocactus, escobarias, etc. The irony with an actual, functional pincushion cactus as seen here is that the "spines"—actual pins or sewing needles—are poking in, not out, like it is doing a voodoo penance for all of the damage its real-life inspirations have inflicted over the years. The common theme in all of these: no light or water required, and you can still pay tribute to your favorite plants in a non-plant-friendly environment. Why not?

Care Basics

This book is about growing these succulents in Mediterranean climates like the one we have in (most of) California. I'm primarily focusing on plants that are available and have proven to be durable growers, both in-ground as well as in containers. There will be a few exceptions, which will be discussed individually. For the most part, consider these to be outdoor, full-sun plants. Most can handle quite a bit of inland summer sun, but very few can endure a prolonged freeze. The Old World plants here—euphorbias and pachypodiums—fit that bill. Many of the cacti will accept desert conditions, which will include winter freezes. However, quite a few cacti are of Central American or tropical South American origin, and those also are cold sensitive. Again, I'll try to give you all I know about each plant individually. Be aware that older, established plants are much hardier than younger specimens.

Some of the more rare and sensitive plants might need to be kept in pots in order to be moved out of the rain in exceptionally wet and cold years, or perhaps protected from sun and heat during the hot and dry Santa Ana winds that California occasionally experiences from fall through spring. Succulents generally are low-maintenance, but as mild as California's climate is, we can still experience dramatic temperature shifts that a plant might never have evolved to endure where it is originally from.

SOIL: Cactus mix needs to be light and fast-draining. Please see the section on soils for containerized plants on the facing page. In-ground plants sort of have to get used to the soil you have, but you can amend your native earth if it is hard sandstone or clay, or anything less than hospitable to organic life. Consider building a mound of new, fresh soil rather than digging into hard-packed inhospitable ground, both for the fresh mix as well as the visually more appealing and natural look of succulents growing in a varied topography, including rocks and boulders. Most soil shops will have a basic landscape mix of amended topsoil—just good brown dirt or sandy loam mixed with some organics—that will work fine as long is it is mounded up somewhat and has good drainage. I don't recommend traditional succulent mix for in-ground applications, mainly because the pumice or Perlite tends to float to the top and make unattractive "snow drifts." For more of a desert look, you can use decomposed granite as either a partial component, or a top dressing.

WATER: I like to water most of my succulents about once a week when it's warm and dry (late spring through early fall), and then back off to less frequent, even to zero waterings in winter, assuming a "typical" winter rainy season. Containerized plants dry out quicker than larger in-ground plants, and may need more frequent watering and feeding. For the most part, the succulents in this book are solid-bodied living canteens, and the older they are, the longer they can hold out between waterings. But we tend to baby our plants to keep them fat and happy, and most will accept regular summer water, provided they have a cactus/succulent mix, good drainage and some full sun. Quite a few are from summer rainfall regions and love water at that time of year, but might be more used to dry winters, so be sure they have excellent drainage to survive wet winters. California is notorious for its alkaline municipal water supply, and ideally water should be more acidic, which helps the roots absorb nutrients. An ideal pH should be in the 5 to 5.5 range. There are a number of ways to get there, but the easiest is to add about a tablespoon of distilled white vinegar per five gallons of tap water; you can buy a pool kit to test the water. Some growers also like to add trace amounts of ammonium, nitrogen, or phosphate as well, and expert grower Elton Roberts has what he considers to be the ultimate system to adjust your water, but it was too complicated for lazy me. Just occasionally use the vinegar method.

FEEDING: You can and should occasionally fertilize cacti and succulents. You certainly don't need to fertilize with every watering. A few times, spring through fall, will likely be enough. I don't fertilize my in-ground plants, mostly because I don't want to give the weeds a head start. When choosing plant food, the three numbers on the label (nitrogen, phosphorus, and potassium) should all be mid-range, 10 to 15 percent. Then I'd recommend diluting the recommended dosage by at least half. Err on the side of going light. Some growers prefer a diluted fish emulsion. You can use granular time-release or soluble fertilizers. Too much feeding can make a plant look temporarily great, but it is analogous to steroids, and ultimately can have the opposite of the desired effect and weaken the plant.

A *Pachycereus pringlei* (above far left) exhibits habitat stress due to poor soil and competition with other plants—still looks kind of cool, but shouldn't be so red. The same problem is also evident in the beautifully sad ferocactus in the far right image. A mammillaria (second from left) exhibits indoor houseplant stress. It is stretching and leaning towards the window, dreaming of outdoor sun. The "frosting" on the green skin of the *Ferocactus latispinus* (second from right) is actually scale—an insidious barnacle-like pest. You'll have to pick your poison to get rid of it, along with some detailed scraping.

Far left: A stressed-yellow *Neobuxbaumia polylopha* growing in Northern California. The stress is likely because it is living at the very northern limit that it can.

Near left: An equally stressed *Euphorbia trigona* in Southern California. This is more likely due to a watering or nutrient-poor soil issue. It is still growing but probably should be put out of its misery soon.

Right: A *Euphorbia lactea* 'White Ghost' variegate, showing the burn marks of an albino plant exposed to too much sun. This should really be a greenhouse or indoor plant.

I get a lot of questions about yellowing plants, and I don't think there ever is any single, particular answer to what is causing the bleaching—it could be poor soil/nutrients, weather conditions, or watering schedule. I'm not a plant doctor and I'm not inclined to try to get into the molecular biology of it all. I like succulents because you can generally be blissfully ignorant of the cause and effect biology. So I just call it all "yellow cactus syndrome" (technically they are "chlorotic") as seen in yellowed and scarred but nevertheless still cool looking crested *Trichocereus pachanoi* at left or the *Cereus peruvianus* below left (it applies to euphorbias too, as seen above), and ask about watering frequency (water after allowing the soil to dry out, once every week or two works in most situations). Have you tried fertilizing, a few times over a month or two, diluted to half strength of whatever plant food you have? How long has it been in that location? Was it growing happily in the same spot before it yellowed? Maybe it is stress from a new move? Did you amend the soil? Have you tried moving it into a larger pot with a good cactus/succulent mix? Is it still growing at the tips? If so, it might work out of it. And of course, I own a nursery and might suggest that if you've tried everything else, just toss it and buy a new one. Have you tried a *Euphorbia grandialata*? I happen to have a nice specimen right over here....

Notice the gray-brown lower portion of the *Euphorbia meloformis* at right. This is a natural occurrence that is common in euphorbias and other succulents. It is called "lignification," or becoming "woodlike" (see the whimsical example of this phenomenon on the background image on page 10). Older established tissue at the base of the plant simply becomes more solid and "dead" looking, while new vibrant growth still continues at the growing meristems. This is most likely a way of solidifying and protecting the base as the plant grows. From a sheer aesthetic perspective this might take away from the perfection we seek in plants, and I tip my hat to the judges of this euphorbia at the San Diego Cactus and Succulent Society show that they overlooked the natural lignification in this otherwise healthy (and old) plant and gave it a blue ribbon. The takeaway here is that if you see this woodiness on your plant, don't think it is something you've done wrong, providing there is no sign that tissue death is due to bugs, and as long as the growing apex is still healthy. I have stood at the base of large tree euphorbias and even the "pencil plant" (*Euphorbia tirucali*) and if I hadn't looked up I would have thought they were some type of traditional tree, with large brown and almost barked trunks that were almost too wide to reach around. Lignification also can occur at branch junctures, likely to strengthen a point of constriction that has to support weight above. It is a shame when the woodiness runs up the stem farther than you'd like.

Pest issues usually are pretty obvious—you can see them, or evidence of them, on your plant. Step one, if the plant is large enough, is to blast them off with a strong spray from a hose, for aphids or mealy bugs—that won't work as well with scale insects. Then spray or treat it with the irritant of your choice, depending on your personal sense of organic obligation. Any spray you buy that says it works on aphids, mealy bugs, mites, etc., should do, and you can apply it several times over a few weeks. They'll get the message. Most of these potions are either poison, oil, or citrus based, and are not as nasty to work with as some of the now-banned products from past decades. With small, directed squirts onto infected areas there shouldn't be concern about getting into the water table; at least I've convinced myself to be okay with it. Scale is a different issue—they are essentially little plant-eating barnacles that need to be scraped off and then sprayed, or else you need to go the systemic route—a last resort for me. I will toss the plant if it is too bad. (I apologize to it and thank it for its service first).

Succulents usually are low maintenance, but they are not immune to predatory pests. Above left is a rather extreme example of scale run amok on a cactus, in this case a monstrose/crested version of *Myrtillocactus geometrizans*. When it is this bad, you might want to just toss the plant, or at least cut off and discard the worst parts. If you want to try to save it, follow the steps outlined above—blast it with a power nozzle on a hose, then spray with whatever poison you're comfortable with. Wait a few hours or days, spray again, and you may need to finish by using a plastic knife to scrape away the survivors, which can hide in the crenulated folds of a crested plant, making it a difficult task. Then you might need to repeat the process in a few weeks.

Speaking of bugs finding a way, the middle left image shows an example of a bug really carving out what you would think would be a pitiful niche to survive—cactus spines. I was amazed to learn early on that there are mealy bugs that actually make their living sucking on spines, sometimes called the "cactus mealybug." It seems like anything nature produces, a predator will develop to work against it. I haven't personally witnessed actual damage done to spines long term, and perhaps these creatures retreat later back into the plant under the spines at some point, where you think the dining would be a bit easier. There are root mealies as well, which must be treated with a systemic insecticide. There are a lot of recipes for dealing with the various types of cottony mealybugs, most involving a spray bottle and either a diluted solution of isopropyl alcohol, or that combined with a certain amount of dish soap or even Tabasco sauce. You should do a bit of internet research and experimentation, but you can win the war if you're willing to work at it.

Middle right above is a minature monstrose form of cereus that has suffered snail or slug damage, or possibly even varmint bites by mice or rats. Spines on this particular plant are minimal, so it wasn't that hard of a dining project, but you would be amazed how snails and slugs can find their way through the spines to dine on the fleshy plant beneath. Snails are generally only a problem during the wet months, and you just need to keep an eye out and pick them off one by one. I like to roll them out on the street, figuring they've at least got a chance. Or try a nine iron or pitching wedge. Do what you gotta do.

Above far right: Opuntias are susceptible to a particular type of cottony scale insect called a cochineal mealy. It will, surprisingly, produce a type of acid that makes a red dye that has been used as fabric colorant for centuries.

When a cactus soaks up a little too much water, it can go from plump and happy to too plump and happy. Stems sometimes can swell to point of splitting. It can lead to further rot and perhaps the death of the plant, but more often than not, the split will scar over as seen here. Your plant likely will survive but bear the scars of good times.

Quite a few of the plants in this book can be propagated by cuttings, particularly the branching or multi-column types. The columnar euphorbias and clustering cacti are best suited for this method, but the downside is the temporary defacement of your plant. I lament this process, particularly with crested plants, as it is so hard to take a knife to such a wonderful living sculpture. The professionals have no problem with it, particularly if they have a large stock of plants dedicated to cutting. The general rule is to let your decapitated new cutting "scar off" for at least a few days, apply a rooting hormone if desired (cinnamon powder to prevent fungus is used by many), then place it upright and staked in a pot of cactus mix, but don't bury it too deep—an inch or two deep at most. Then water once a week like a typical plant and it should root. If you have access to a greenhouse, that can be an easier environment (diffused light, more humidity) to establish new roots. Of course, some plants can be more difficult to start vegetatively than others, and you will have to experiment and endure some failures. Or buy something new from your local nursery.

Above: *Lophophora fricii*, a 3-inch mature specimen at left, and a gaggle of its seed-started progeny to its right. You can see the small, black seed cases from whence the plump little infants germinated.

Above and below: When a grower's seed flats go a little too long without being thinned out, they can end up forming these tremendous patterned mounds of prickly beauty. I've bought a few, and they are fun to look at but not fun to separate.

Many succulents must be started from seed. This is the case with many of the slow-growing cacti and smaller euphorbias that really don't offer much to cut without ruining a prized specimen. Many, such as the ariocarpus or pachypodiums, seldom, if ever, branch or offer offsets, so there is nothing to cut; seed starting is our only option. Seed collection and successful germination is a bit of art backed up by some science, and is worthwhile if you have access to both of those qualities, as well as a good amount of patience and the ability to deal with a lot of failure. As I mentioned earlier, I'm limited in both of those characteristics (and lazy), and despite selling succulents for a living, I rely on others to do the germination. If I have something rare or desirable that is offering seed, I'll get in contact with a few friends who are eager to collect the seed and get to work, and I buy some of the babies back a year or two later. There are some excellent succulent seed sources online.

Propagation

Above is an example of a newly rooted cutting of a crested *Euphorbia kibwezensis*. After a clean cut was made, it was allowed to scar off for a few days to a week, perhaps dusted with a rooting powder, and then planted in cactus mix.

Many succulents—aloes, agaves, and many of the soft succulents—make it very easy by surrounding themselves with easy to detach offsets or "pups." Few of the plants in this book make it so easy. The terrestrial bromeliads do sport a lot of offsets, but you need gloves and a sharp knife to detach them, and it is not easy. There will be blood.

Grafting is done for a few reasons. Some plants are difficult to grow on their own roots in cultivation, but growers have found they will sometimes be more vigorous if the plant body is attached (grafted) to the stock of a related plant. This will allow a grower to get a larger plant faster, either to use for further propagation or simply for the sake of keeping a specimen alive and healthy.

If you cut a large crest into sections, they can sometimes be more difficult to establish with their own roots. By using grafting stock, you can propagate many more crests, illustrated in both images at right.

Despite their occasional visual similarity, cacti and euphorbias are way too far apart genetically to be hybridized or even grafted with each other. Below left at first appears to be a *Euphorbia suzannae* hybrid grafted onto a myrtillocactus, but in all likelihood the stock is a blueish euphorbia. In the case of the colorful "hot-head" or "moon cacti" gymnocalyciums (below middle), the grafting stock allows the normally spotty or capricious color anomalies to grow more vigorously. Over the long term, however, "the hot-head" (*scion*) often ends up dying and the stock plant can take over. Below right: A trichocereus is playing host to a number of different genera in what can only be considered a whimsical chimera (or Frankenstein's monster) example of fun with plants.

Like most succulentophiles I know, I'm not a huge fan of the look of a grafted plant. If I have one in my personal collection, and if the stock plant is short enough, I try to hide it with rocks when staging. Grafting has an obvious purpose and is useful for propagation and keeping difficult plants alive, and is an art form that you can grow into if you are so inclined. In my thirty years of playing with succulents, I've only dabbled with the process a few times, with mixed results—it's really not my thing. If you have a botanical engineering bent, this is a subject worthy of further study, but I'm personally not enough of an authority to give you a "hands on" tutorial here.

Kingdom: *Plantae*
Phylum: *Magnoliopsida*
Class: *Malpighiales*
Order: *Euphorbiales*
Family: *Euphorbiaceae*
Genus: *Euphorbia*
Species: *sepulta*

Euphorbias

Right: I think you can make a case that euphorbias as a whole have more dramatic and variable shapes and structures than cacti. However, cacti win the flowering category hands down—check out the cactus flower images in that section. Probably the best blooming euphorbia group are the various forms and hybrids of *E. milii*, but in general, euphorbia flowers are small, usually yellow to chartreuse in color, and cluster along ridges, as seen on the *Euphorbia abysinnica* at right. Indeed, the subsequent seed pods are often larger and more dramatic than the flowers they replaced. In euphorbias, flowering—start to finish—can last several weeks to over a month, which is quite a bit longer than the several days, at most, that most cacti flowers last. In Southern California, euphorbias tend to bloom anytime from spring through fall, often several times over the warm period (excepting the *E. milii* group, which can often bloom year-round).

Above: The stunning and aptly named *Euphorbia tirucalli* 'Sticks on Fire.' As with all euphorbias, beware the white sap, particularly any contact with your eyes.

Left: The prolifically and perennially blooming *E. milii* 'Crown of Thorns.' The thorns aren't that bad.

Right: One absolute in the plant world is that there are few absolutes. Most euphorbias aren't supposed to thrive in triple-digit, dry desert heat, but this big *E. ingens* is happy to hang in Palm Springs heat with his cacti cousins. It's been there for a while.

Photo: EW&C

Above left: *Euphorbia ferox* has some of the most significant and almost cactus-like spines in the genus. The newest spines at the apex emerge in a fuchsia-purple color, slowly fading as they age. Photo: Brian Kemble.

Middle left: *Euphorbia inermis* (or possibly *E. esculenta*—plants in habitat don't come with labels) photographed by Jeremy Spath. He speculates that the cleaned up lower stem was done by goats. If so, well done!

Below left: An unidentified euphorbia growing on a Moroccan sea cliff. Without looking closely at the plent, at first glance you might think this was an echinocereus growing in coastal Baja California.

Above: *Euphorbia avasmontana* mimics quite a few of the columnar cacti of the New World. Or vice-versa. As with many others in the genus, you will see images purported to be this same plant in cultivation that have a similar look but seem to be of smaller stature, or maybe hybrids. This is the real deal at home. Photo: Mike Hackett.

Euphorbias in Habitat

Haven't been to Africa yet? Yeah, me neither. It is big on my bucket list. Most Americans think of going on safari to see the African fauna, which would be nice, but I would spend most of my time scrambling through the bush and up rocky hills looking for succulents. That is what Mike Hackett did with Tim Harvey in Namibia some time back. He has a wealth of fantastic images, such as the *Euphorbia virosa* (dig that African sky!) above and *Euphorbia avasmontana* on the facing page. I am a bit more familiar with the cacti and fouquieria of the U.S. southwest and northern Mexico, and these African and Madagascan plants offer up similar sculptural statements in the places they evolved.

The 10-volume series of *The Euphorbia Journal* is the definitive treatment of this huge genus. Published by Herman Schwartz of Strawberry Press, this lushly photographed series is long out of print but still available. Each book is like an excellent hardcover magazine, with articles by authorities in the field. The design and overall feel of the books was ahead of its time. Released over a 10-year period, there have been some name changes and reclassifications over the 30 years since the first volume, but this series would be well worth the sizable investment if you are a fan of euphorbias or well-done plant books in general.

Publisher Herman Schwartz founded Strawberry Press and put out some wonderful succulent books in the eighties and nineties, and *The Euphorbia Journal* may have been his crown jewel. He also operated the Euphorbia Reference Collection in Bolinas, California, and conducted research and collecting trips to Africa and other overseas succulent hot beds. He had a dedicated staff of designers and plant folk, and the volumes have articles by some legendary "succulenterati" such as Gordon Rowley, Seymour Linden, Susan Carter, Frank Horwood, Werner Rauh, John Trager, Ernst van Jaarsveld, and others. For years, I only owned Volume 5, but finally knuckled under and bought the other nine volumes to help with this book. It doubles down on my bucket list wish to see Africa.

Despite the great variety of look and structure of euphorbias, there are some common features that can clue you in to the genus. Flowers generally are small and form in clusters, sometimes spectacularly as in the *E. milii* group, often inconsequentially as with many of the columnar or pencil varieties. On some columnars, such as *E. ammak*, the seed pods that follow the flowers are larger and more impressive than the blooms themselves. If you see a large columnar succulent with a large bloom, it is certainly a cactus and not a euphorbia.

Another characteristic of euphorbias is a sort of latex feel to the skin, and for those with thorns, you'll find them to be less intimidating than those of the cactus family. They generally are thicker, not quite as sharp, and less likely to detach and get stuck to your skin (read about the opuntias of the cactus family later in the book). That's not to say that spiny euphorbias won't make you bleed, but if you handle them with care, you'll find you can almost "pet" the spines without harm. They look worse than they are in most cases.

I lament the moniker "crown of thorns" for the *E. milii* group. A customer at my nursery will often be sold on the lush foliage and flowers of a compact form of *E. milii*, as the "spines" are rarely even visible, but once I tell them the common name, they take a step back. Then I show them how you actually can stroke your hand along the interior "spiny" branches, which you'll never see or touch anyway, but once they start thinking of grandkids or dogs.... I end up showing them an echeveria or some type of soft succulent instead.

Left: *Euphorbia ingens* has very small and inconspicuous flowers, but the subsequent fruiting decorates the growing heads with a dense coating of ball-shaped seed pods. At right are the red-blushing seed pods of an *E. abyssinica* hybrid. Too bad you can't eat them—really, don't try to eat them.

Above: *Euphorbia abdelkuri* is reputed to be the most poisonous of poisonous euphorbias. It is known only from a single small, rocky location on a tiny island off of Yemen but has been in cultivation for some time. Rarely available for sale (perhaps due to its reputation), it is a unique plant, with yellow rather than white latex, and is highly valued by collectors.

Right: There are significant differences in the body structures of euphorbias and cacti. Euphorbias tend to have rigid, almost woody spines, with sharp tips that can detach into your skin if handled roughly, but nothing like cactus spines. The well-armed *Euphorbia grandicornis* (near right) is a nice example of a spiny euphorbia. Not something you would want to fall into, but you can gently touch the spines with no adverse effects.

Cacti, on the other hand, are a different deal. The *Trichocereus (Echinopsis) terscheckii* (far right) shows the abundant and finer spines that you really want to avoid at all costs. With opuntias, if the large primary spines don't get you, the fine glochid spines below might. Cacti spines will get stuck into your skin much more readily and can be a pain to remove—take it from a guy who deals with them for a living.

The **"poison thing."** It is true that the white euphorbia sap is poisonous and something to be avoided. Some plants (*E. abdulkuri* and *E. virosa*) have more toxic sap than others, and some people are more sensitive to it than others. I've worked with all manner of euphorbias for years, and like most people, the sap causes no issues with skin contact, other than making a stain that needs to be washed out later. But I've talked to a few folks who break out in a rash not only from the sap, but even from touching the exterior of the plant. This seems to be a rare condition, but when it happens, it usually seems to involve the pencil plants, *E. tirucalli,* or the 'Sticks on Fire' version of that plant. I'm not sure if it is because that variety has a more potent latex or that there is just so much of it around and it breaks so easily that sap contact is more likely.

One thing everyone should avoid, however, is getting sap in the eyes. It stings pretty badly, and I know of a few folks who needed hospital visits to take care of it, but no permanent eye damage that I've heard of. Wash your hands after you've been dealing with euphorbias, sap or no sap, to be sure. If you're cutting on a larger plant, wear a hat. I've had euphorbia sap dry in my hair, then leak into my eyes later in the shower, which led to an hour of eye drops and misery, but it passed.

Then there is the issue of internal poisoning if the sap is ingested. From what I've ascertained (not from direct experience), it is that euphorbias taste so bad, nobody or nothing will take a second bite, and the amount you'd have to ingest would be basically impossible to gag down, so it just doesn't happen, even with animals (unless your dog is of the extra stupid variety). The poinsettia has been battling this "poisonous plant" albatross for a long time. So yes, euphorbias are poisonous, but if you're comfortable with a poinsettia in your house for the holidays, you should be okay with most of the other euphorbias.

Having said all that, I really shouldn't soft-peddle the fact that there are a few euphorbias that are very poisonous, and some individuals are much more sensitive to them, so always handle with care. That is the best of my advice from 30 years of dealing with euphorbias—handle with care and you should be fine. But I'm neither a doctor nor a lawyer (sorry, Mom and Dad), so if you're worried, get a cactus instead. Of course, then you have the nasty spines to deal with .... The sacrifices we make for beauty!

One of my favorite books is a true celebration of the magnificent oddities of the succulent world. *Teratopia* by Gordon Rowley (Cactus & Co.) takes you on a tour of some of the spectacular crested and variegated succulent specimens, including many of the cacti and euphorbias. Rowley spent a lifetime in the succulent world, and the book is now out of print and hard to find but may be available from the lending library of your local cactus club. Try to hunt it down if you can. I wish I had some of its images to show you here.

Above: a textbook example of crested growth in a euphorbia.

Left: A show-quality specimen of *Euphorbia kibwezensis*.

Cresting in euphorbias

Cresting is an aberrant growth form where the usual growing meristem contorts into a kind of fan or crenulated shape rather than the typical columnar or globoid fashion. It is analogous to a programming malfunction, but it is one we plant nuts love. Cresting is rare in nature and does happen occasionally outside of the succulent realm, but most of the crested (or "cristate") plants you will encounter will be succulents. Euphorbias and cacti are among the best of the best at this.

In cultivation, growers will isolate a crested portion of a plant and cut it up to make more crests. To my knowledge, nobody has yet figured out how to make a plant reliably form a crest, but when it does, a good grower with a sharp knife will hack away and make more. I have difficulty with this myself, as it goes against my nature to cut into a beautiful beast like the plants on these pages. But sometimes you just have to dig in.

Occasionally a crest will revert to the more normal columnar growth, as evident on the right side of the *Euphorbia ledienii* crest (bottom right). I think it is wise to remove the reverted growth, as you want to direct the growth into the crested portion. However, I have seen the "normals" eventually begin to crest as well, so you might want to wait a bit. I have also removed the normals and rooted them, only to have them begin to crest at a later time—apparently the cresting genetics can remain in them.

Euphorbia obesa

Euphorbia pseudocactus

Euphorbia mauritanica

Euphorbia suzannae

Variegation in euphorbias

There are not nearly as many stunning variegated examples in the euphorbia family as there are with cacti (see pages 132-133). When you do see variegated euphorbias, it is usually a white or milky color. The active growing tips or edges, as seen in the crested *E. lactea* (above left) will often take on a vibrant reddish pink color. On occasion, variegation will show up in an artistic flow against the green portions of the plant, particularly with *E. ammak* (above right and on the facing page). Occasionally you will find a two-tone variegation with some yellow, as seen in the variegated version of *E. milii* (below left). There are a number of attractive variegates of the bushy euphorbia varieties, such as *E. characias*. Below middle is the white variegated version of *Euphorbia mammillaris*, with some indications about thinking of reverting to green. Below right is a yellow variegated version of the same plant.

A whimsically variegated example of *Euphorbia ammak*.

The large, arborescent euphorbias that are so dominant in the Southern California landscape have been here for quite some time. They are frost sensitive, so large specimens are less frequently encountered in the central and northern portions of the state. In the proper climate, they grow rapidly and can overtake a small yard, so be aware of where you plant one.

We have two primary forms, *E. ingens* and *E. ammak*. *E. abyssinica* is less common and, at times, perhaps, is a hybrid parent to some of the tree euphorbias. Most are grown easily from cuttings, but I have observed seedling volunteers growing in the shadow of large plants. I've grown a few of these seedlings to some size, and I notice variations from the parent plant, meaning they may be hybridizing unassisted. I'm not sure if their African species parents look exactly like the plants we have here or whether we are slowly evolving our own forms that are adapting to their new climate. Regardless, these spectacular "not a cactus" succulents are dominant, sculptural players in our landscapes.

The large tree euphorbias don't seem as prone to forming crests as much as some smaller euphorbias, but they will on occasion (see page 54). Another fantastic phenomenon is the weeping or pendant (monstrose) forms of *E. ingens*, seen at left and above left in San Diego's Balboa Park. There are some famous examples of this at Lotusland in Santa Barbara. The fantastic and very full specimen above right could be either of the two prominent species discussed above. One way to tell might be via the seed pods. Round would indicate *E. ingens* while a triangular or triploid shape might indicate *E. ammak*.

Arborescent (candelabrum) tree euphorbias

We can't really grow saguaro cacti well in California, but some of our big alternative succulents are the tree euphorbias. Many wrongly assume they are big cacti, but these African succulents grow wonderfully in a Mediterranean climate. They are not as happy with the heat and cold of desert conditions and are not as suitable as landscape plants for those regions. When I sell a cute little 3- or 4-foot specimen with an arm or two at my nursery, I tell the customer to first look up at the giant, 30-foot euphorbias that have become permanent fixtures at Solana Succulents so they are aware of what they are getting into. While a pot will limit their growth, once you plant one in the ground, you'll end up after ten or twenty years with something like the big *Euphorbia ingens* on this page. They grow much faster than cacti.

Euphorbia ammak

Euphorbia ammak is better known in its yellow variegated form, as seen in the huge tree at left. It also occurs in the green form, below, which can easily be confused with *E. ingens*. One way to distinguish between these two large relatives is the density of the canopy. *E. ammak* arms tend to form thicker clusters, creating a profile that very little light can show through. *E. ingens* can grow that way as well, but is generally a bit more airy, with more space between the arms. *E. ammak* also has closer spaced and more pronounced thorns, while *E. ingens* has spines that almost retreat into little brown spots along the edges. Seed pods (inset below) are more like a 3-lobed pumpkin shape, as opposed to the rounded ball shape of *E. ingens*. The *E. ammak* below is in full seed stage at my house, and on warm afternoons towards the end of the cycle, I'll hear audible "pops" followed by the sound of little, dry, brown shells hitting the ground around me. Like a number of euphorbias, this exploding popcorn method of seed dispersal does the job, and I'll later find a few volunteer seedlings growing among my other plants. It's nice when they do the work for you.

Left: A variegated *E. ammak* somewhere between crested and monstrose growth.

Below left: Another and larger example of cresting.

Below right: *Euphorbia ammak* has more closely spaced and slightly more pronounced spines than the otherwise similar *Euphorbia ingens* (facing page).

Euphorbia ammak seed pods

Euphorbia ingens

This is the dominant form of the large, arborescent or candelabrum euphorbias. "Ingens" is usually pronounced with a hard "g" but many use the "j" version of the "g" as well. It can get massive, exceeding thirty feet tall and just as wide across the canopy, with the trunk eventually resembling a brown woody tree trunk. Spines are very small and recessed, looking more like brown spots along the ridges, as seen near right. It grows in a bit more airy, less dense form than *E. ammak*, but individuals vary. Seed pods are ball-shaped, larger than the small flowers, both seen in the image at far right. An interesting pendant form exists as well (see page 52). Like all the others, it is easily grown from cuttings, but smaller cuttings (2-4 feet) will root more easily than large ones. Be aware that wherever you remove a branch, multiple new ones will form at or near the point of decapitation, eventually giving you a top-heavy tree that is prone to lean and break. Crested specimens exist but are rare, and I have yet to knowingly encounter a variegated *E. ingens*.

Euphorbia abyssinica

There is some confusion in the literature and on the web about this plant. Occasionally it is listed as synonymous with *E. acrurensis*, which looks more like the plant on page 58. *E. abyssinica* in its best form should look like the plants in the two images above right, with many rows of wavy edges or "fins." While the other large green tree euphorbias have four to five fins, *E. abyssinica* can have many more; the plants above right have eight or more fins. The corky spines are packed so close together that they almost touch, and it is a very enthusiastic leaf producer during periods of warm weather growth. The plant above also is supposed to be *E. abyssinica*, but it looks different, almost like a cross of *E. ingens* and *E. cooperi*, and is four-finned; without DNA analysis, it's all a guess. The plant in the image at right has lived at my nursery for over twenty years (it rooted through its plastic pot as a 4-footer and claimed permanent squatter's rights) and was identified as *E. abyssinica*. It may, in fact, be a cross with *E. ingens* or *E. ammak* as it displays similar spination but is not as wavy or leafy, and the large seed pods will blush pinkish red, as seen on page 46. There is a form that leaves fuzzy dimple-spots around the spines that occasionally goes by the name "chocolate drop" or "cinnamon."

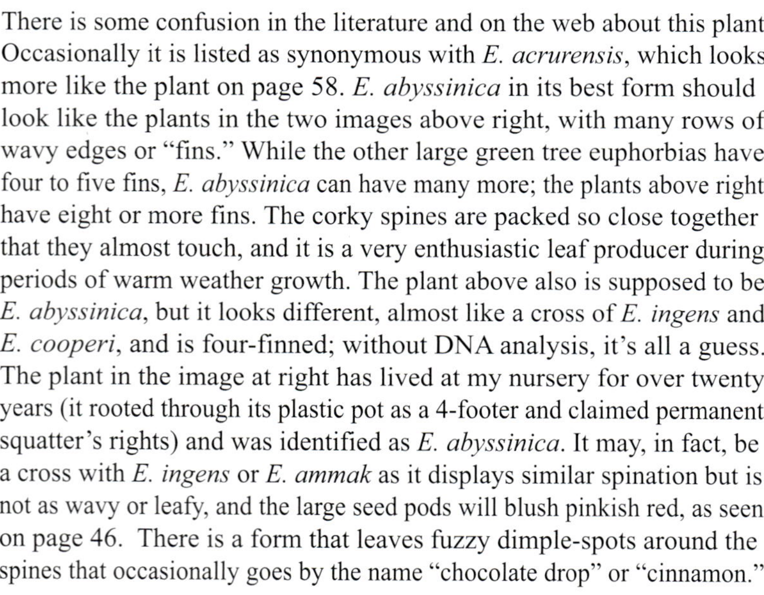

Euphorbia amphiphylla

This is one of the most interesting, yet not frequently encountered, of the large euphorbias. The Latin species name refers to the large leaves that are omnipresent on the growing tips of the plant. It is rare likely because of it being more of a tropical plant, very averse to the occasional hard freezes we can encounter in California. Having said that, there are some obviously long-lived examples such as the two shown here at Pitzer College in Claremont, California, along with others at Lotusland and The Huntington Botanical Gardens. Reputed to be a fast grower in the proper conditions, I think it would make an excellent indoor specimen for a tall foyer room with skylights or plenty of window light.

Euphorbia acrurensis

Euphorbia acrurensis is a true species from Africa, and there is an image of it in *The Euphorbia Journal* that looks a bit like the plants here, which are what we call by that name in California. However, if one were to create a hybrid of *E. trigona* and *E. ammak* or *E. ingens*, I think it would look pretty much like what you see here. Whether it is true to the African species or not, this is a nice plant for containers or landscape. The unidentified plant in the image at left looks like *Euphorbia acrurensis* but also could be a particularly branchy example of *E. ammak*, or a cross. It also appears to have more compacted spinescence, but whatever it is, it is a fine representative of its genus.

E. acrurensis (be aware of that first "r" when you say it out loud) doesn't seem to grow more than ten to fifteen feet tall, but it can grow almost that wide and very dense, to the point of being top-heavy, particularly in green-house conditions. Its relatively smaller size as compared to the other large candelabrum euphorbias makes it an excellent candidate for a large potted plant.

Euphorbia trigona

The somewhat arbitrary and superficial way I've categorized plants based on appearance maybe means I should have placed *Euphorbia trigona* in the cactiform rather than arborescent section as it does look a bit like a dense columnar cactus, but it also has a vertical tree appeal. It is a wonderful container plant, one of the better indoor euphorbias if given bright light. It also will serve as a landscape plant, as you can see with the 6-foot specimen at left gracing the succulent landscape of the Fullerton Police Department.

The redder form "rubra" is shown below middle. The red/burgundy color is most evident in the leaves and the growing tips, not as much in the greener body. It tends to show more color in greenhouse conditions than in the elements. The small, bright burgundy specimen, below right, is a new and apparently much more color saturated cultivar just entering the market. Hopefully, growers will keep this one going.

The plants here have full shapes as they have been grown in sun. An image I wish I had was of a *Euphorbia trigona* that my high school friend's family had brought from New Jersey to California in the seventies, and it moved around the state with them over the years. It was a tall, single stem growing out of a cowboy boot, had always lived in the bathroom with indirect light, and had just the slightest of side branches with a few little leaves at the tip; it eventually hit the ceiling at their last house. They must have had it for over thirty years, always in the same boot, and it endured, let's say, less than ideal conditions, but it was their baby and had a will to live. I love succulents.

I remember first seeing this orange version of the ubiquitous green pencil plant in the early '90s and wondered if it was sick. It wasn't. Just the first introduction of a plant that would soon catch fire (pardon the pun) in the botanical world. Apparently, it all started with one green *E. tirucalli* in South Africa that had a little piece come out orange. It was isolated and propagated, and has since made its way around the world. The late Gary Hammer was credited with bringing the first cuttings to the U.S. in the '90s.

This bright orange form is now much more popular and in demand than its green parent. Although technically the same plant, it does have a slightly different growing habit, generally more bushy, with thinner and floppier stems than the larger, trunk- forming green form. I have seen "Sticks on Fire" reach close to twenty feet in height but have yet to see any approach the massive size and thick trunk of the green form. Perhaps it just needs more time.

Be wary of over-using it as a landscape plant. I've made the mistake of planting too many little 1-gallon orange cuties, then watching them grow and just dominate a garden. I'd recommend just one, or a few at most, and plant them in back, mindful of how big and overpowering they can get.

The color seems to be best in the cool winter months. The plants can go through a period of yellowness, perhaps due to soil, water, or fertilizer conditions, or time of year. I've had individuals fade and come back, others maintain the color year-round. The best color is usually in the new growth at the tips, enhanced by strong direct sun, with the interior more yellow to yellow-green. Flowers are basically nothing, and it is very sensitive to frost.

As mentioned in the introduction, this plant has a toxic latex sap like the rest of the genus, so avoid eye contact if you encounter the white sap.

Stick or Pencil Euphorbias

If you just flipped open to this spread, I bet your eye went first to the burning bush on the facing page. That is the orange version of the plant on this page, *Euphorbia tirucalli*, which has been in cultivation in California for over a century. You can read more about "Sticks on Fire" on the facing page, but it is a shame that the green form is now playing second fiddle. It is a stunning architectural plant but has a couple of downsides. First, it gets BIG. It can become tree-like, so plant accordingly. A potted specimen will only get as big as the pot allows, but that still might be more than you bargained for. Secondly, like all euphorbias, it has a caustic white latex sap, so you need to beware of eye contact. Some folks are more sensitive, and even touching the plant can cause problems for them. I've yet to hear of a story of a human or animal taking more than one bite, which would preclude taking a second, and it is not so poisonous that the one bite would do any harm, other than mouth swelling. So don't take a bite. Flowers are tiny; you get it for the structure.

In addition to the two primary forms of *E. tirucalli*, there are a number of other pencil types on the following pages. The same cautions would apply. All are easy Mediterranean climate growers but don't take well to a prolonged frost or too much triple digit heat. At the end of this section, we'll take a look at the closely related genus of *Pedilanthus*, another group of pencil-type succulents that may end up being reclassified back into the euphorbias, if the lumpers win this battle.

Below: A crested specimen of *E. tirucalli*.

There are a handful of pencil or stick succulents that you might, at first glance, confuse with the euphorbias of that same description. At left is *Ceropegia dichotoma*, which can reach several feet in height. It is differentiated from the euphorbias by its pinched segments, much different flower (you can see a few in the upper part of the picture), and by its lack of caustic white sap. There is a nice variegated version of this plant, as well. At right is another non-euphorbia pencil plant, *Senecio anteuphorbium*, which even gives a nod to euphorbias in its species name. It is a more vigorous grower, again with differing flowers and sap.

*Euphorbia
leucodendron*

Euphorbia leucodendron is a bit smaller and more graceful in appearance in comparison to the larger plants on the previous pages. It has stout, cylindrical stems with more rounded tips that tend to transition from dark to light. It can put on a nice show of yellow blooms clustered at the tips. I have used this plant in "undersea" succulent gardens, as it somewhat mimics aquatic eel grass—if you choose to see it that way. It rarely forms crests (inset).

Euphorbia antisyphilitica has a wonderful name that suggests a folk remedy for syphilis—fortunately, I have no firsthand experience. It is a new world euphorbia that grows well in desert climates. Inset of flowers by Russel Ray Photos. *Euphorbia aphylla* is a smaller pencil type, which naturally forms an almost bonsai tree-like shape as it ages, with a woody trunk. I have found it to be self-fertile, with seedlings popping up in the vicinity of the parent.

Euphorbia enterophora (xylophylloides)

This Madagascan shrub is essentially a stick or pencil euphorbia with flattened, ribbon-like branches. It grows for many years as a full shrub but eventually can reach a small tree size. There is a form known as *ssp. crassa* (above right) that is characterized by rusty brownish red leaf tips, a quite attractive variant rarely found in cultivation. The image of the *Euphorbia stenoclada* with the brown fuzzy leaf tips on page 65 may well be a hybrid with this form.

There are a number of pencil-type and bushy Madagascan euphorbias in cultivation, but identification is dicey at best, and there may be a few hybrids or cultivars that have been bouncing around unidentified. The plant at right has been around for a while, and it appeared to me to be an inferior substitute for *E. tirucali* 'Sticks on Fire' as it is more airy and brambly, with a brownish/burgundy, less flashy color. Over time, I'm beginning to appreciate subtlety more, perhaps because I'm a bit over the bright orange one. This unidentified plant may be either or *E. intisy* or *E. intisy v. mainty*, or something else.

The exceptional *Euphorbia stenoclada* specimen above is commonly referred to as the Silver Thicket for obvious reasons. It offers a stunning silver/white profile, particularly if featured with a darker backdrop as seen here at the Cal State Fullerton Arboretum. Images from its native Madagascar show colonies shaped like small trees, growing in the sand by the ocean. It is as hard and stiff as it looks, so handle with care.

This is a variable plant, likely due both to natural variation and hybridization. The form above left has zig-zag branching with golden brown cinnamon fuzz along the new growth (see inset). This may be a cross with *E. enterophora ssp. crassa* (previous spread), or possibly the subspecies *E. enterophora ssp. ambatofinandrahana* (say that one five times fast). The little beastie above, and much larger on the facing page, is an extra spiny, more blueish-white version. It is Madagascar's answer to the new world chollas. At left is the most-encountered greener form, and the unusual burgundy meteor flower below belongs to what I believe is a hybrid of *E. stenoclada* and *E. tirucalli*. There is a hybrid on the market of exactly those two plants, called "Briar Patch."

There are a number of succulents that you'd think, after twenty-five years of operating a succulent nursery, I would be able to name upon sight, as they are staples of cultivation. You might understand my difficulty after looking at the plants on this page. All are somewhat tree- or shrub-forming around a central trunk with thin green stems creating an occasional full and bushy look. The plant above right looks to me like *E. tetragona*, or possibly *E. evansii*, but other candidates would include *E. grandidens*, *E. quinquecostata*, *E. triangularis*, or *E. zoutpansbergensis*. None of these are commonly grown in the trade or usually identified when sold. If you find a plant that looks like one of these in a six-inch pot, you may be in for a happy surprise down the road. All are relatively easy landscape plants and worth tracking down.

Euphorbia tetragona, Euphorbia evansii, and their allies

The plant at left and the larger specimen at right at the Ruth Bancroft Garden are identified as *Euphorbia tetragona*. I have no doubt those are accurate identifications, but if you look up images of *Euphorbia evansii*, you will see a very similar plant, just perhaps a bit more airy and with slightly larger spines. They both usually develop a large conical main trunk and develop a small tree profile with age. Check out the twenty-foot plant in the group shot on the Title page.

Cactiform euphorbias

Quite a few euphorbias have a cactus-like profile—or, depending on where you're from, some cacti might have a euphorbia-like profile. Once again, this is a purely subjective lumping of plants based on visual similarities for the purposes of this book, and you can certainly make an argument that some of these plants might belong elsewhere, but here they are.

There actually is a species known as *Euphorbia cactus*, and habitat images look quite a bit like the plant at right. Others I've seen have been labeled as *Euphorbia grandialata*, but plants identified by that name look more like the plant on page 68. Good luck googling "Euphorbia cactus" as you'll get a bunch of "euphorbia vs. cactus" articles.

Left: *Euphorbia fortissima* is a Zimbabwean species that is visually similar to a handful of close relatives. The happy individual shown here holds a prominent position in the Princess of Wales Conservatory at Kew Gardens in London.

Euphorbia cooperi

This wonderful African sculptural succulent is a borderline tree form, as it can get tall, but it typically grows tight and lower to the ground, as seen here. The defining characteristic is the stacked "onion-dome" sections, a bit more in evidence on page 41. Habitat photos show an almost cartoonish-looking plant, a form I have yet to see in cultivation in California. There appears to be a slightly variegated or patterned form or hybrid (x *E. grandialata*, below?), seen at right.

Euphorbia grandilata has to be one of my favorite euphorbias, both for the cactiform shape, the fantastic flow of the thorns, the rows of yellow flowers, and especially the reptilian skin pattern. It can get six to eight feet tall but is generally more of a bush/clumper in nature. As always, there are hybrids out there to confuse us.

At left: Check out the new red tip growth. Some euphorbias have new growth that emerges red or pink/red, and it feels like an artificial rubber or latex to the touch. As it ages, it reverts to green, and the spines to a white woody look.

Euphorbia grandialata

Red and ripe seed pods.
Photo: Michael Buckner

Have I mentioned too much already about the variability of euphorbias? Well, the plants in cultivation labeled as *Euphorbia pseudocactus* usually look like the plant at right, which you'll notice looks a lot like the *E. grandialata* on the facing page. This plant generally is smaller yet has similar teeth and markings. Some of my favorite forms look like the tight, smallish, and nearly spineless types seen in the bottom right images. There is a regional form called *v. lyttoni* or *lyttoniana*, but my guess is that a number of the types we encounter are hybrids. A possible hybrid parent here is *E. grandicornis*. All are typical of euphorbia culture, preferring a temperate climate and water during the warm season.

Euphorbia grandicornis

Characterized by its rather spectacular cow-horn spines, this plant can form a sizable bush or almost a hedge over time. It is one of the most impressively armed of all the euphorbias and is likely a hybrid parent to a few of the similarly-spined plants on the previous pages.

The bizarro example at right deserves an explanation. This plant started life with proper sunlight (lower portion). Then it ended up in very low light (middle section) and stretched itself into a *Euphorbia trigona* mimic. It was then rescued by a savvy plant guy and given proper light and is once again happy. Long term it may get top-heavy, but this was a nice save by Art Scarpa.

Euphorbia coreulescens

This clustering columnar looks cactus-like as an individual or small cluster of plants, but over time will grow into more of a mounding shrub or series of columns. It has a somewhat turquoise-green skin color (the Latin "coeruleus" means "blue"), with orange-ish tips where the new spines form, and impressive seed pods that ripen to a beautiful burgundy, as seen at right. It is from South Africa and is one of the more cold tolerant of the succulent euphorbias. I have seen it happily growing in Northern California and desert areas that experience more frequent freezing conditions.

The euphorbia above is unidentified but looks very similar to *E. virosa* (or possibly *E. avosmontana*) with a nice turquoise/ green skin and red spines.

Euphorbia virosa

Reputed to be one of the nastiest succulent euphorbias due to its significant spines and caustic, milky, latex sap, *Euphorbia virosa* (the name refers to a supposed bad smell produced by the sap) nevertheless is an impressive ornamental plant. It occupies a large swath of southern Africa, and the indigenous people have used the potent latex as a spear-tip poison. It is a very low-water plant but is fairly rare in cultivation where you seldom see a specimen as large as the plant at right. Habitat images show some large head-high clusters.

Euphorbia ferox

This spiny clumper seems to be an old world mimic of an echinocereus cactus (or you could argue vice-versa). "Ferox" translates to "ferocious," and the spines are quite sharp and sturdy for the genus. Newer spines arrive in a lovely purple hue, which can hold color in a pampered greenhouse situation, but older and more neglected specimens may exhibit more bleached spines. Brian Kemble contributed both of these images. The plant at left was photographed in African habitat, the one at right in the California collection of Peter Walkowiak.

Euphorbia royleana

This desert-friendly euphorbia often looks like a cactus, as you can see in the image at left. The giveaway is the large green leaves when in the growing phase, as seen here. It has small clusters of yellow flowers, typical of most euphorbias. This plant hails from central Asia and may be considered subtropical, but it is very heat tolerant. I have seen it growing in semi-protected areas of Phoenix.

Euphorbia tortilis

As I am only familiar with this plant in the spiral form, I did an online search, and it seems that is just about the only form grown in cultivation (for obvious reasons I suppose—it is pretty cool). Then I looked up what "tortilis" means in Latin, which is "coiled" or "twisted," so I assume that this is the only form. One of several of the genus with the moniker "African Milk Tree," it shares at least a visual kinship with *E. lactea* as well as the rarer *E. antiquorum*. The images I've seen of the crested form of *E. tortilis* do look quite a bit like crested *E. lactea*. It is a slow grower, but if you can provide a nice greenhouse environment, you may end up with a show plant like the one at right. Collection of Steven Lysaght.

Euphorbia canariensis

Hailing as you might surmise from the Canary Islands, this plant is an easy grower in the similar coastal California climate. It typically forms a four- to five-foot high cluster branching mostly from the base but occasionally up the stem as well. It has typical small yellow flowers, and once established can be considered a "vacant lot" type of plant. The growth habit of the plant here is typical after several years—new arms will radiate out from the base, curving upwards as they find their way clear to enjoy a more vertical lifestyle.

Euphorbia lactea

Euphorbia lactea is more commonly seen in the crested rather than regular form. The image at left shows the variegated white cristate form, with a reversion to regular green emerging. The plant below right is the green crested form, also showing reversions to regular form.

E. lactea, particularly the white form seen below middle is also known as "white ghost" or "dinosaur bones" and can be subject to sunburn, so plant with partial sun exposure if possible. The unusually and exceptionally variegated specimen below left is a new cultivar coming out of Asia, not yet widely available.

Above right is an example of the popular crested grafts, in this case the white form. Note the brown damaged section. As mentioned above, the albino forms can burn and generally are more difficult growers. The plant at right is sort of a miniature crested version. When it reverts to normal, the reversions appear to also be a minima form of the regular plant.

Euphorbia kibwezensis

Euphorbia kibwezensis (technically *K. bussei v. kibwezensis*), much like *E. lactea* on the facing page, is more commonly seen in cultivation in the cristate form. The large specimen at left shows a reversion to regular emerging from the crest, but unlike some other crested plants, the cristate portion tends to win out on this one, with the "regular" portions often reverting back to cristate. It frequently is displayed as a container specimen but can become a significant landscape plant, as well.

Euphorbia ledienii

This narrow, cactiform euphorbia has a nice profile in its normal phase (left), and will, in season, have typical clusters of small, bright yellow flowers at the growing tips. But the real attraction with this plant is the crested form, at right. I've always favored this as one of best of the convoluted crests, and it is a vigorous, sun-tolerant grower, less prone to burning than *E. lactea*.

Euphorbia atrispina

This little red-spined plant will become "moundy" over time, but individually the long spines make it very cactus-like, so I'm including it here. It is almost impossible to distinguish from *E. enopla* but equally easy to grow.

Euphorbia opuntioides

This is a dainty little mat-forming small plant with somewhat flattened stems that give it a visual kinship with the paddle-forming opuntia cacti. Flowers are small but bright red and attractive.

Euphorbia confinalis

This obscure gem is *Euphorbia confinalis ssp. rhodesia* (or *rhodesiaca*), rarely seen in cultivation but worthy of more propagation. Though rare, it is sort of a classic representative of the genus—wonderful body patterning, typical double-horned spines, and just a marvel of botanical engineering to the point of almost looking fake.

Right: There can be some fantastic patterning in euphorbias. At near right is *E. confinalis ssp. rhodesia* (also shown above). Far right is an even more obscure plant, *Euphorbia quadrangularis*. Both of these species are known only in cultivation as container specimens, but images of them growing in Africa show them as surprisingly large trees, growing in the candelabra or "inverted umbrella" form of so many mature euphorbias. It should be noted that the patterning seen here is much more evident in the juvenile form, or only at the newer growing tips. However, in cultivation there are few if any large landscape specimens, so we tend to only see the more attractive small plants.

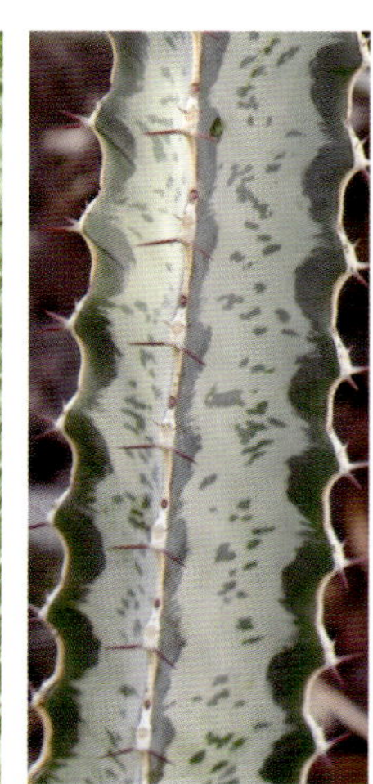

Euphorbia tortirama (*x. schinzii*?)

Shown here is an older specimen grown into a cascading shape, displaying the typical spiral stems. Not shown here is the large root/caudex that surely is at the base of all that growth. This is one of the euphorbias that may have its roots partially raised over time to give it the appearance of a trunk—see the other similar varieties so displayed on pages 113.

Euphorbia aeruginosa var. minor

As you would gather from the name, this is the smaller—and more interesting—form of a slightly larger plant. It has the profile of a dwarf clustering cactus, with blue and black stems and very bright flowers. It is a delightful miniature for small containers or dish gardens. A visually similar plant is *Euphorbia greenwayii*.

Euphorbia knuthii is a compact, smallish, upright stem plant that develops a thick root system over time. Growers like to raise it for a bonsai effect. See the similar plants on page 113.

Euphorbia baioensis is just a cute little plant that mimics saguaros or other larger cacti or euphorbias.

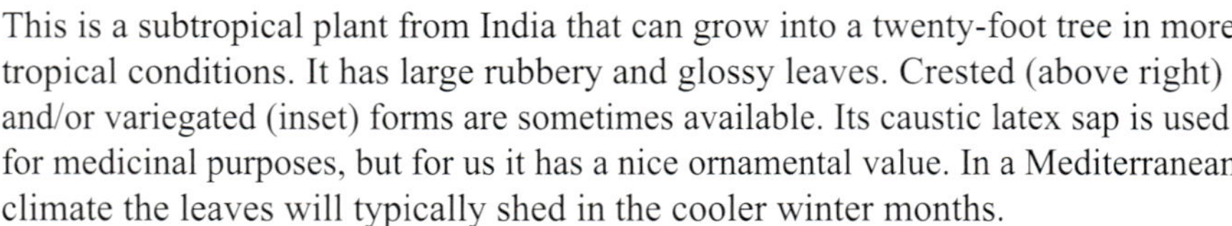

This is a subtropical plant from India that can grow into a twenty-foot tree in more tropical conditions. It has large rubbery and glossy leaves. Crested (above right) and/or variegated (inset) forms are sometimes available. Its caustic latex sap is used for medicinal purposes, but for us it has a nice ornamental value. In a Mediterranean climate the leaves will typically shed in the cooler winter months.

Euphorbia loricata

This is an easy-growing, mid-size plant, best suited as a large container plant. The tips resemble small palm trees with a corn-cob-like series of green trunks emanating from a central stem. Older plants are prone to gray, wood-like lower portions. The form shown here is the most common in cultivation, but habitat images in *The Euphorbia Journal* show a somewhat different looking plant with more pronounced spines. That may indicate our variety is, indeed, a hybrid or cultivar of the true species.

Euphorbia poissonii, E. unispina, E. venefica

I can never tell the difference between these plants. The one at right is *E. unaspina* (meaning it can be identified by a single-forming spine). Below left with the dark background is *E. venenifica*. These are rare subtropical African collector plants, unique with large leaves and stout whitish stems. They should be considered container specimens rather than landscape plants. Another closely related and visually similar plant is *Euphorbia poissonii*, below left. It can exhibit interesting veined and crinkly leaves. Below middle is a staging of all three at the Palomar C&S Show: *E. venenifica* at left; *E. poissonii*, top; and *E. unaspina*, bottom. You can see the leaf differences. All are reputed to have some of the more caustic euphorbia sap, so handle with care.

Euphorbia clandestina and its allies

Volume 2 of *The Euphorbia Journal* has an article about the *Euphorbia clava-loricata* complex, of which *E. clandestina* doesn't merit a name in the complex title but seems to be the most prominent in cultivation. I'm quite sure the top left image is *E. clandestina*; the other three I'm not as sure about. The other similar allies are *E. clava*, *E. pubiglans*(!), *E. cylindrica*, *E. loricata* (facing page), and *E. tugalensis* (even more are listed). All have similar vertical palm tree profiles, with clustering flowers among the leaf fronds. *Euphorbia bulbalina* and *E. clandestina* can be prolific volunteers via seed in California gardens.

Left: The undulating ribs of one of the many iterations of *Euphorbia horrida*.

Right: *Euphorbia anoplia* in late winter bloom, in-ground specimen in Piedmont, California. This plant is easy to confuse with *Euphorbia polygona* and is sometimes referred to as *E. polygona v. anoplia*. To further complicate matters, there is another clumper with more pronounced spines called *Euphorbia enopla* (page 83). I know, I know....

Left: A show plant specimen *Euphorbia fruticosa*, collection of Jim Hannah.

Globoid, mounding, and clumping euphorbias

The mounding cactiform here looks to me like *Euphorbia horrida*, variety 'Snowflake.' It also is considered a form of *E. polygona* by some. Rancho Santa Fe installation by Rogue McNeal.

I've cast a pretty wide net with the three descriptive terms I've used for this section, and you will find plants here that also could be lumped into the previous cactiform section. You'll have to humor me a bit with the arbitrary classification system, but it's the best I can come up with to lump these plants into categories of visual and functional similarities that make sense if you're new to the genus. Plants aren't aware of the classifications we put them into, either Linnean or genetic or visual. They just exist as they always have, although we do end up creating new ones to suit our fancy. Some of those are found in this section.

Above left: Another example of *Euphorbia fruticosa* in bloom, this one showing more pronounced spines than the example on the previous spread.

Above right: This happily-growing landscape plant in a private garden near Ensenada in Baja California is probably *Euphorbia polygona*, with puffy green striped globoid columns and nearly non-existent spines. It has an almost artificial feel and look. You will notice the similarity to the plant on page 80, which looks just like it. The only difference is that plant, reputed to be *E. anoplia*, makes just a bit more of an attempt to form some thorns along the ridges. Both have small clusters of burgundy flowers.

Left: It always is a relief when I photograph a plant that is properly labeled at a botanic garden, so I can tell you confidently that the plant at left is *Euphorbia horrida v. striata*, as shown on the accompanying tag. If you have any issues with that, take it up with the folks at the UC Berkeley Botanical Garden. I highly recommend a visit to that wonderful place.

Whether you see this as an alien plant or undersea colony animal, there is just something otherworldly about some of the euphorbias—in this case, a perfectly grown mature clump of *Euphorbia enopla* either in flower or just post-bud. This plant closely resembles several other euphorbias, including *E. atrispina* (page 76). As discussed a few pages ago, it also at times is confused with *E. polygona v. anoplia*—but that is due to the similarity of the names, not the overall appearance.

Above left: *Euphorbia polygona* in-ground planting near Ensenada, Mexico.
Above middle: *Euphorbia horrida* displays seed pods in African habitat.
Above right: *Euphorbia polygona* 'Snowflake' in a grower's field stock in Southern California.

Below left and middle: *Euphorbia stellispina* (not to be confused with *E. stellata* on page 113) is unique with its star-shaped spine clusters, almost looking like sharp jacks attached along the ribs. Note the new growth showing bright red in the middle habitat photo. Like most euphorbias and cacti, new spines emerge colorful and almost soft, then will lose color and become more rigid and white as they age and take their place in line along the growing ribs. The characteristic spines of *Euphorbia stellispina* are actually persistent peduncles—the stalk that attaches a flower or fruit to the plant body—like the spines on many euphorbias. So while cactus spines are essentially modified leaves, euphorbia spines may often be leftover flower stems. This can be seen in action on the plant at left.
Below right: *E. polygona* "Snowflake" crossed with *E. horrida* displays some exceptional radial saw-toothed "lizard back spines" or "fin ridges," for lack of better terms. This hybrid is part of the collection of Santa Barbara collector John Bleck.

This outstanding *Euphorbia horrida* has been growing for many years in the relatively benign climate of the UC Berkeley Botanical Garden. You won't see too many specimens like this outside of its African habitat.

The "Moroccan Mound" makes an unmistakable statement in the landscape. Given time, it will create mounds several feet high and even larger in circumference. It has been established in California and Arizona gardens since early in the last century, and along with being extremely low-maintenance, *Euphorbia resinifera* also handles desert high temperatures as well as the occasional frost. The specimen above is on display at the Los Angeles County Arboretum. At left is a residential plant in Phoenix.

E. resinifera has a particularly high content of resiniferatoxin, which can be synthesized for mediating pain. This compound acts via the same mechanism as the active ingredient in hot chili peppers—capsaicin—but it is 500 to 1000 times more potent, so be wary of the sap of this plant in particular.

Euphorbia makallensis

Euphorbia makallensis looks somewhat like a minature version of the larger *E. resinifera*. It also creates pillowy mounds but with a smaller and more compact series of stems.   *Photo: Viggo Gram*

Euphorbia mauritanica

This vigorous and easy-to-grow euphorbia technically could be in the "pencil" section, but the usually compact profile you see here makes it more of a mounder to my eye. The stems are long and soft and bendable, but the overall effect over time is a large mound. This is an example of a plant that might be a cute little thing when you plant it, but it will quickly overwhelm anything within a six-foot radius. I have seen quite a few placed in new succulent gardens that I wish I could have warned the owner about before they started.

As an example, check out the giant blob below left. I planted that in my neighbor's yard years before, at maybe eight inches across, not realizing what would happen in only a few years. He still likes it as it is, but I know for a fact that there are some nice aloes and large ornamental rocks now buried under this oversized tumbleweed of a euphorbia. Cutting back these types of euphorbias isn't easy either—they have the messy and noxious sap, and it will look bad for quite a while. See the sidebar below about trimming. Having warned you, it still is pretty cool if you have the right spot to accommodate its eventual size.

Trimming euphorbias

Euphorbias and most other succulents don't usually require or need the maintenance that other bushy plants demand. In fact, I don't think the terms "gardening" and "succulents" really belong together in the traditional sense. With most succulents, you plant it and let it do its thing over the years. A succulent garden is more of an installation project that evolves on its own without too much help. You shouldn't have to "deadhead" or hack back new growth or some of the other routines that many other types of plants require. The primary concession to maintenance gardening is pulling weeds, and of course the fun part of finding a place to add a newly acquired plant.

Having said that, some succulents can get out of control and get big or in the way faster than you anticipated when you stuck that little one-gallon thing in the ground. This is particularly true of the pencil euphorbias, which grow relatively fast. As mentioned above, the large mound at left might have taken ten years from a ten-inch plant to reach this size, but it was in need of cutting back (or removal) in half that time. To cut back a plant like this, you should have long sleeves, glasses or goggles, and a big lopper, and just go to town, mindful of the sap. If you can cut it back to a little globe perhaps a foot or two across, it will look pretty ugly (I love that oxymoron) for quite a while, but given time, it should eventually look nice and green like the plants here. But it will just get big again. Best to plant it way in back or up on a hill so it can just grow unimpeded. Who wants to get all sappy? We're not gardeners.

Above: The "Lion's Spoor," *Euphorbia clavarioides*. This compact gem from Southern Africa is a cold-tolerant plant that is excellent in a rock garden situation as seen above. There is a subspecies *v. truncata* that tends to grow extremely flat and low but also has a very deep and substantial taproot, so be sure to use a deep pot if you're keeping it as a container plant. The little euphorbia Christmas tree, above right, is the very similar *Euphorbia multiceps*. This specimen is a prized plant from the collection of Naomi Bloss in Santa Cruz, California. It looks much like *E. clavaroides* but tends to push into much more of an upright, vertical form.

Euphorbia echinus is a substantial mounding/globoid euphorbia. It is an attractive plant, mimicking a clumping cactus, with maroon or yellow flowers, and is tolerant of extreme temperatures; it can take some cold. The excellent specimen shown at left is growing at the Arizona Desert Botanical Garden in Scottsdale, Arizona. The proper name is *Euphorbia officinarum ssp. echinus*, but it is commonly referred to by its subspecies name. The slightly spinier iteration below is at the Ruth Bancroft Garden in Northern California.

Left: *Euphorbia submammillaris* is a dainty, nearly spineless form of the slightly larger *Euphorbia mammillaris* seen in the white variegated form below.

Above: *Euphorbia* 'Twinkle Twirl' is an old hybrid by Ed Hummel, thought to be a cross of *E. bupleurifolia* and *E. pulvinata*, but I've seen other speculations as well, including *E. suzannae*, which looks likely to me. At any rate, it is a very easy grower, as you can see in this happily overgrown pot. The only thing I don't like about it is that I have to say "Twinkle Twirl" when I talk about it. Having said all that, the plant above may in fact be *Euphorbia spiralis* or a hybrid of. I wish people would keep their labels.

Left: *Euphorbia mammillaris variegata*. New growth can make the stem tips blush pink in season. Although variegated plants are sometimes shy about too much direct sun, I have seen the variegated form grown in all-day full sun in inland climates, and seems to enjoy it.

Above left is a delightful plant that appears to be a hybrid of *E. symmetrica*. The plant above right looks much like *E. obesa* (page 92), but the clustering nature indicates it is either a hybrid or anomaly.

Below: *Euphorbia meloformis* is often confused with *Euphorbia valida*, and depending on which taxonomist you read, *E. valida* is either a subspecies of, or variety of, *E. meloformis* (or sometimes you'll see *meloformis* as a subspecies of *valida*). Both forms can have striking stripes or banding, as seen below and on the facing page, with the *valida* variety often exhibiting persistent flower peduncles that will dry and remain on the plant, as seen below middle. The burgundy caste, below right, may be an example of a temporarily stressed but still fine and happy plant. With more pampered conditions, it may revert to more of the greenish stage seen at left.

Globoid euphorbias

Most of the plants on the following several pages can be considered to be "globoid" or ball-shaped, at least until they age into more of a columnar shape. Perhaps the best-known member of this group is *Euphorbia obesa*, also known as the baseball plant for its round shape. Old specimens will eventually stretch into columns, such as the specimen on the following page, but it takes many years. A closely related and visually very similar plant is *Euphorbia symmetrica*, and naturally there are hybrids between those and other globular euphorbias, making identification a challenge at times. Most of these plants are best suited as container specimens due to both their relatively smaller size and occasional sensitivity to wet and cold. These are, for the most part, spineless or very gently armed.

Euphorbia obesa

Always a hit when first seen, the "Baseball Plant" is a favorite among succulent collectors. The true species rarely, if ever, forms offsets (see a possible exception in the image below), and old specimens will grow into a columnar shape as seen at left. It can exhibit differing degrees of stripes, patterning, and colors. A very similar plant is *Euphorbia symmetrica*, seen middle right, which has more pronounced ribs. To confuse matters, there are hybrids between the two. These little globoids are best kept as container plants, as harsh in-ground conditions can eventually lead to scarred or dead plants. They are not good candidates to survive wet and cold California winters and should be protected from too much rain. Most of these plants must be grown from seed, so availability is often scarce.

Euphorbia obesa with crest.

Photo: Viggo Gram

Euphorbia bupleurifolia

This little beauty is a favorite among euphorbia enthusiasts. Young plants have a round trunk with radiating leaves that gives it a profile reminiscent of a cycad. Chartreuse/yellow flowers are frequent in the spring and summer. Older plants can reach up to a foot or more in height. It can shed leaves during the winter and is best kept as a container plant so you can protect it from wet and cold.

Euphorbia millotii

Photo: Mike Hackett

Euphorbia millotii is a charming miniature, endangered in its limited Madagascan habitat but sometimes available in cultivation. New leaves have a dark purple underside. Flowers are numerous and either capitate or nodding. It is happiest in a greenhouse or protected environment during the cold/rainy winter. *Euphorbia schoenlandii* has been described as a small green pineapple-shaped plant which will cluster over time. Other euphorbias that I don't have room for here but belong in this group of miniature collectibles are *E. neohumbertii* and *E. pachypodioides*.

Top images: Two examples of stem cresting in *Euphorbia flanaganii*. It has a tendency to contort itself into a smile or puckered grimace.

Middle images: Two more medusoids, both probably *Euphorbia flanaganii* in early red-bud stage at left and opening into yellow flowers at right. Note the central Fibonacci spiral at the heart of the plant at far left and on the facing page—a pleasing and frequent occurrence with these plants.

Bottom images: *Euphorbia caput-medusae*, which has a remarkable and long-lived flowering period. The older clump, near right, shows how it can migrate over time, in this case mimicking a den of snakes with heads poking up.

Medusoid Euphorbias

Nicknamed "medusoid" for their medusa-like halo of snaky tentacles that radiate out of a hypnotizing apex, these are some of the most prized of the euphorbias among enthusiasts. The most common form is *E. flanaganii*, seen above and on the following pages. The reason for its availability is that it will form new plants on stem tips, making propagation easy. Most, including such prized specimens as *E. esculenta*, must be grown from seed as they never form offsets. To complicate matters—as always, but in a happy way—is that there also are myriad hybrids in cultivation, and some will offset, likely due to *E. flanaganii* parentage. Flowers are small but often quite abundant and long-lasting, mostly yellow but sometimes white or reddish. Prized specimens are often kept as container plants, but quite a few are suitable for in-ground planting.

Identification of the medusoids can be tricky. There are a few that are easy spots, although even the ones I think I can identify on sight have a couple of visual allies, and then there are the hybrids. By far the most common medusoid, as previously mentioned, is *E. flanaganii*, as it is one of the few that freely offsets new plantlets (usually at the ends of its tentacle-like limbs). However, *E. woodii* and *E. superans* look very similar in my opinion. *E. caput-medusae* also stands out due to its longer arms and unique blooms. And you can spot an *E. esculenta* and be at least fifty percent sure you are right, as it could also be *E. inermis*. So as always, we do the best we can. The plant above left is unidentified by its owner. A guess would be *E. gorgonis* or *E. pugniformis*, or a cross of at least one or both. Above right is an example of a leaf (or "arm" if you prefer) crest of *E. flanaganii*. Contrast this with the stem crest of the same plant on the previous spread. Below are examples of various medusoids at succulent plant shows, artistically presented in hand-built stoneware pottery. Plants like this deserve to be displayed singly, as seen here.

Above and below: *Euphorbia esculenta* and *E. inermis* are both outstanding ornamental plants, with thick, finger-like tentacles emanating symmetrically around a central core. I just wish I could tell them apart. I believe the plant below is *E. esculenta*. The one above I'm not positive about. Over time, these plants can form an almost two-foot radius, and in the true species will never form offsets. That is why some of these plants are rare, not because they are hard to grow (in fact, both of these are very tolerant of extreme temperatures and indifferent watering schedules), but because you must grow new ones from seed. You can see an African habitat specimen on page 44.

Above is a mature, clustered example of *Euporbia woodii*, mimicking an undersea anemone cluster.

If I may indulge you with a look into my book-making process for a moment, the aim with this and all of my books is to be both inspirational and informative—a "coffee table" book that also works as a reference guide. I really want to get all the names right, or as right as I can get them—that is my job, both as a nurseryman and author. Having said that.... I take a lot of photos of plants in private collections, nurseries, botanic gardens—wherever I see them (thank goodness we live in the digital age and I can afford to indulge in my hobby). However, most of the plants I'm shooting are unidentified. I'll ask owners if they can confirm what I think it is, but I often get shrugs. Either the tag was lost, or it never had one, or quite often the owner just wasn't into the names. I'm spitballing with best guesses quite often.

In case you haven't noticed, I tend to bombard the reader with images, and I really shouldn't be just throwing out scattershot multiple images of the same plant or plants just for the heck of it, as I've done here. I'm not sure if the images on this spread will add to your knowledge of the medusoids. But getting back to the inspirational part, ain't they cool?

So let's spitball! Top left: *E. pugniformis*. Top middle is *E. esculenta* in flower. Photo and identification courtesy Brian Kemble. Top right: *E. inermis* or *E. esculenta*. Left: *E. suzannae* or hybrid thereof. Below left: An unnamed hybrid, likely *E. esculenta* or *E. enermis,* or a cross of one or both.

Left: Powdery mildew is an occasional unwelcome visitor to euphorbias, particularly the medusoids. It seems to appear on plants in more shady and wet winter conditions. One home remedy is Tinactin antifungal spray. Really. Peter Walkowiak recommends applying a horticultural oil via a spray bottle, followed by a systemic pesticide. With both remedies, repeating the process after a few weeks is a good idea, along with getting the plants into a sunny and dry location.

Above is an example of *Euphorbia flanaganii* showing its tremendous propensity to multiply, and also exhibiting the beginnings of a leaf crest.

The large image at left is an unidentified medusoid (possibly *Euphorbia inermis v. huttonce*) I planted at the San Diego Botanic Garden's "Undersea" exhibit in 2006, where it has been happily growing ever since. It is over three feet across and I've noticed it is in flower more often than not.

Below: Peter Walkowiak is one of the premier growers of medusoid euphorbias (among many other succulents and cacti). This is just a slice of the plants he shows and sells.

Above: There are quite a few cultivars of *Euphorbia characias*, but I believe the plants above are of the naturally-occurring subspecies status, *ssp. wulfinii*. It is an outstanding mid-size garden shrub for Mediterranean climates, with showy flowers in late winter and spring, as seen above. It seems to be a more vigorous grower in Northern California but grows fine down south, as well, perhaps with a bit extra water. You will see a few other examples of some of the cultivars of this "Mediterranean Spurge" on the following pages.

Below left and middle is a plant I acquired years ago. It was supposed to be *Euphorbia regis-jubae*, another Canary Island native. While it shares a similar profile to that plant, it has much finer and thinner leaves. I believe it is more likely *E. lamarckii*, or *Euphorbia broussonetii*, or *E. obtusifolia ssp. broussonetii*, depending on which taxonomist you talk to and when you talked to them. It is self-fertile, and I find quite a few volunteer seedlings close by, much like the more common *E. lambii*. Below right is the Silver Spurge, *Euphorbia rigida*. It is repulsive to browsing creatures such as gophers and is sometimes referred to as the Gopher Spurge. *Euphorbia rigida* will eagerly spread via seed without help, so be aware you may need to thin it out.

Leafy Euphorbias

Euphorbia lambii seems to be very happy to spontaneously crest, although the cristate sections seem to come and go on any given plant.

There are just thousands of euphorbias, succulent and otherwise. Seen on these pages are some of the more leafy varieties that still have succulent stems and are considered succulent, dry-climate plants. Some are sometimes referred to as "shrubby spurges." *Euphorbia lambii*, above, is very common in California landscapes. I have found it to be self-fertile, and volunteer seedlings may populate around the parent plant. A Canary Island native, it thrives in winter wet and will partially defoliate over the summer dry season. It begins as a single head on a stem, similar to the burgundy flowered close relative at left (*Euphorbia atropurpurea*—which will branch in a similar manner with age). At right is a smaller cousin from the Canaries, *Euphorbia balsamifera*, which can make a fantastic bonsai specimen. There also are some related forms of *E. balsamifera* from North Africa and the Arabian peninsula with similar form but larger leaves, such as *E. balsamifera ssp. adenensis*.

Above and inset right: The wonderful chartreuse flowers of *Euphorbia charachias*.

Below left: The "Mediterranean," "Silver," or "Gopher" Spurge, *Euphorbia rigida*, described in more detail on the previous spread.

Below middle left: *Euphorbia myrsinities* is an attractive blue creeper that is very cold tolerant. It can be an invasive "weed" in colder climates as it will readily re-seed but is less invasive in Mediterranean regions.

Below middle right: The dark burgundy cultivar known as *cv. 'Blackbird.'* There are similar dark-leaved cultivars known as "Red Wing" and "Black Pearl."

Below far right: There are a number of variegated versions of *E. characias*, with names like "Tasmanian Tiger," "Emmer Green," "Ascot Rainbow," "Glacier Blue," "Silver Swan," and more. This brief section is just the tip of the iceberg for all of the cultivars and hybrids of these herbaceous euphorbias.

Euphorbia xanti

Euphorbia xanti is a native of Baja California and is an easy grower in California landscapes. It is sort of a cross of a pencil/stick type and a leafy mounding plant and can reach over twenty feet in height, going deciduous in winter months. It awakens to tiny-leaved foliage in spring, along with a profusion of small white and pink flowers. I have found it to be self-fertile so you may end up with more than you want. Owing to its eventual size, be sure to plant it at the back of the garden as it can become an effective hedge or plant wall if so desired.

Euphorbia cotinifolia

The "Caribbean Copper Tree" is considered to be a succulent and dry climate tree, but the succulence is in the stems, not the paper-thin leaves. It is deciduous and easily grown from cuttings. It can be treated as a large shrub but can reach twenty-feet-plus tree-sized dimensions with age. It has small, creamy flowers as it wakes up in spring, as seen here. The species name refers to the "smokebush" (*Cotinus* sp.), which have similar deep burgundy leaves.

Left: This old hybrid is one of the original *Euphorbia milii* 'Crown of Thorns' known in cultivation. Lacking a better, or at least older, name, I call this one "Apache" since the more compact form that is now so much more popular first burst onto the scene in the '90s as "Dwarf Apache" (facing page, although this also might be a cultivar called "Jerry's Choice"). The original seen here is also a prolific bloomer but grows taller and more rangy, with the spiny stems visible as part of the overall look of the plant. This version is not as available nowadays, as the compact dwarf versions have overtaken the market. It may be one of a number of early hybrids by Hummel or Crosby, possibly crossed with *E. milii v. hislopii*. There is an old pink-flowered form, as well.

This perennial bloomer has large cream-colored flowers, somewhat smaller than the "Thai hybrid" forms.

Above: Another old-time "crown of thorns" is *Euphorbia milii v. splendens*. More of a low-growing, bushy plant with thinner and more flexible stems, it is an excellent bloomer. This plant is not a hybrid but rather a subspecies that does exist in this form in its Madagascan habitat (although this plant has naturalized throughout Africa and the Indian subcontinent). Due to the popularity of the newer compact hybrids, such as "Jerry's Choice" and others, it is much less frequently grown now, but is excellent as a long-blooming, bushy landscape plant.

"Crown of Thorns" euphorbias (*E. millii*)

One of the mantras for those of us who sell succulents for a living is that you need to like the plant more than the flowers, as most succulent blooming events—as spectacular as they sometimes can be—are very brief. Your plant will be out of bloom most of the time, so look at the flowers as an occasional happy bonus.

Exceptions to this rule are the various iterations of *Euphorbia milii* (along with a few similar species) known collectively as the "Crown of Thorns." Some of these plants hold flowers as much as eleven months of the year (I'm pretty sure I know of a few that are never out of flower). Original species forms display spiky stems with clusters of flowers and leaves at the tips, but newer hybrids can look like compact green mounds dotted with little red flowers, and people are surprised to find the benign spines underneath.

If you appreciate oxymorons, there is a "thornless Crown of Thorns"—*Euphorbia geroldii* (right), which is critically endangered in Madagascan habitat and also rare in cultivation. It has the appearance of a more typical shrub or houseplant but offers a year-round spray of small red flowers, in line with rest of the milii group. It is rarely encountered in the succulent trade.

Euphorbia milii in its various forms all derive from tropical to subtropical species, and while they can handle quite a bit of heat, they are not happy with cold, so treat them as a tropical.

The plants here have been potted patio dwellers for their happy owners for many years, and they look like this pretty much year-round in Southern California. An extremely wet and cold winter might cause a temporary cessation of flowers and/or leaves. There are cycles, as seen in the plant below, when they can dedicate so much effort into blooms that the leaves can't compete and drop off for a while. At a later phase, the leaves will make a comeback, with fewer flowers.

The plant below was picked out of a batch at Home Depot by Peter Walkowiak, who has an eye for a cultivar that stands out from its kin. A closeup of the flowers is seen below left.

Giant Thai hybrids

There are several giant-flowered forms of *Euphorbia milii*, generally referred to as the Thai hybrids, as some of the original crosses came from growers in Thailand in the '90s. Most thrive in warm and somewhat tropical and wet climates (like Thailand), and can throw out some amazing flower clusters, almost resembling hydrangeas at times. Most of the giant hybrids are in more subdued reds, pinks, and yellows. Their stems also are larger and thicker than the regular forms and hybrids.

The majority of cultivated *E. milii* hybrids have reddish to red-pink flowers but, of course, growers have tinkered with nature and developed hybrids and cultivars with other colors. There are several in the white to creamy yellow range, some with mottled or splotched flowers, a few shading into more orange or pink, and I'm sure there are more in the works. There also is a divergence in leaf type and fullness, as well. At present, many or most are making their way into the trade either nameless or with conflicting names. The plants on this page were not identified, and I've grown comfortable just knowing they all are permutations of *E. milii*. All are generally easy growers and enthusiastic bloomers.

Most of the vigorous flowering *Euphorbia milii* are hybrids or cultivars. There are some similar flowering varieties that are seen less often, such as *E. milii v. imperatae*, *E. milii v. hislopii*, *E. milii v. breonii*, and a few others that look much like the milii complex but have their own species name. Many of these plants are native to Madagascar, and some are likely genetic contributors to our currently available *E. milii* varieties. Some of the crosses were done many years ago by such succulent luminaries as Ed Hummel, but the parentage data is long gone.

This variegated form of *E. milii*, sometimes called 'Fireworks,' can be a show-stopper when in full leaf and flower. It offers a two-tone green against a creamy yellow leaf, contrasted with bright red blooms. It seems to like it hot and does well with water, meaning it will thrive in a greenhouse, but outdoors you need to find a hot sunny location and be liberal with water in the warm months. I wouldn't consider it an easy plant to grow unless you can find the right conditions.

Top Left: *Euphorbia spiralis* is highly sought by collectors for obvious reasons. Top middle: A particularly brainy-shaped crested version of *Euphorbia suzannae*. Top right: *Euphorbia bougheyi* is a flattish, small brancher. This form might be considered variegated, but I think it is just the more popular variant skin pattern seen in cultivation.

Bottom left: *Euphorbia misera* is endemic to a small area extending from southern San Diego County into northern Baja California. It is a leafy, shrubby plant that can form a natural bonsai. Bottom right: A hybrid in the *Euphorbia obesa/symmetrica* complex.

Container creatures

Euphorbia bupleurifolia

There are, quite literally, thousands of succulent euphorbias in cultivation. The previous pages have highlighted many of the more available and mostly larger and durable varieties. There also are some fantastic, mostly smaller euphorbias that are more suitable for container culture—either owing to being too small to appreciate in the landscape, or because they require more pampered care. If you ever attend a cactus and succulent show, you will see some expertly staged specimen plants, as seen here.

Euphorbia multifolia

Euphorbia capsaintmariensis

Euphorbia squarrosa

Here are some smaller euphorbias, best suited for container culture and displayed as show plants. Above left: *Euphorbia francoisii* is a variable miniature with twisting trunks and roots and sometimes remarkably patterned leaves. Middle: Unidentified, possibly a form of *Euphorbia polygona*. Right: A nice double-headed specimen of *Euphorbia suzannae*. Below left: A beautifully staged example of *E. francoisii*. This individual has remarkable patterned leaves, complemented by a somewhat similarly artistically made pot. Below middle: *Euphorbia mammillaris*, yellow variegated form. Below right: A twisty-trunked *Euphorbia squarrosa*.

While it is true that "the plant is the thing", if you want to properly show off a specimen plant, part of the art form is finding the appropriate, and hopefully handmade pot. The examples in this section are showcased in some fantastic pieces of art, often with subtle textures and patterns, but primarily in earth tones without gaudy colors. You don't want the pot to distract from its occupant. The late Juergen Menzel had one of the finest cactus collections ever curated, but he disdained fancy pots and preferred square plastic or simple terra cotta flower pots. So there is that school of thought as well. I like cool pots.

Left: *Euphorbia squarrosa*

Right: *Euphorbia francoisii*

There are a handful of euphorbias that are fine with letting you expose their roots. As you have probably ascertained from the images here, there is a legitimate reason for such a risqué move. The large and sometimes bulbous or twisted roots can take on the appearance of a trunk over time. As the plant matures out of the juvenile phase, you might notice the plastic pot it came in beginning to swell, and inside you'll find a significant root ball. On the first move to a new container (plastic or otherwise), expose the top inch or so. In subsequent transplants over the next few years, repeat the process, leaving the bulk of the fine, lower roots in the soil. Eventually, you end up with a show specimen as you see here. This technique also can be used with several other types of succulents, such as fockeas and mestoklemas.

Left: *Euphorbia stellata*

Right: *Euphorbia stellata*

Synadenium grantii v. rubrum

As far as I can tell this is the only cultivated plant under the genus name *Synadenium* and, in fact, may be more properly identified as *Euphorbia umbellata*, but as of now, it is still called a synadenium in the trade (although the species name *compactum* also is used. Confused yet?). At any rate, the form we encounter is called *var. rubrum*, due to its propensity to frequently throw burgundy or burgundy splotched leaves. It is a subtropical plant that will leaf out in warm weather and will accept water in the growing season, going deciduous in the cool months. Some plants will offer green sections as well, seen at left. Flowers are inconspicuous, and it is typically seen as a four- to six-foot shrubby plant. I have seen older specimens reach a tree height of over twenty feet (right), but that is a process that will take many years. The only common name I know of is "African Poinsettia." Its sap is reputed to be particularly caustic, and since it is a plant that can easily break, handle with care.

Many people are surprised to find that the poinsettia is in the *Euphorbia* genus, or even allied with succulent plants. It may reside on the fringe of even being a succulent (there are a number of euphorbias that are not succulent at all), but it is a drought-tolerant plant from that genus. You may have found that store-bought Christmas poinsettias rarely, if ever, survive as in-ground plants, likely due to years of greenhouse breeding (there are some amazing new varieties introduced every year). In my experience, only the old-growth early hybrids or cultivars will survive in the California landscape, or even long-term in outdoor containers. The Paul Ecke Ranch developed the original plants from Mexican species in Hollywood in the early part of the last century, moving south to Encinitas in the forties. In older parts of Southern California, you may still see landscape examples of such old cultivars as "Magdalena Ecke" or "St. Louis Red." If you can locate older landscape plants and get permission from the owner, cuttings will root, and you can grow your own Christmas plant outdoors.

Right: A close relative of the poinsettia is the "Desert Poinsettia," *Euphorbia heterophylla*. Native to Mexico and into the southwest U.S., it is an annual that volunteers via seed to the point of being a semi-invasive "weed." It does offer red bracts similar to its larger relative, usually in the spring/summer months. There is a nice variegated form as well (near right), but at present still rarely seen.

Euphorbia heterophylla

Monadeniums

The genus *Monadenium* overlaps euphorbia habitat in Africa. For the most part, they look like they should be euphorbias, with the visual difference lying primarily in their flowers, which often show a hood-like structure. There are only a handful seen in cultivation. One of the nicest ornamentals is *Monadenium ritchei*, seen at left in the variegated form (and temporarily leafless), with the regular green form inset.

Monadenium ellenbeckii is a spineless, bright green, snake-shaped plant that very much resembles a small euphorbia. There are a few others that look very much like *Euphorbia clandestina* and its allies, and *M. spectable* almost resembles a small new world fouquieria—at least in stem until it leafs out.

Another euphorbia-related genus is *Jatropha*, with most species from Central and South America, although there are some old-world jatrophas as well. I am not including them here as they are mostly in the caudiciform or "bushy" category, and don't align visually with the plants in this book.

Monadenium guentheri is a subtropical that grows upright and columnar at first, then multiplies into a cluster and even will form a cascading medusoid over time.

Monadenium guentheri v. mammillare

Pedilanthus bracteatus

Fairly rare in cultivation until recent years, this wonderful statement succulent offers an excellent architectural touch, either in pots or in-ground. Euphorbia-like stems will grow to four to six feet over time, with dull salmon-red flowers that look somewhat like clamshells holding a pearl inside appearing off and on over the seasons. It can have a more sparse and leafless look, particularly during cool and/or dry times, as seen below. In warm periods with regular waterings, it can become a very full and leafy bush, as seen at left, with an almost tropical look. *Pedilanthus bracetatus* has proven to be an easy and rewarding plant to grow, providing an excellent vertical element.

There are a few more obscure varieties of pedilanthus, including the "Devil's Backbone," *P. tithymaloides*, which might be considered to be more in the unusual "houseplant" realm, and a few others that are, at present, found only in botanic gardens. To confuse matters, sometimes the former genus name *Euphorbia* is still used in place of *Pedilanthus*.

There is some more nomenclatural monkey business going on at present. *Pedilanthus* may soon be subsumed (back) into the genus *Euphorbia*. In this case, the plant discussed above will become *Euphorbia bracteata*, and the plant on the facing page may become *Euphorbia lomelii*, losing both its current genus and species name.

Pedilanthus cymbiferus

This is a rather small and unremarkable shrubby succulent with gray/green stems, but it does offer bright red flowers that somewhat resemble a bird's beak. It is small, usually less than a foot or two high, but it is very heat and cold tolerant, making it an excellent softer accent plant for dry desert gardens.

Pedilanthus

Plants in the genus *Pedilanthus* are euphorbia relatives from Mexico into Central and South America. The few we see regularly in cultivation do resemble the African euphorbias, including the white sap. The flowers, however, are definitely different. *Pedilanthus macrocarpus* (on this page) is a nearly leafless variety that is sometimes called the "Lady Slipper Plant" due its unusual but attractive red-orange flowers that somewhat resemble a slipper. In fact, the Latin name translates roughly to "shoe flower," and the moniker is also used as a common name for *P. bracteatus* on the facing page. New stems will radiate out from the base as it grows, eventually forming a shrub nearly three feet high and nearly as wide. There is some variability in this plant, as seen in the example above, with wandering and contorting stems. At right are some examples of unusual cristate forms, which can occasionally form something that looks like a spiraling extrusion. These are rarely encountered but highly coveted by fans of unusual and/or crested plants. *Pedilanthus macrocarpus* is indigenous to the Sonoran Desert of northern Mexico, including Baja California, and is an easy grower in both coastal California as well as desert climates.

Kingdom: *Plantae*
  Phylum: *Magnoliophyta*
   Order: *Caryophyllales*
    Family: *Cactaceae*
     Genus: *Mammillaria*
      Species: *spinosissima*
        cv. 'Un Pico'

The low winter sun enhances an already dramatic cactus tableau at Mojave Rock Ranch in the California desert. *Photo: Maureen Gilmer.*

My personal journey into the world of succulent plants began when I saw a display of bonsai caudiciform succulents, including crests and unusual variegated plants. Cacti were always there around the periphery but not my main focus. Shortly after opening the nursery, I talked with an old timer in the business about how my main interest was in the non-cactus succulent realm. Cacti just didn't hold a big attraction for me. So many looked alike, and they were pretty nasty to work with. But the gentleman said my view would evolve, and it has.

Over time, I couldn't help but notice how nice a large Golden Barrel, or preferably a group of them, could frame a garden. And with the sun behind them, they would just glow in backlit splendor, as did some of the "fuzzy" columnars such as the cleistocacti. Then there are the flowers. Although cactus flowers can be very short-lived, some are among the most glorious in the botanical world. And the contrast of the wicked spiny plant and the delicate flower that emerges from it is truly remarkable.

Aside from the sculptural quality that the larger specimen cacti provide, there can be great beauty in the architecture—in the formation of colorful new spines, evolving flower buds, and geometric ribbing. Compact, clustering mammillarias, angled among rock outcroppings, can bring a little slice of the natural desert to your yard. Lastly, as you'll see on the following pages, some of the most wonderful of the crested or variegated succulent deviants belong to the cactus family.

There are three primary subfamilies of the broad cactus family: *Cactoideae* (where, by far, the most varieties reside), *Pereskioideae*, and *Opuntioideae*. Those words are rarely used in conversation, or even uttered out loud, but you should know that opuntias generally are seen as just part of the larger cactus family. Pereskias are, indeed, quite different. The South American pereskias are considered to be the most primitive members of the family, and most don't really resemble cacti at all ("cacti" is the proper plural term, but I've found it to be discretionary— I occasionally use the word "cactus" in the plural sense, and it sounds fine to my ears). Pereskias are more leafy and shrublike plants, although most do have spines, which is your first clue of their relationship to the larger group. You will see examples of the subfamilies at the end of this section.

Earlier in this book you saw "cactus/not a cactus" examples of convergent evolution. Remember that all cacti are succulents, but not all succulents are cacti. *Cactoideae* is its own New World family with nearly, but not quite, all united by their overall spininess and some botanical technicalities of how the spines are formed via areoles— a diagnostic feature of all cacti that separates them from other spiny succulents. Areoles have evolved as abortive branch buds from which vestigial "leaves" emerge as spines. In the ferocactus image at left, the areole is the cluster of fuzz and spines that dot the plant body in an orderly and geometric pattern. In addition, most cactus flowers are quite large, showy, and soft or papery compared to those of euphorbias and many other succulents.

Above: A large grower's stock field of *Trichocereus* (*Echinopsis*) hybrids in glorious spring bloom in Valley Center, California. Stock plants are field grown, then cut and divided, potted up, and, after rooting, are ready for sale. Trichocereus such as those seen above have been hybridized over the years for their vigorous and colorful flowers. There usually is an initial spring bloom, as seen above, where each plant has a crown of multiple flowers that can, at times, obscure the entire plant. Each flower might be open for a day or two, the entire blooming event lasting a few days to maybe a week if the buds stagger a bit. Then the plant shuts down for a while, and you'll have a few more blooming events over the spring and summer, but usually not as prolific as that first spring awakening. You rarely see a flower from late fall through winter, although nothing is absolute with plants—I have seen some offseason flowering.

Brent Wigand stumbled onto this glorious tableau a few years back on a visit to the wholesaler's yard. No one was there to see it except him and a few workers. I'm so glad he took his camera.

For our stroll through cactopia on the following pages, I've tried to lump the various cacti into groups with a similar feel, again based on size or morphological similarities and not necessarily according to botanic kinship or alphabetically (which presupposes that you know the name of the plant you are looking for; there is an index for that). I like to work large to small, so the first grouping will be the large columnar types. Following that will be the midsize columnars and candelabrum-shaped plants. Then we'll examine some of the hairy or fuzzy cacti—most of them columnar. Next are the blue man group—the various blue cacti, most of which are also columnar but stand apart due to their skin tone (it's politically correct to segregate that way with plants). Some of the "blues" also are hairy, so I just had to pick a place for them. Then we'll look at the various barrel-type cacti, including the ferocacti (my favorites). Next, we'll examine midsize to small globular clumping cacti—the mammillarias are the king of that category. We also will look at some of the orchid cacti—tropical tree dwellers with gorgeous flowers. Then we'll follow with a catchall for a few that stand apart and also a look at some of the rarities that are much more in the miniature, container culture/plant show realm. Following that will be a section on the opuntias—the round-padded cacti of cartoon lore. A distinct group that fits the previous description but sort of stands aside from the rest due to the dense spination are the cylindropuntias (chollas). Lastly, a look at the pereskias. This will be my best attempt in 150 pages to give you a taste of what could easily be 500 pages to be more thorough. You can check out the *New Cactus Lexicon* or several other outstanding books (several are shown on the following pages) if you want thorough.

Hopefully, you already have read in the preceding section on euphorbias (I'm assuming that, by now, you've looked at all the pretty pictures and are now getting into the learning part—thank you!) that euphorbias are, for the most part, averse to harsh, full-sun desert conditions. While there are exceptions, most cacti don't have that problem—they love full sun and triple digit heat. The majority in cultivation are from the southwest U.S., down into Mexico and Central and South America. Some are from more tropical conditions and do have a difficult time with the cold. I'll do my best to let you know of any special needs for a particular type of plant as we go. There are some very cold hardy cacti, either from the high elevation Andes or even South Dakota or the Pacific Northwest. These are not among the most ornamental of cacti, however, and few of those will be discussed here.

Despite being desert plants, most cacti will live along the coast, but ideally would prefer to be inland, outside of the fog and overcast zone. We can grow nice, white, fuzzy espostoa cacti by the beach, but on visiting a client in the inland foothill region, I saw how they were supposed to look. His were much fatter and almost glowing white. I don't think it was an issue of care or fertilizing or soil (maybe a little bit soil)—it just liked the heat. So if you live in the Inland Empire or the desert, these should be your plants. Embrace the spines (figuratively speaking).

Right: Occasionally an individual specimen will break from protocol and do something unexpected. In the case at right, a *Trichocereus terscheckii* decided to bloom in a magenta tone rather than in the typical white, similar to the aberrant red-flowering Golden Barrel cactus on page 176. (It should be noted that although the owners of both plants claim the seed came from the attributed species, there is a good chance hybridization may have occurred.) This makes an already desirable cactus even more coveted, and the owner has collected seed in hopes of creating a new clone to make its way into cultivation. It can take a few years to reach flowering size, and you never know if the new batch will hold the color, but it's always worth a try. We're still waiting on this batch.

Above: A tasteful garden of mostly cacti backlights beautifully in the early morning sun in Vista, California.

An echinopsis is in autumn bloom at ground level of a cactus forest at Cal Poly San Luis Obispo. This old, established garden features some lower story cacti, including many Golden Barrels, along with small agaves and aloes. One level above are a multitude of head-high, clustering cacti, including various trichocereus and several blue or white fuzzy varieties, with some euphorbias for contrast. And all are under the dappled shade of some twenty-foot high *Cereus peruvianus*. Gravel blank spaces allow a gardener some access to pull weeds, but the overall statement is "enjoy the view, but stay out."

Above: succulents can provide little moments of happy surprises when they flower and/or the light hits them just right.

Left: a collector's happy little world of treasures provides a daily dose of inspiration.

There are a lot of excellent cactus books. Some are collectible classics almost one hundred years old, but the books below are more contemporary and feature wonderful color images and proper technical information and nomenclature—at least at the time of their publication. The *New Cactus Lexicon* is out of print, hard to find, and expensive but has some of the best habitat images of cacti I've ever seen. Anderson's book is comprehensive and presents quite a bit of useful and historical information, along with some great images. The *Illustrated Encyclopedia of Cacti* pretty much is what it says it is (although less comprehensive than the Lexicon or Anderson books). If you can't find your exact plant in one of these books, well, maybe you've got something special.

Probably the best website for cactus identification is the very thorough *cactiguide.com* by Daiv Freeman. In the limited space I have here I might show you the most prominent three to five species of each genera—Daiv's got them all, with lots of great images. Some other websites worth a visit for further research are *worldofsucculents.com* and *llifle.com*, along with a number of individual nursery websites.

Specialty nurseries are always fun to visit, and cactus nurseries are among the most enchanting if you're a nature lover. These plants have just adapted so many forms and appearances as they evolved in their respective habitats. That is true for succulents as a whole, and most of these nurseries often will offer all manner of succulents, but you really know when you're in the cactus section. You need to move a little slower and be more careful as you examine plants. Spines demand respect. I've always speculated on whether I could thwart a robbery or assault at my nursery by tossing cacti, or pushing an intruder into a nasty one. Hope I never have to find out. It might be a good idea for an action movie chase scene though.

At right is wonderful collection of red, white, and yellow cacti at a nursery in Mexico. *Photo by Viggo Gram.*

Left: Most nurseries have a "not-for-sale" display section of specimen plants that can give you a heightened case of the "wants." This rustic display is at Moorten Botanic Garden and Cactarium in Palm Springs, California, one of the oldest cactus nurseries anywhere. Established in 1938 by Jack "Cactus Slim" Moorten, an original Hollywood Keystone Cop, it has been in family hands ever since, long operated by son Clark Moorten.

Cacti can live a long time. The image at left was sent to me by Tucson Bill. The carpet of flowers between the barrels covers a cluster of echinopsis hybrids created by Harry Johnson of Paramount, California, way back in the 1930s and '40s. The same plant seen here arrived by mail in Arizona sometime in the '60s, and Bill mailed me a cutting a few years back that is now living once again in California in a form of assisted immortality.

Below is an excellent arrangement of spinies at B&B Cactus in Tucson, Arizona. It has height, color, and wonderful contrasting architecture. You want to plant a bowl like this in the location you plan for it to live out its days as it will be very heavy and difficult to move.

Left: A cactus snowman. A couple of cherry tomatoes for eyes and a chili pepper nose would complete the illusion.

Below: A tightly compacted conglomeration of cactaceans captured a blue ribbon at the San Diego Cactus and Succulent Society annual show.

As I mentioned earlier in this book, despite being the owner of a succulent nursery for over 25 years as of this writing, cacti have never been my strong suit. I've always had some favorite genera or varieties—the various barrel cacti and ferocacti, blue columnars, and blooming trichocereus/echinopsis hybrids, to name a few. And I've always admired some of the fantastic smaller collector cacti that I've seen at shows or in collections, such as astrophytum, ariocarpus, and copiapoa. But even after putting this section of this book together, there are still quite a few globular spiny critters that just have a generic "cactus" look, and the best I can do is throw out some of the more obscure genus names in hopes of maybe getting it right. Then I ask friends who likely have a much better idea.

How many primary cacti genera are there? That depends, at any given moment, on how the battle between lumpers and splitters is going. Different cactus books go into different depths on this question, but I thought for our purposes, I would take a look at how a cactus and succulent club might break them down with regards to show plant categories for its annual show and sale. In the case below, I lifted a section of the Palomar Cactus and Succulent Society's (north San Diego County) website to show you how they approached categorizing cacti for their 2018 show. You will notice some genus names not even discussed elsewhere in this book, largely due to space constraints.

> ***North American****—Ariocarpus, Astrophytum, Aztekium, Coryphantha, Echinocactus, Echinocereus, Encephalocarpus, Epithelantha, Escobaria, Ferocactus, Gymnocactus, Hamatocactus, Leuchtenbergia, Mammillaria (straight or hooked spines), Neobessya, Neolloydia, Obregonia, Opuntia, Ortegocactus, Pediocactus, Pelecyphora, Sclerocactus, Stenocactus, Strombocactus, Thelocactus, Turbinocarpus*

> ***South American****—Ancanthocalycium, Blossfeldia, Borzicactus, Buiningia, Copiapoa, Discocactus, Echinopsis, Eriosyce, Frailia, Gymnocalycium, Horridocactus, Lobivia, Melocactus, Matucana, Neochilenea, Neoporteria, Notocactus, Opuntia, Oroya, Parodia, Pyrrhocactus, Rebutia, Submatucana, Sulcorebutia, Uebelmannia, Weingartia*

> ***Other Cacti****—Ceroids - columnar types, Epiphytic cacti - Rhipsalis, . . ., Opuntioides, other genera*

The first two categories above—North vs. South American cacti—cover most of the smaller, container-sized plants suitable for bringing to a show. The "Other" category is, by definition, broad and not complete but also represents a good number of the larger plants that are too big to bring to the show, at least in their most impressive mature phases. What I hope is that this book will give you a good starting point to jump further into the hobby, do your own research, and figure out what niche inspires you the most, either from an "art-in-nature" appreciation or from a more scientific/botanic angle, or both.

If you're a serious aloe collector, you eventually procure *Aloe pearsonii*. If you're a serious cactus person, at some point you will likely track down and procure plants such as the cluster of little buckyballs known as *Tephrocactus geometricus,* at left, or the cartoonish *Eulychnia castanea f. spiralis,* at right. Both of these are very slow growers and not very easy to find for sale. At present, they are just about impossible to find at a retail nursery. You'll have to pay a lot of money online, and they are probably better off in greenhouse culture, as well. I guess I'm not a serious cactacean yet, as I don't have either. Always something for the want (need) list.

So you've got your huge cactus and your trippy wigged-out crested cactus, and your cactus covered in chili peppers.... It sort of runs the gamut. Here are a few more examples of the diversity of the genus. Above left is a huge *Pachycereus weberi* in Scottsdale, Arizona. It probably was planted as a little guy when the house was built in the '60s, and I bet they had no idea what lay ahead. This happens in California with the large arborescent euphorbias. Above are some nice fatboy saguaros growing a bit out of their natural range but happy enough as street plants in the California high desert suburbs. Enjoy the plants, and get a haircut and some ammo while you're at it. At left is a glorious *Cleistocactus winteri* crest in Piedmont, California. Below middle is a *Mammillaria limonensis* with its trademark post-flower, chili pepper-like seed pods. Below right is a winning show plant presentation of *Mammillaria bocasana* 'Fred' in crested form.

Mammillaria magnifica

Echinopsis hybrid

Neoporteria sp.

Astrophytum asterias
Photo: Paul Lawson

Echinocereus sp.

Rebutia atrovirens 'Haefnerian'
Photo: Elton Roberts

Neoporteria senillis(?)

Ferocactus wislizeni

Coachemiea setispina

Cactus flowers

Echinopsis sp.

Lobivia sp.

It almost seems that some cacti are overcompensating for their menacing and spiny profile with some of the most gorgeous flowers imaginable. They are built to keep herbivores away but still need to pull pollinators in, and they do so with a stunning diversity of flowers, from large, shimmering, technicolor fuchsia to a halo of miniature yellow-gold. You need to love the plant for the plant since flowering events are brief and far between. Like orchid enthusiasts, some cactus owners will plan their vacations around peak blooming times. You'll see some more stunning blooms in the echinopsis section.

Notocactus (Parodia) sp.

Left: What's better than a variegated version of your favorite plant? How about a crested variegate? This cristate/variegated *Myrtillocactus geometrizans* offers two glorious anomalies in one plant.

Inset: *Gymnocalycium marquezii* (*saglionis*?) in the variegated form.

Below left: *Astrophytum ornatum x myriostigma* with particularly nice, horizontally banded variegation.

Below middle: A hybrid of *Echinocactus grusonii* and a ferocactus exhibits strong variegation and appears to be considering forming a crest, as well.

Below: A rare variegated cutting of the monstrose form of *Cereus peruvianus*. I had never seen this until Julien of Earth Wind & Cactus showed me this photo. I sure hope the cutting takes.

Astrophytum myriostigma

Astrophytum myriostigma

Cereus 'Fairy Castle'

Gymnocalycium

Variegation in cacti

The wonderful botanical aberration of variegation is even more frequent or pronounced in the cactus family than in euphorbias. Collectors will pounce on all things variegated, and what you see here is just a small sampling of what they lust for. Some variegated cacti go for ridiculous prices online.

Astrophytum myriostigma

Echinofossulocactus fissuratus

Ferocactus fordii

Mammillaria marksiana

Above left: *Myrtillocactus geometrizans* 'Elite' or minima crest is a compact, tighter form of the regular crest of this plant (see more on page 156).
Above middle: *Cleistocactus winteri* crest.

Right: The rarely available crested form of *Stenocereus marginatus* might be the coolest, and you could argue the most unbelievable (i.e., it almost looks fake), of the crested cacti. It looks like someone made dotted line tracks on it with a white marker. As of this writing—and as of basically forever—this is one of the rarest and most difficult crests to obtain.

Below left: This gem was identified by the grower as *Notocactus scopa* (monstrose crest). It also bears a resemblance to *Cleistocactus strausii* 'Quantum Leap.' Without a DNA test or a reversion to normal growth, it is difficult to be sure.
Below middle: *Lobivia desnsispina* crest, one of most crenulated and brain-like versions.
Below right: The extremely compact and rock-hard crested form of *Mammillaria compressa*.

If you were impressed with some of mutated beauties in the section on crested euphorbias, I'm sure you'll agree that cacti hold their own in terms of offering some stunning cristate works of botanical art. The various iterations of the crested blue *Myrtillocactus geometrizans* (facing page, upper left) are almost a must-have for succulent collectors. Cresting does occur in nature, albeit very rarely. There are some amazing large crested saguaro cacti in the Arizona desert. But in cultivation, bold propagators will take a knife to some of these beauties and cut them up in order to root new plants. That really is the only way to create new crests—you need to deface your beautiful specimen, something I hate to do, but you have to take the long view.

Another delightful mutation similar to cresting is "monstrose" growth, which is usually an aberrant undulating or bumpy way of growing, but not as crenulated or fan-forming as seen in cristate forms. The "Totem Pole" form of *Lophocereus schottii* (page 147) is an excellent example of this, as well as the various mutant forms of cereus and a few other genera you will see on the following pages. Often the monstrose growing mechanism will suppress spines as well as flowers.

Left: *Monvillea (Cereus) spegazzinii.*
Below middle: An extremely crenulated *Mammillaria geminispina.*
Below right: A wonderful example of an unidentified wooly cactus.

Above: In this habitat image of *Copiapoa dealbata* by Ron Regehr, you can see how crested growth can spontaneously occur. There may be a genetic predisposition to crest in certain individual plants, but the root cause is still somewhat of a mystery.

Echinocereus pectinatus v. rigidissimus

Lophophora williamsii

Aztekium valdezii

Above left: Nick Deinhart and Jeremy Spath botanizing in Baja. I didn't ask them to stand next to the cactus that best describes their body type, but that's Jeremy next to the thin columnar *Pachycereus pecten-aboriginum* and Nick by the more robust *Ferocactus diguettii*. Hey Nick, I trend fero myself.

The remaining habitat images on this page were taken by Jeremy on some of his Mexican field expeditions. He has a way of finding plants that almost look staged in their presentation, but I guess that is what staging really is, trying to mimic nature in the best way possible.

Cacti and succulents are often *saxicolous*, Latin for "living among rocks," which provide excellent cracks or fissures for seeds to germinate and young plants to become established. Over generations, many take on the colors of the rocks themselves as a means of camouflage; check out the tiny *Epithelantha micromeris,* below middle.

The famous hallucinogenic plant *Lophophora williamsii* ("peyote"), above right, can, at times, become submerged in mud.

Mammillaria muehlenpfordtii

Epithelantha micromeris

Mammillaria crucigera

Cacti in habitat

Ferocactus pilosus
Photo: Jeremy Spath

As of this writing, my personal succulent habitat trips have been few and local. I've been able to do a bit of amateur botanizing in Northern Baja California and parts of California and Arizona, but my more typical "habitat" experience is a really nice botanic garden or grower's backyard in Southern California. My whole frame of reference for most succulents are the introduced foreigners that live in our benign local climate.

I dream of Africa, but at least I've managed to have the pleasure of seeing a few of my favorite plants growing right where they always have, pre-humans. A quote I love that I attribute to Brian Kemble is that seeing a familiar plant actually growing in habitat is like seeing an old friend for the first time. It sort of blows you away, and I remember seeing a big clump of *Myrtillocactus cochal* on a ridge just south of Ensenada and at first wondering who planted it way up there. Oh yeah....

Jeremy Spath makes it a point to visit his old friends as much as possible and brings back the images and occasionally seed (only seed!) to prove it. Desert trips are a grind, but the reward for us plant geeks is worth the effort.

Photo: Jeremy Spath

You'll see cultivated examples of the *Ferocactus pilosus* above and the *Echinocactus grusonii* at left later in this chapter, but here they are in habitat. The Golden Barrel specimen at left is very old and responded to some meristem damage by multi-heading. We have millions of these in captivity, but the wild population is endangered.

Right: Jeff Chemnick is an inveterate habitat plant stalker—he leads tours to see specimens like this in the places they evolved. This is a giant *Echinocactus platyacanthus* in Mexican habitat, a specimen that must be five times larger than anything I've seen in cultivation.

Ariocarpus kotschoubeyanus

One of the things that may save certain collector plants, such as the Ariocarpus in habitat here, are how difficult they are to find. On this page we have a "Where's Waldo?" gallery of what are the New World's version of "living rock" succulents, nestled into and blending in with the native rock, or almost covered in dried mud as seen above. Below right: I have to take Jeremy's word on the *Ariocarpus scapharostrus*; that one is rare, and I can just barely see it inside the red box. Right: A crested specimen of *Ariocarpus fissuratus* in Mexican habitat. Compare this with the spectacular cultivated specimen on page 223. Photo by Jeff Chemnick.

Ariocarpus retusus

Ariocarpus fissuratus

Ariocarpus scapharostrus

Above: I've never seen this plant in cultivation, and for all I know it is a one-of-a-kind tease, but Jeremy Spath took this photo of a spineless *Melocactus guanensis* in Columbia. I've seen fake plastic or ceramic plants where a designer dreamed up something like this, likely riffing on images they had seen, but this is one time that the real thing looks more fake than the fake thing. Life imitating art, which was imitating life, which imitates....

Below: *Aztekium hintonii*, photo by Jeff Chemnick.

Above: *Ferocactus cylindraceus (acanthodes)* settling in for a cold winter in the California high desert.

Below: *Ferocactus chrysacanthus* nestled in a protected spot in a rockery with an ocean view on Cedros Island in Baja California, Mexico.

Both photos by Jeremy Spath.

Above left: Crested saguaros (*Carnegeia gigantea*) occur rarely in habitat, but there are a few on public display, such as this beauty at the Desert Botanical Garden in Phoenix, Arizona.

Above middle: An exceptional flowering event captured by Rich Zeh's camera.

Above right: An unusual monstrose form of growth that almost resembles a drip sand castle cactus.

Left: The saguaro, along with opuntias and ferocacti, is the prototypical cartoon cactus, famous for their profiles. This one is pretty much how you draw them.

Right: Two giants battling for supremacy at the Desert Botanical Garden. The *càrdon* (*Pachycereus pringlei*) at left is winning the altitude race against the saguaro on the latter plant's home turf. The *càrdon* will always win the battle for height and mass, but the saguaro usually wins out on sheer aesthetics.

Inset right: If you live in California, this is about the most you can hope for out of a saguaro. They will live but not grow much.

Tall columnar cacti

Let's get this out of the way up front: If you want to grow a full-sized saguaro, you need to move to Arizona or the desert southwest. The best we can do in California (desert regions excepted) is keep them alive, but they won't really grow. If you buy a small plant, and if you manage to keep it alive, it will never grow big enough to actually sprout arms in your lifetime. Mature and branched specimens have been imported over the years (large ones are very expensive, as is the cost to move them), and in hot inland parts of the state they usually manage to stay alive for years, but I know of a few old imports that eventually gave up the ghost. Just take a trip to Tucson and enjoy them in their native habitat. Some of fattest and most branched specimens in Tucson are growing in town, sometimes the last survivors of an abandoned Circle K or gas station. The extra bit of water they have received over their suburban lives have given them their robust and often comical excess growth.

You can enjoy them in habitat at the Saguaro National Park just west of Tucson, the Desert Botanical Garden in Phoenix, or the Boyce Thompson Arboretum in Superior (about 60 miles east of Phoenix). Or you can just drive around the local neighborhoods and you'll see some monsters that grandma planted in the fifties.

The saguaro (don't pronounce the "g") is the only member of the genus *Carnegiea*, which is actually an old artificial genus made up to honor the Carnegie family. There is some debate as to which genus this plant would otherwise belong, but it is iconic enough to have its own genus.

In Mediterranean climates, some stand-ins for the saguaro might be *Trichocereus terscheckii*, *Pachycereus pringlei*, or even certain large euphorbias.

Below: A serious flowering event is about to happen.

"Saguaro"
Carnegiea gigantea

Photo: Chuck Rietz

Pachycereus pringlei

According to the literature, old habitat specimens of *Pachycereus pringlei*, known in Mexico as the "Càrdon" cactus, are among the most massive of all cacti (alongside *Pachycereus weberi*). In cultivation, they do indeed get large but are relatively slow growers, at least compared to euphorbias. They don't branch higher up the trunk like the classic saguaros do, but rather from closer to the base, resulting in multiple columns like the plant in the middle image on the facing page. That plant, however, was a specimen removed legally from its Baja California habitat and imported to the San Diego Zoo Safari Park in Escondido, California. In cultivation, most *càrdons* that I'm aware of are tall singles.

Young plants are very spiny along the margins, but older plants tend to lose the spines on lower parts of the trunk, as you can see on the facing page background image or at right, and even develop a cottony series of tufts as seen on this page. Mature specimens will bloom laterally along the ribs with white flowers. If you ever drive through the Catavina desert region in Baja California, you will see some majestic specimens of the *càrdon* alongside the equally tall boojums (page 291).

The awesome specimen at right was photographed in spring bloom in the Catavina desert and is displaying one of the finest examples of fluffy rib tufts I've seen.

Pachycereus pecten-aboriginum

Pachycereus pecten-aboriginum is a thin columnar from Baja California and mainland Mexico. Rows of attractive white flowers yield fuzzy seed pod "balls" attached to the plant, as seen at left and above at the San Diego Zoo Safari Park. One of several common names is the "Hair Brush" cactus, for obvious reasons. Over time, individual fruits will emerge, as seen above, and will float down and attach to animals in order to spread themselves around.

Also sometimes identified under the genus *Isolatocereus* or *Stenocereus*, this large Mexican native is an excellent landscape plant with a classic candelabrum form and greenish-white nocturnal flowers, which may last through the day in cloudy conditions. There are a few more members of this genus in cultivation as well.

The stem of the *P. marginatus* above was cut and responded by growing a four-fingered cartoon hand.

Formerly classified under the genus *Stenocereus*, then *Pachycereus*, now perhaps to *Lamaireocereus*—this is one situation in which I think we should just default to the common name for good—the "Mexican Fence Post." It is one of the most elegant of the columnars. Spination generally is short and compact although there is some variability. Flowers are small, but it is otherwise an iconic cactus.

Pachycereus marginatus has small and infrequent white to pinkish or greenish flowers. The attraction of this plant is its very straight and rigid upright form, especially when grown as a clump of varied heights as seen above right near Duarte, California. It can remain a singular and tall individual (up to 20 feet) or occasionally branch from the base with time. There are a handful of different clones in cultivation that vary in thickness and branching habits. It can be a bit susceptible to scale and is not very cold tolerant, but it does seem to grow well in most desert conditions. There is a stunning crested form that, at present, is still very rare in cultivation (see page 134).

Trichocereus (Echinopsis) terscheckii

Sometimes referred to as the "Golden Saguaro" or the "Argentine Saguaro," this wonderful columnar is as close as we can find to a saguaro surrogate that will grow well in California. It tends to branch out closer to the base, more like *Pachycereus pringlei* than the saguaro. The spines can be very large and menacing, making it one of several cacti that occasionally are referred to as the "Toothpick cactus" or "Devil's Toothpick" (*Stetsonia coryne* is another). The fine specimen at left is one of many impressive columnars at The Huntington Botanical Garden in San Marino, California.

"Totem Pole" *Lophocereus schottii*

It doesn't seem possible that the knobby and spineless "Totem Pole" cactus at left and below is the same species as the one with the almost hairy spines below left and middle left, but it is in fact the monstrose or mutated form. This aberration is known only to occur in a few isolated Baja California locales, in both the fatter and preferred form seen here, as well as a thinner clone known as "mieckleyanus." As is often the case with crested or monstrose forms, flowering is inhibited, making vegetative propagation the only way to produce more plants. Growers are good at doing that, but it must occur in nature only when plants break or fall over and root themselves.

By far the most impressive Totem Pole specimens I've seen are growing in Arizona, such as the stand at left at Bach's Cactus Nursery in Tucson. In California, locate this plant in the sunniest and warmest part of your yard. It is a very slow grower, even in its favored hot and sunny locations.

To add a dose of cool aberration on top of an already cool aberration, there is a spiral growth form, seen below at Serra Gardens in Fallbrook, California.

Monstrose growth forms in *Cereus peruvianus*

Seen on this page are several of the monstrose forms of *Cereus peruvianus*. Monstrose growth is sort of a wavy, aberrant or wigged-out growth form, similar to cresting, but not quite as dramatic or fan-forming. It can manifest itself in a variety of forms. The image at top left shows a thick manner of growth, more contorted and leading to a plant that grows into almost a fat, solid-looking creature, like the one at bottom left. The middle left image at the Leaning Pine Arboretum at Cal Poly San Luis Obispo shows a bit more rounded and tall columnar form, not quite as blue. The large image, inset above, shows a veteran plant that has developed a character elephant foot. The image at bottom left has a sentimental attachment. No, I have no idea who the kid is—I think his mom just told him to go over and stand by that cactus—but this was the first photo, or at least the first color photo, I ever received on a computer. It was 2001 (we were a little late on the digital bandwagon) and a customer sent me this shot of *C. peruvianus* monstrose (we had dial-up so it took a few minutes of beep-beeping and the slow scroll-down reveal) to see if I wanted to come dig it up. It was an awesome specimen, but guess how much that thing weighs! My back told me to pass. A word of warning: Convoluted growth as seen here can provide safe harbor for scale insects. Be vigilant.

Cereus peruvianus

This large and robust cactus has long been established in California and around the world, but its true identity is still a mystery. Technically, there is no cactus properly named *Cereus peruvianus*—no native wild population in Peru. It closely resembles several South American species, namely *C. hankeanus*, *C. jamacaru*, and *C. hildmannianus*, but it is a bit different from each. In Europe, they usually refer to this plant as *Cereus repandus*. My guess is that it is either a hybrid or selected cultivar that made its way into cultivation a long time ago, with no known documentation. Now that that is out of the way....

Cereus peruvianus is the accepted name in the U.S., and once established it is a vigorous grower and will become massive with age—over 35 feet high and equally as wide. It has large flowers off and on in spring and fall, and has a glaucous blue-gray color, with relatively minor spines. There are a number of monstrose forms, seen on the facing and following pages. The monstrose growth can simply cause wavy undulations along the normal columnar stems, or at times create a much more dense, compact, and twisted form. I have yet to see a true fan-crest example. And to complicate things, there are a number of miniature monstrose forms (following page), although many of those are identified as *Cereus forbesii*.

You often can spot ancient monsters poking over backyard fences as you drive around older neighborhoods, such as the beauty at left, visible from the freeway in Carlsbad, California. Below left is the flower, always large and white. Old specimens, below middle left, can develop trunks that almost look melted under their own weight, similar to old yuccas. Below middle are large, post-flower seed pods splitting open and asking for birds to eat the fruit and broadcast the seeds. Below, second from right, is the rarely encountered spiral form dubbed "Vortex" or "Twisted Sister." There are a few images of the spiral form online that look too good to be true. One large plant in particular that is supposed to be somewhere in South America looks like the most amazing succulent of all time. While I've never encountered anything quite like it, the image below, far right, was a spiral form of cereus at a collector's garden in California. This is a digital copy of a film image I took in the '90s. Unfortunately, the plant no longer is there. The owner said it succumbed to some type of beetle or larvae infestation and collapsed in a hurry. But as you can see, this is a real phenomenon and something to shoot for.

Photo: Brooke Parkin

Photo: EW&C

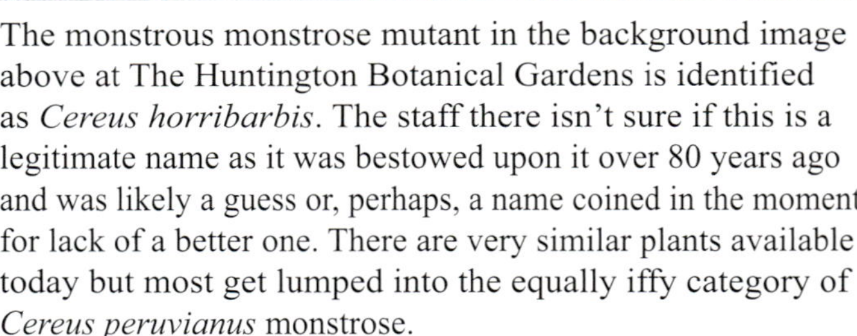

The monstrous monstrose mutant in the background image above at The Huntington Botanical Gardens is identified as *Cereus horribarbis*. The staff there isn't sure if this is a legitimate name as it was bestowed upon it over 80 years ago and was likely a guess or, perhaps, a name coined in the moment for lack of a better one. There are very similar plants available today but most get lumped into the equally iffy category of *Cereus peruvianus* monstrose.

Far left images are some of the miniature cultivars, often called *Cereus forbesii*, that are more suited to container cultivation. The top and middle of the three are likely the little treasure known as "Ming Thing." Second from top appears to be a cultivar known as "Rojo." Second from bottom is the diminutive *Cereus* 'Fairy Castle,' a much beloved cultivar that has a bonsai cactus appeal. Bottom image is the fantastic spiral form of *Cereus forbesii*, which can easily be confused with the spiral form of *Cereus peruvianus*. In truth, I can't tell the difference unless the label tells me.

Left: One of the best specimens of *Cereus peruvianus* monstrose I've seen is this sculpture of a cactus at Poots Cactus Nursery in Ripon, California.

Pachycereus weberi

Stenocereus thurberi

Commonly known as the "Organ Pipe cactus" because mature plants resemble a large pipe organ, *Stenocereus thurberi* is the most prominent of a genus with at least 23 species. Native to the Sonoran Desert of northern Mexico, Baja California, and southern Arizona, you can see some amazing specimens at its namesake national monument south of Ajo, Arizona, near the Mexican border. It grows well in desert climates but is not as vigorous or prominent in California landscapes.

I have always confused *Pachyereus weberi*, seen here in Mexican habitat, with *Stenocereus thurberi*, at right. This may be due to both plants assuming an "organ pipe" shape in maturity, and also because there has been a bit of reclassification of plants between the genera *Pachycereus*, *Stenocereus*, and *Lamaireocereus* over the years. *P. weberi* has the reputation of becoming one of the most massive of all cacti, as you can see with the huge cultivated specimen on page 128. It prefers a desert climate. *Photo: Brian Kemble*

Cereus jamacaru (I love that name) is almost indistinguishable from the more commonly encountered and probable hybrid *Cereus peruvianus*. This mature specimen at a grower's field exhibits slightly thinner columns than the latter, with similar large, white flowers that quickly wilt in full sun, making it one of several cacti referred to as "Queen of the Night."

This might be the place to address the "Night Blooming Cereus" common name. There are a number of cacti that flower nocturnally. Some have flowers that wilt at first light, others with blooms that will persist through a cloudy but not sunny day, and others that will hold through for a day or two regardless of the sun. There are columnar cacti with such nocturnal opening flowers like some of these cerei, and also a number of epiphytic cacti that at times are bestowed the title "Queen of the Night" moniker. The true queen might be *Epiphyllum oxypetalum*, but *Selenicereus grandiflorus* might have an issue with that.

The columnars in this section are a sampling of some of those available and willing to grow in California, but be aware that there are lots of other amazing tall cacti that you likely will have to travel to Central and South America to see at any size. The books I mentioned earlier—or the internet—will show you fantastic examples of magnificent specimens of armatocereus, browningeas, cereus, eulychnias, neobuxbaumias, neoraimondias, pilosocereus, polaskias, stenocereus.... Okay, I'm going to run out of room here. There's a bunch.

Stetsonia coryne, the "toothpick" cactus from South America, usually is seen as a smaller container specimen (inset) and can tend towards a blue phase near the growing tip when small. However, given years in the ground, it can become a massive columnar like the one at the grower's field in the larger image. *Stetsonia* is a monotypic genus, meaning this plant is the sole member.

Photo: EW&C

Stetsonia coryne

Neobuxbaumia polylopha is a wonderful, multi-ribbed columnar from a very small native range in Mexico, rarely forms arms or offsets, and is rare in cultivation. The grower of the regiment above has done well, and has a nice cash crop that looks like they are all standing at attention and ready for assignment.

There are at least nine related species, but the only other type occasionally seen in cultivation is *N. euphorbioides*, which has thicker spines, and only one to three spines per areole, which somewhat gives it the appearance of a euphorbia, particularly as the plant ages.

The "neo" prefix means "new," as the genus *Buxbaumia* refers to a group of mosses—you can't be much further apart in the plant kingdom than moss and cactus. This also is a fun, ten-syllable Latin name to toss out to impress your friends.

Neobuxbaumia polylopha

Sometimes a plant—a cactus in this case—can look almost too perfect, like it was aesthetically designed (make your own religious interpretations). If you were going to make a realistic knock-off cactus, you couldn't have a much better real-life model than a *Neobuxbaumia polylopha*. Old specimens can get scarred or burned, but a young plant in good condition just has a perfectness about it, seen at left. The habitat beauty on this page shows the almost hairy-looking spines of a mature specimen.

Photo: Brian Kemble

Above: Over time, *Trichocereus pachanoi* will form a tall and dense stand, similar to large euphorbias.

Above right: I'm not sure if this is an aberrant form or one that has endured multiple stress episodes. Whatever it is, the drip-castle effect is cool. Left: A properly placed crested specimen will rival any piece of art you might choose to place on your patio. And it just grows and gets cooler.

Below: A spinier iteration of the plant (or possibly *Trichocereus bridgesii*).

Below right: The monstrose form of the plant exhibits bumpy or wavy growth. This seems to be an intermediate state of the plant, as it is more prone to form crests, and crested specimens sometimes will revert to this phase (see the image of the crest with a reversion on the facing page). Viva variability!

Trichocereus pachanoi

This wonderful plant gets a two-page spread because it is an excellent green columnar with large white flowers and can exhibit one of the best crested forms, along with an excellent monstrose phase. I have a pet nickname for it. I call it the "Dude, got any?" cactus. This is because it is also known as the "San Pedro" cactus, one of the more popular of the psychedelic cacti. When I get a phone call at the nursery that starts with something like 'Dude, got any ...?' I always know where they're going with that. For an old guy like me that covets my remaining brain cells, I prefer it as an ornamental, although I think you'll agree that the crested and monstrose forms have a psychedelic appeal. It looks like they may have self-medicated.

At left is the typical phase as a large landscape columnar, exhibiting the large white flowers in late winter and into spring. You will notice that this plant is only nominally spined—one of the least threatening of the columnar cacti. The form shown inset is more stout, known as "Jule's Giant," and is perhaps six to eight inches thick. The normal form is closer to four inches across.

Below is an excellent landscape specimen presentation of a crested *T. pachanoi*—even the columnar section popping up on the left side of the image appears to be monstrose, with a crest beginning to form on the top. If you want to maintain a crest that has some "normals" sporting out, you should cut those off so the growth continues in the crest. If you root the normal arms, there is a good chance that they will maintain the crested genetics and form a crest in time. This is true with other cacti, such as *Myrtillocactus geometrizans*.

There are quite a few ways that *Myrtillocactus geometrizans* can mutate, all of them nice. Far left is the miniature form, sometimes called "Elite" (see also page 134). This is a reversion from a crested form of the plant (image near left). As this came from a crested plant, there is a chance that it has the cresting genetics in it and may yet form a crest. The middle image is the larger form of the plant growing in an extra plump, monstrose, and more spiny manner. Near left is the minima or "Elite" dwarf form exhibiting a purple blush, which it is prone to do, for reasons as yet unknown (to me). I do know that it isn't necessarily indicative of a sick plant— it can and should turn blue again—and it can be more of a light green in warm times.

At left is the most impressive specimen I've acquired at my nursery in over 25 years. It is the large form, with no reversions and a complete suppression of spines, with hardly any dings or cuts. It was about three feet tall and two feet wide, looking like blue lava extruding into convoluting fans—a Picasso of a plant. I should have kept it, or just put a "not-for-sale" sign on it, as it was a show-stopper for the nursery. Instead, I put a "Don't buy me" price on it (not a normal practice for me) but I honestly didn't think anybody would pay....—Let's just say we were into four digits for it (not that it wasn't worth even more than that, looking back). In fact, if you read the attached sign, I didn't even post a price and said it wasn't for sale. Of course, I caved, and commerce won out as somebody just had to have it, so off it went. I gave him ten percent off.

As mentioned earlier in the book, the only way to get more crests is to cut up larger crests. Can you imagine taking a knife to this plant? I hate to do it, but I finally have started hacking up some crests in order to make more. It feels like sacrilege, but the end result is more plants to make more people happy. I'd be happier if I had that big plant back.

Myrtillocactus geometrizans and *cochal*

Almost anyone with a cactus-centric landscape will have some form of *Myrtillocactus geometrizans*, either a common or crested form. Sometimes called by the common name "Blue Candle," it is a variable plant, based on both genetics and growing conditions, but generally is a wide clumper with a menorah-shaped series of ascending candelabra arms. It can be green, as seen above, or more of a glaucous-blue as seen at right, and can also offer various degrees of spination, from significant (left image) to subdued. Large plants can reach ten feet high, but it typically grows wider than tall.

The two-species genus *Polaskia* has a visual and likely genetic similarity to plants in the genus *Myrtillocactus*.

Myrtillocactus geometrizans is indigenous to northern Mexico, mainland as well as Baja California, where the species name is sometimes referred to as "cochal," which also is a name for the small, edible fruit that follows its small, white flowers. Many consider *M. cochal* to be a separate species, but they look a lot alike to most of us. There is a spineless form referred to as v. 'Gil Tegelberg' for the famous cactus man. As you drive south from Ensenada, you will begin to encounter large specimens on the hillsides. It always is a bit of a trip to see such specimens existing where they always have lived when your frame of reference has been seeing them planted as part of a man-made garden.

Above left is another species of myrtillocactus, *M. schenkii* from mainland Mexico. It has a fatter column, more recessed spines, and pink rather than white flowers. It is less often encountered in cultivation, although is perhaps often misidentified. It flowers along the stem as seen in the middle image. The fruit is called garambullo, a delicacy in Mexico.

Above right is a very confused plant. This example of *M. geometrizans* exhibits both the "Elite" (i.e., the compact or minima) crest form, as well as the beginning of a larger/fatter crest. Then there are reversions to "normal," with thinner "normals" in front exhibiting a purple blush along with the larger, normal growth in back. I suppose the proper term for this plant's genetics is "unstable," but it sure makes it fun to look at, and maybe to relate to a little bit.

Right: One of the more peculiar and comical forms of *Myrtillocactus geometrizans* is the feminine yet phallic monstrose variety nicknamed the "breast cactus" or "booby cactus," for obvious reasons.

Left: I'm not sure what this poor deformed creature is. It looks like it is a comically monstrose form of *Myrtillocactus geometrizans*. One of my editors thinks it is an exceptionally monstrose form of *Lophocereus schottii*, and he may be right, but I'm leaving it here anyways. If the plant could think or talk, I'm sure it would prefer to grow up normal like its relatives (or maybe whisper "Please kill me"), but I know collector Joe prizes the weird ones, and this is a weird one. He gave it a good home in a greenhouse.

Above: A grower's field stock of crested *Myrtillocactus geometrizans* oozing up out of the ground. A good
propagator will take a knife to it and turn it into more plants. Note the reversions to normal growth at right.

Here is a sample harem of hairies. In some cases the "hair" really resembles hair, different and ancillary from the actual spines. In other cases, the spines are so fine and white that they provide the illusion of hair, but are, in fact, quite stiff and sharp.

Above left is an opuntia that appeared in cultivation a while back, and most of us were stumped as to its name or origin. Mark Sitter of B&B Cactus Farm in Tucson, Arizona, has done the research, and he says it is *Opuntia pailana* from the Sierra de la Pailana in Mexico. This variety is apparently stuck in a permanent juvenile form, unable to flower. It does better in desert heat and away from the coast, and is sometimes referred to as the "ghost cactus."

Top middle is *Lobivia formosa*, and below middle is *Denmoza rhodacantha*. Above right is *Pilosocereus palmeri*, which can trend to blue, but you wouldn't know it for all that fuzz. At right is a naturally white/cinnamon and cresting form of *Espostoa mirabilis*. Left is a crested specimen of *Espostoa lanata* at Kew Gardens in London.

Pilosocereus pachycladus
Pilosocereus palmeri

There are quite a few hairy cacti. This sometimes comical characteristic has several functions—it keeps plants in very dry climates from transpiring moisture in hot conditions and also serves as a reflective surface, using the white covering to bounce away excessive solar radiation. Some may also serve as moisture collectors, but for us, the benefit is that they are just weird and cool little (sometimes big) conversation starters. Quite a few are called the "old man" or "old lady" cacti (more on that later).

Featured on this page are two of the pilosocereus species from South America, *P. pachycladus* and *P. palmeri*, which I find hard to differentiate. Technically, these plants are supposed to have the prefix "pseudo" in front of the genus name, but in practice most of us dispense with the extra two syllables—it's enough of a mouthful with six. Most of these are also blue-skinned cacti, which will be covered in more detail in a few pages in their own section. Younger plants generally don't display so much cottony hair, but older ones, as seen here, tend to bush out extensively on the upper portions of the plant.

Oreocereus and *Espostoa*

The genera *Oreocereus* and *Espostoa* are the predominant hairy groups from South America, and the hairy members of each can be difficult to distinguish. Some are from higher elevations, and many are so covered in "hair" that the stout columnar stems and even the large spines cannot be seen. But beware, as you can see in the image of the new growth at bottom left, there are some nasty spines deviously lying in wait under cover of such softness that you almost want to pet it—but don't.

Several species of these stout, middling height columnars are referred to as the Old Man (or Woman) of the Andes. The most common in cultivation is *O. trollii* from Argentina and *O. celsianus*, which generally has a little more see-through green, as illustrated at right. A shorter but more vigorous clumping form is *O. doelzianus*, below right.

Cephalocereus senilis

Cephalocereus senilis is, perhaps, the best known of the shaggy set. This is the prototypical "old man" hairy cactus with hairs up to five inches long, more prominent on the top half to third of the plant. Rarely over five to six feet tall in cultivation, and usually singular, older plants are less hairy on the lower part of the stem. This native of eastern Mexico is endangered in habitat but often grown in cultivation. Flowers are nocturnal and whitish-yellow. I still have a tough time differentiating it from *Oreocereus trollii*, at least from a distance.

Above: A foggy day at Lotusland in Santa Barbara accentuates the ghostly profiles of this white, fuzzy cacti garden. The tall, thinner columnars at left are the "Silver Torch" *Cleistocactus strausii* (or possibly the very similar *C. hyalacanthus*). The stouter columnars at right are a tribe of *Oreocereus*, and the mounding creatures in front are mature clumps of mammillarias, primarily *M. geminispina*. You will see a few more hairy mammillarias a bit later in the book.

Cleistocactus strausii

The classic "Silver Torch" cactus is perhaps the finest of the fuzzy columnars, particularly for its almost glowing white profile when backlit. It will cluster from the base with age and has a very generous blooming event in late winter or early spring. Flowers arrive in tubular clusters along a considerable length of stem and are usually a bright candy magenta as seen in the bottom right image. It is a South American native from a summer-wet/winter-dry climate, but seems to adapt well to California landscapes.

Cleistocactus hyalacanthus is similar but has more pronounced spines (seen below left) although some sources consider it synonymous with *C. strausii*.

You'll notice a common denominator on the various cleistocacti above: They backlight! There are a number of cactus groups that show this feature, in particular the chollas, but most cleistocacti can really glow when the sun is behind them, so be mindful of that if you're placing them in a cactus garden. They also have delightful flowers in season.

Top left: *Cleistocactus strausii* crested form. Top middle: *Cleistocactus ritteri*. Top right: *Cleistocactus strausii*.
Below left: *Cleistocactus brookeae*. Below middle is a likely hybrid of *C. ritteri*. Below right is *C. samaipatanus*.

The prefix "cleisto" means "closed," referring to the tubular flowers that just barely open at the ends for a short time; they spend most of their brief existence looking more like colorful closed cylinders.

Above: An unidentifed golden-brown "fuzzy,"
possibly a *Haageocereus*.

Cleistocactus smaragdiflorus
Photo: Brian Kemble

Sometimes growers get their hands on an unidentified delight and have to try to figure out what they have. I've owned a nursery for many years and have done a bit of detective work myself, which usually consists of asking anyone that I think knows more than me about certain types of plants. I'll also send out images to get opinions. The opinion on this delightful bloomer above and below is that it is a *Cleistocactus hyalacanthus* (which may be a synonym for, or a species related to, *C. strausii*) hybrid, perhaps crossed with a haageocereus. It blooms several times a year, with large round fruits after the flowers.

Bergerocactus emoryi is the sole member of its genus and is prolific along the west coast of Baja California. Sometimes called the "Golden Cactus," it resembles a sprawling form of cleistocactus, exhibiting a two-tone gold/brown as new growth contrasts with older sections. The habitat image below middle shows it growing alongside *Dudleya brittonii* near Rosarito Beach in Baja California. The stand at left is growing in the splendid Baja Hill of the San Diego Zoo Safari Park. *Cleistocactus icosagonus* (below right) is a warm-colored plant with orange flowers.

The impressive banded cactus above is on display in the columnar cactus garden at Lotusland in Montecito, California. It is identified there as *Haageocereus versicolor*. That genus is rare in cultivation; it is from an extremely harsh and low rainfall part of Peru's Pacific Coast.

Succulents, more so than most other types of plants, can bring a little humor or weirdness into our lives. Some of them just seem like little sentient ambassadors of the plant kingdom keeping an eye on us. This little cluster of *Micranthocereus purpureus* isn't often in bloom. Most of the year they look like a colony of little fuzzy-headed, limbless creatures. Then the purple "eye" flowers pop out, and they look more like a gaggle of alien meerkats on the lookout for predators. Whenever I walk by them in this stage, it really feels like they're looking at me with way too many eyeballs. It sort of makes me smile and feel a little creeped out at the same time.

Micranthocereus are from Brazil and are somewhat tropical in nature. They are not common in cultivation and may have trouble with wet winters, at least as in-ground plants.

Left: Blue *Pilosocereus pachycladus* snuggling up with winter blooming aloes. Cacti and other succulents can cohabitate and complement each other wonderfully in California. Cool winter conditions bring out the color in many plants, and it is also the primary blooming time of year for many succulents, including most aloes. I find I take some of my best images this time of year, for the reasons above and maybe just the angle of the sun and the clarity of the air. And as I've mentioned before, aloes and agaves are certainly excellent statement succulents. I hope you can do some research about those groups, as well. Have I already mentioned my other book about those plants? Just askin'....

When we use the term "blue" in the plant world, we typically are talking about a plant that is sort of grayish-blue, or "glaucescent." Some are truly blue, or at least a vibrant light sky blue. This is the case with a number of agaves, palms, cycads, and conifers, and in particular, some of the columnar cacti seen on these pages. Years ago I installed a temporary blue garden at a local garden show using entirely blue plants such as those listed above, along with an assortment of white succulents and non-succulent shrubs ("non-succulent" is a term those of us in the succulent world use on occasion when referring to those *other* plants). That blue garden was very a pleasing and serene thing to look at, and that is the case with the blue columnars of various genera on the following pages. You can't help but see them and smile.

Above and right: *Pseudopilosocereus azureus* might be the most common blue cactus in cultivation, characterized by its color and short, almost fuzzy yellow spines. As you can see at right, it can get quite large, and like many cacti is an excellent specimen to locate where it can be backlit, as seen here. The low winter sun and cool temperatures bring out the best color and lighting.

The majority of blue columnar cacti are of the genus *Pilosocereus* and are South American in origin. You sometimes will encounter the older and now improper spelling of *Pilocereus*.

The plants in the images above left and right appear to be *Pilosocereus azureus*. The larger colony above middle may be *Pilosocereus pachycladus* as it exhibits a bit more of the fuzzy white hair. The hairiest blue cactus is probably the "Woolly Torch," *Pilosocereus leucocephalus*, seen in the section on hairy cactus on page 161.

Left: *Pilosocereus glaucescens* (?).

Right: *Browningia hertlingiana*, also featured at size on the facing page.

Browningia hertlingiana

Browningia hertlingiana always has been one of my favorite blue cactus. The genus was named after botanist W.E. Browning, and most of the species are, indeed, closer to brown than blue, but not this one. I have seen it labeled on occasion with the genus name *Azureocereus*, which would be a more descriptive name, but I'm not sure if it is accepted yet. Some examples of this plant are much more gray than blue, which might be due to conditions or genetic variability. You rarely will see as tall and impressive an example in a private collection as this eight-foot tall colony at Lotusland in Santa Barbara, California.

Left: A *Pilosocereus azureus* growing happily in a Los Angeles suburb. You can see that the plant had been previously cut or otherwise damaged, resulting in multiple new blue arms emanating from the cuts. This makes for a fuller plant, which may become too top heavy with age.

Above middle: A monstrose and miniature version of the same plant, also showing interesting patterning, above right.

Below: A vertical stem cephalium on a mature *Austrocephalocereus estevesii* (a.k.a. *Micranthocereus estevesii*, a.k.a. *Siccobaccatus insigniflorus*).

Below right: Post-flower seed pods on this pilosocereus will split open to display little black seeds embedded in a dayglow magenta explosion of fruit. Come and get it.

Above left and right: I believe these blue fuzzies are *Pilosocereus palmeri* or *P. leucocephalum*, both sometimes dubbed the "Woolly Torch," but they were not labeled so that is a best guess.

Left: The best (and really only) blue barrel, *Ferocactus glaucescens*, which you will see more of on the following pages. There also are a few blueish melocacti.

Above: A rare example of a red-flowered form of the Golden Barrel, *Echinocactus grusonii*. It likely is an accidental cross with a ferocactus—my guess would be *F. wislizeni* based on the flowers, but the seed parent was definitely *E. grusonii*. Although rare, there are some intergeneric crosses between those closely related genera. From what I've found, this particular plant is one-of-a-kind. We're hoping the owner will collect seed and that it comes up true.

Top right: A spiral assembly line of flower buds on *Ferocactus glaucescens*.
Middle: *Ferocactus diguettii*.
Below right: *Echinocactus platyacanthus* (*E. palmeri*??) shows an impressive bramble of unfolding spines.

Ferocactus glaucescens in the foreground, *Echinocactus grusonii* behind, at Cal Poly San Luis Obispo.

There are a number of genera that can fit into the loose category of "barrel cactus." Implicit in the term would be an exceptionally fat and large plant that would fit the profile of a beachball, perhaps in old age elongating into a true barrel shape. One group in which nearly all the species would fit this description are the ferocacti, a personal favorite of mine. And, of course, the echinocacti, which have one famous member that has the title in the name—the Golden Barrel, *Echinocatus grusonii*. We'll take a quick tour of some of the primary members on the following pages. Most are solitary statement plants, although some will clump with age. If you're planting an in-ground succulent/cactus garden, consider these iconic desert sentinels as some of your foundation plants.

Ferocactus glaucescens

Left: A spring bloom on a rare spineless (enermis) form of *Ferocactus glaucescens*. The same specimen is shown below in full profile. Normally I'd recommend repotting a plant that has so overgrown its pot, but this grower has figured it out.

Below left is a cluster of the more typical spiny form. Older specimens sometimes show a banded pattern.

Photo: Shawn Perkin

Top left and above is *Ferocactus diguettii*, endemic to Baja California. It eventually will grow out of the round beachball shape (seen top left at the Baja Garden at the San Diego Zoo Safari Park in Escondido, California) and grow as a fat columnar. Old habitat specimens can grow to over ten feet in height, but that is rarely seen in cultivation. The vertical cliff configuration above is a natural phenomenon in northern Baja California. The image actually looks more believable if it's flipped on its side, but this is how they sometimes grow.

Left middle and bottom: *Ferocactus schwarzii* displays a symmetrical perfection.

Above left: *Ferocactus pottsii*.
Above middle: The very impressively armored *Ferocactus emoryi v. rectispinus*, also a Baja California native. I guess if you're going to have spines, why not go all in?
Above right: I can't remember where or when I took this image and am not entirely sure if it is a ferocactus, but I love the plant and include it here unidentified just for the mystery of it.
Right: After a number of years, many globose cacti will stretch into chunky columnars, as this *Ferocactus gracilis* has done at the San Diego Zoo Safari Park.
Below: *Ferocactus macrodiscus*. Nice flowers! Photo: Michael Sousa, Plants for the Southwest.

Top left: *Ferocactus herrerae* often displays a spiral growth pattern.

Top middle: *Ferocactus pilosus*.

Top right: *Ferocactus acanthodes*.

Left and below: *Ferocactus wislizeni* is a robust grower from the southwest U.S. with excellent flowers followed by copious yellow fruit (inset). There is quite a bit of regional variability with this species in terms of spines and body shape, as there is with the genus in general.

Ferocactus pilosus (stainseii)
Photo: Steve Rausch

There are a handful of different red-spined ferocacti. The best and brightest forms are *Ferocactus pilosus*, *F. gracilis*, and *F. latispinus*. There are a few others that have outlier reddish iterations, such as *F. chrysacanthus*. *Ferocactus cylindraceus* usually has a nice red profile, particularly with the new spines on top. This is true with all of these plants—new spines show more color. Within the *F. gracilis* complex, there is also some variability, both in the color intensity, size, and profusion of the spines, which can flatten out to rival those of *F. latispinus*.

Top left: *Ferocactus gracilis* in habitat, Cataviña Desert, Baja California. *Photo: Viggo Gram.*
Second from top: *Ferocactus pilosus* showing a star spine pattern. *Photo: Gerhard Bock.*
Middle: A habitat shot from the Cataviña Desert, possibly a young *F. gracilis v. gracilis.*
Second from bottom: *Ferocactus gracilis*. *Photo: Viggo Gram.*
Bottom: *F. cylindraceus Photo: Viggo Gram.*

Ferocactus pilosus

Ferocactus pilosus is a popular red barrel, which can become columnar with age (see the habitat example on page 137 or the mature cultivated specimen on the facing page). There are several different varieties and other names associated with it, including *F. stainesii* and *F. pringelii.* It is endemic to a large swath of northern Mexico. One distinguishing feature of this plant vs. the similar red barrel *F. gracilis* is that it usually displays fine "hairs" around the spines, as you can see above.

Ferocactus gracilis has several synonyms and a few subspecies, so identification is not always easy. It also is called *F. viscainensis,* or that name is sometimes referred to as a subspecies, along with *ssp. gracilis, coloratus, gatesii,* and *peninsulae....* What I can say with certainty is that most iterations are impressive and easy growers, usually with red spines and yellow or red/yellow flowers. Its native range is primarily the central Baja California peninsula.

Ferocactus pilosus

Ferocactus gracilis v. coloratus

One of the most popular and available of the ferocacti, *F. latispinus*, boasts rigid, wide ("*flat*-ispinus") and downward-curving spines, emerging red but eventually fading with age to orange and then to gray-brown. It usually has beautiful purple flowers (above), giving it a terrific one-two punch of nasty and pretty. There is a creamy yellow-spined version occasionally available (below; identified as *v. flavispinus*) that displays yellow flowers as well.

Ferocactus latispinus

Ferocactus cylindraceus

If you take a walkabout in the desert, at times you will stumble upon what looks like a natural arrangement with an eye to design. Attribute it as you will, it is wonderful to stumble upon these random tableaus. Michael Buckner found this bouquet of *Ferocactus cylindraceus*, echinocereus, and agaves in the Colorado Desert in eastern San Diego County. A synonym or older name for this plant is *Ferocactus acanthodes*. It is one of the finest of the cacti from the California desert regions, extending into the neighboring southwestern states. It usually is a red barrel, but some individuals lack color, or the color has dissipated due to stressful conditions. If you see one of these in the wild, take a picture but leave it be. Not only is it unethical to dig a plant up from habitat, but habitat plants don't generally do well when brought into pampered or more coastal conditions. They are sometimes available as seed-grown starter plants.

Above: A habitat image of *Ferocactus cylindraceus* resplendently red against the desert sky.

Known as the San Diego Barrel Cactus, *F. viridescens* is our precious little native cactus from my neck of the woods. It may not be the most ornamental of the ferocacti, but it's ours. The name refers to the green-yellow flowers. There are two recognized subspecies, *ssp. viridescens* and *ssp. littoralis*, the latter of which is from coastal northern Baja California. This cactus is rarely available, but should be grown more often from seed to meet the demand of the nativists.

Ferocactus pottsii is a smaller barrel from a subtropical, deciduous pine forest region in Mexico. New spines on juvenile specimens appear long and, sometimes, red, but older plants have shorter spines, as seen in the photo above right, where the plant seems to have acclimated nicely at the Ruth Bancroft Garden in Walnut Creek, California. I'm looking for someone to name another new species *Ferocactus ralphmalphii* or *Ferocactus richiecunninghamii*. Get it? Happy Days? *F. fonzii*?? See, if I wasn't self-published, an editor would have made me delete that punny attempt at humor.

Left: Unique among the ferocacti, *Ferocactus robustus* is a dense, clustering plant that can occupy a significant portion of real estate after a time.

Below: *Ferocactus histrix. Photo: Gerhard Bock.*

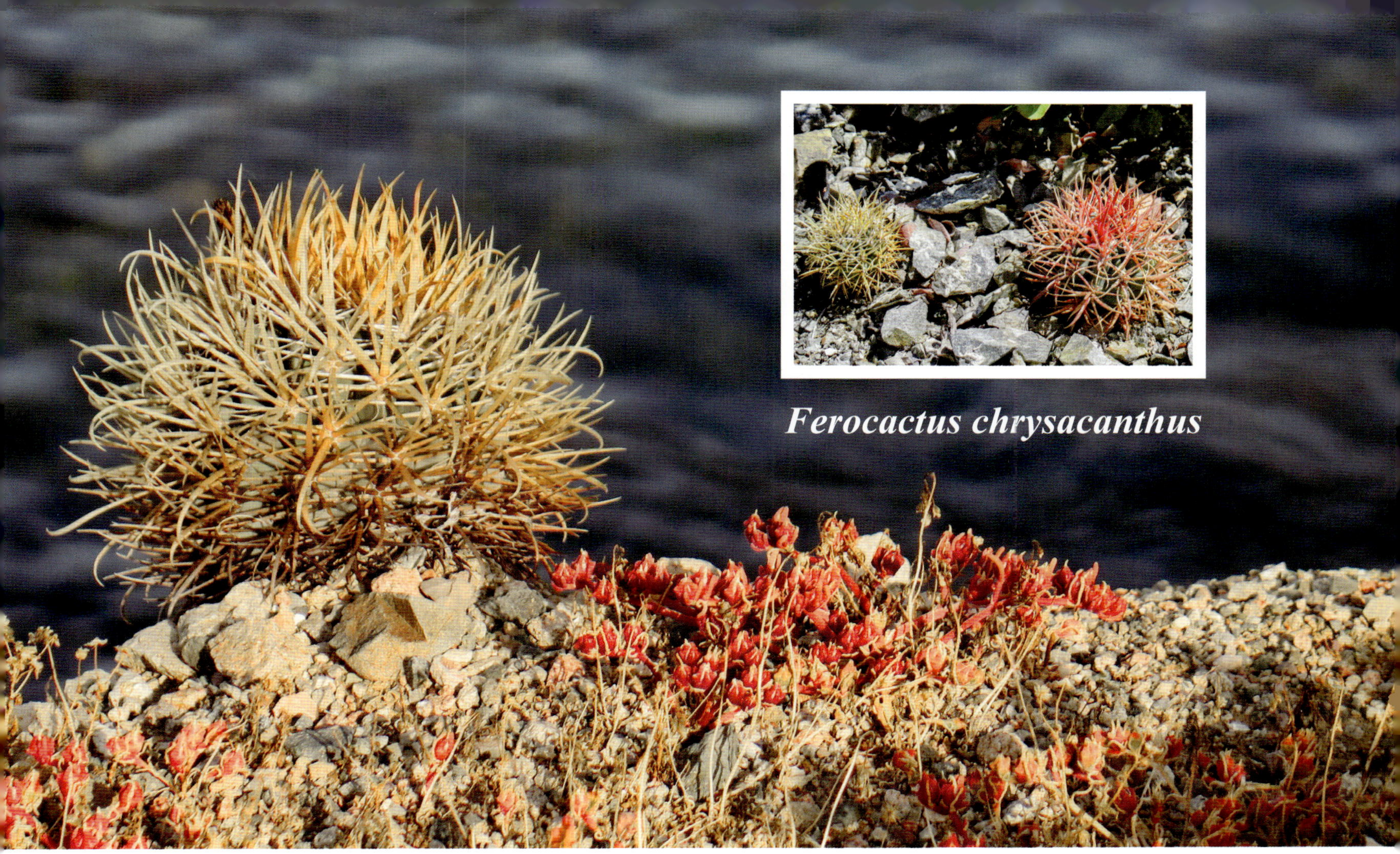

Ferocactus chrysacanthus

Ferocactus chrysacanthus is endemic to Cedros Island off the west coast of Baja California. It rivals the Golden Barrel with dense yellow-gold spines but has more of a hooked tip. It still is rare in cultivation but is a favorite of collectors. There is an even more rare red-spined version of this plant as well, shown in the inset above as seedlings in habitat. The young plant above overlooks the Pacific on a leeward cliff on the island; erosion someday may deposit it into the sea. Below right is a densely spined youngster, also in habitat. Below left is a happily cultivated specimen, greenhouse-grown in Tucson, Arizona. Below middle are the flowers.

Photo: Viggo Gram

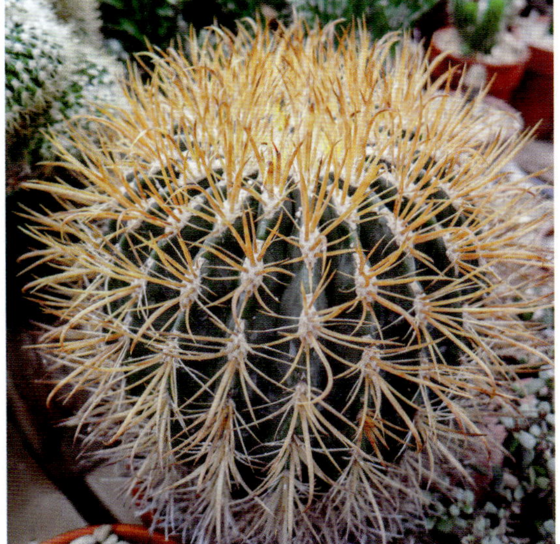

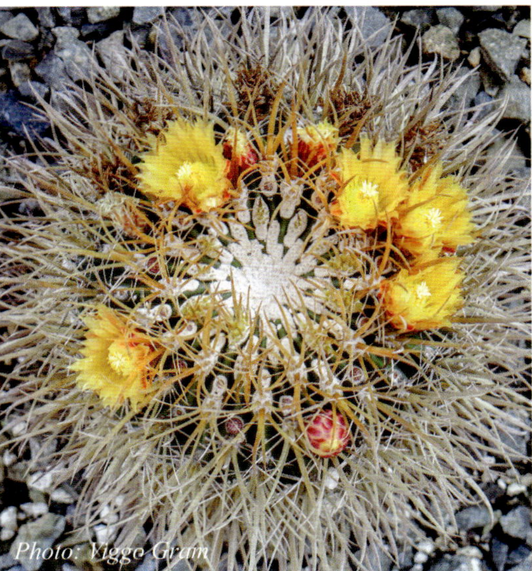

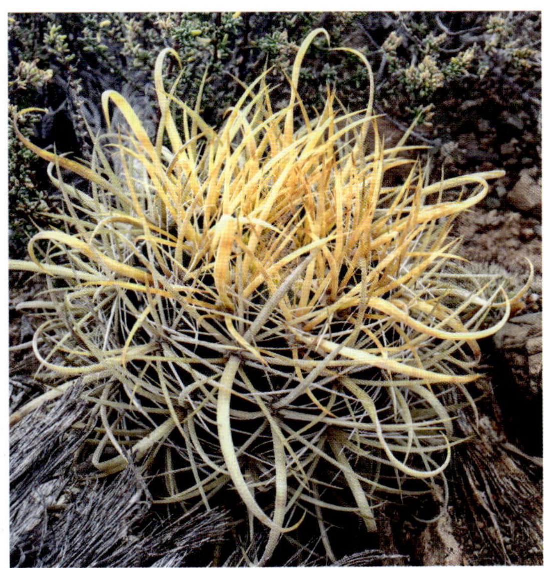

Echinocactus grusonii may be rare in the wild in its native Mexican habitat, but growers produce them by the tens of thousands in the southwest U.S. They are easily grown from seed, remaining solitary plants until they reach at least beach ball size in perhaps ten to fifteen years (faster if you like to water). Older plants will begin to form pups around the base with age; pups can be separated off with great difficulty if you want to try. When you see a clump like the one at left, age may have been the trigger, but occasionally smaller plants will experience some damage at the growing tip, resulting in multi-clumps such as this. I wouldn't want to try to make more out of this guy.

E. grusonii really likes the sun. The intense UV of the Arizona sun makes the barrels there just a radiant yellow-gold, and they are generally fine with maximum desert sun, although a poorly hydrated plant might suffer during an extreme triple-digit event. Check out how bright the Golden Barrels on page 119 look in the extreme desert sun of the Mojave Desert in California.

At left is a crested example from the collection of Gene Joseph of Plants for the Southwest and Living Stones Nursery in Tucson, Arizona. Aberrations always are a fun thing—more to follow.

Echinocactus

The genus *Echinocactus* (ee-KINE-o-cactus or EK-in-o-cactus; both pronunciations seem to be in use) used to be one of the primary genera classifications that included many barrel-shaped cacti. Over the years, most of the members have been shaved off to other genera, including the ferocacti. There are roughly nine species left in the genus, only a few available in cultivation. A common characteristic is the barrel shape and pronounced spines. What sets them apart somewhat from ferocacti is the propensity to form a woolly mat of "fur" on top, from which the (usually) yellow flowers will emerge. The two genera are close enough that there are intergeneric crosses. I always have to pause a moment when I'm discussing echinocactus vs. echinocereus, which are two very different groups, connected just by the Latin prefix "echino," which simply means "prickly" or "spiny"—a bit redundant in the cactus world.

If you own just one cactus, in-ground or containerized, I'd recommend the classic Golden Barrel. When I help customers plan their succulent landscapes, most prefer a more lush, less "cactusy" look, which is fine, but I almost beg them to consider one—or several, hopefully—strategically placed Golden Barrels. They can lend such dramatic architecture to an otherwise soft and leafy landscape, and they absolutely glow with the sun behind them. True, they have nasty spines like most cacti, but if you tuck them off the garden path, perhaps nested in front of a rock where nobody should run into them, you'll be glad you did.

Planting a barrel cactus isn't as difficult as you might think. I don't even wear gloves (they give you a false sense of security). Just cradle the plant in an old towel (see the photo on page 14), lay the pot over, kick the sides, and it will pop out—a big sphere with some scraggly little roots. The hole you dig need only be a slight depression as they are so shallow-rooted. Make it more of a shallow crater, drop it in, and back fill some soil around the base. Try slightly tilting for dramatic and habitat-style effect.

The grower's hillside at left has become quite a nursery, and needs to be thinned out soon before they begin melding together.

If you grow enough new generations of a plant, there will be some surprising deviants, which us plant folk jump on. We tend to step in with our enthusiastic form of unnatural selection based on eye-catching aesthetics—selective hybridizing or, in the cases here, selective culling for spontaneous abnormalities—to create new wonders. We do it with dogs, fish, almost anything. Golden Barrels are among the most frequently grown cacti from seed, and here are a few of the weirdlings that sometimes pop up. Above left is an adorable, short-spined form that looks, at first glance, like a well-done fake plastic cactus, which first popped into existence at Bach's Cactus Nursery in Tucson, Arizona. Miles Anderson calls it *Echinocactus plasticus*. That's not an official name, but I like it. It is such a slow grower that it is almost never available. Perhaps it should be called *E. grusonii v. brevispina* ("short-spined"), but that label sometimes is used for the essentially spineless form, above middle, which is properly known as *v. enermis* (or sometimes "subenermis." The proper spelling is "enermis" with an "e," but it seems to be spelled "inermis" or "subinermis" with an "i" more often than not, myself included). Above right is a plant that has thrown off almost tumor-like clusters of confused growth.

Below left is an unusually thin-spined form. Below middle is a long and abnormally dense and wavy-spined version. It looks remarkably similar to the similarly aberrant form of *Ferocactus chrysacanthus* on page 187. Below right is the occasionally available white-spined form. In my experience, the white form rarely looks as nice as the field-grown specimen seen here but has more of a dirty brown look. Earlier in the book you have seen examples of this plant in both a crested and red-flowered (and likely hybrid) form.

Echinocactus platyacanthus

At first glance, *E. platyacanthus* (*ingens*) looks a bit like a golden barrel that got gypped in the spine department, but it is its own plant and makes a statement in its own right. It will develop a substantial creamy yellow, hairy apex with age, and juvenile plants display a wonderful burgundy patterning (shown inset), that, sadly, fades with age. In fact, the plant may be more popular as a small potted plant but eventually will make a classic desert sculpture in-ground. It can get huge with age (see page 137). The extra spiny form seen below (see also page 176) is a particularly attractive type—assuming you like spines—which may have a subspecies name "*palmeri*," but I have yet to confirm if that is correct.

Left: *Echinocactus texensis*, known as the "Horse Crippler" for its thick spines, is from, you guessed it, Texas. It has salmon pink flowers and is cold tolerant. *Echinocactus horizonthalonius* (above) is a small, usually singular barrel with beautiful flowers as seen above shown in Coahuila Mexican habitat. *Both photos by Brian Kemble.*

Above is a habitat specimen of *Echinocactus polycephalus*, including a crested section in the middle. This plant has a reputation as difficult to grow in cultivation—it evolved in very harsh, hot/cold, and dry conditions, including Death Valley. Nasty nice. *Photo: Jeremy Spath.*

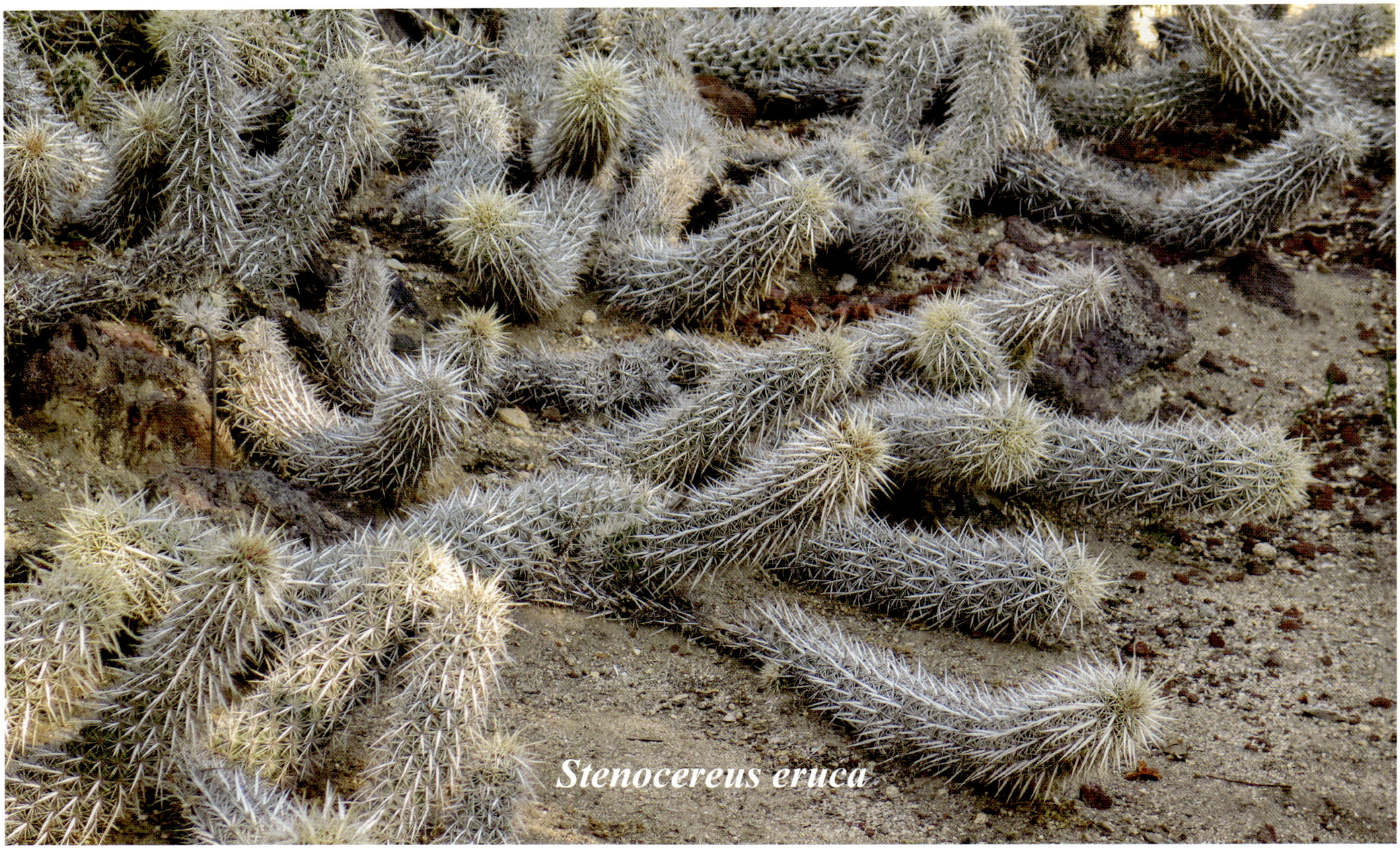

Stenocereus eruca

The famous and aptly named "Creeping Devil" of the southern Baja California Pacific Coast is a favorite among cactophiles. It grows mostly prostrate in very sandy soil with the tips always pointing up. As these tips grow, the back end of the plant slowly dies off while the "belly" crawls along the ground as it forms new roots, allowing the plant to slowly creep forward at a glacial pace. This traveling chain of growth is reflected in the Latin species name "eruca," which means "caterpillar." This plant will grow in California gardens if provided full sun and not watered much. It is a must if you are creating a "Baja" garden, and you can see extensive examples at The Huntington Botanical Gardens and a few other California botanical gardens. Owing to its spiny nastiness, Debra Baldwin has correctly observed that botanical gardens are, indeed, the best place to see this plant.

The other spiny devil at right has made its way recently into cultivation, but it just seemed to appear with no identification. I was at a loss to even guess the genus. It was plump and spiny enough that I thought it might be an echinocactus, but it turns out it is *Corynopuntia invicta* (after bouncing around through a few other genera until the molecular biologists got involved). For the purposes of this book, it rightfully belongs in the following cylindropuntia (cholla) section, but I'm placing it here next to its equally nasty Southern Baja California regional neighbor just based on looks. The new spines come in vivid red, and the skin can blush pink, as seen here.

Corynopuntia invicta

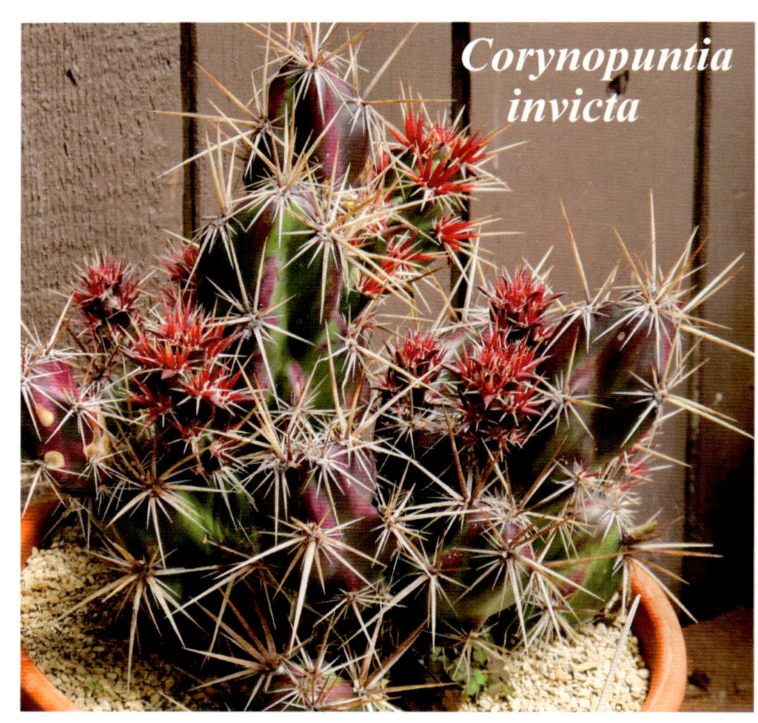

Echinocereus

Above: *Echinocereus triglochidiatus* (*coccineus?*)
Left: The "strawberry hedgehog cactus" of the southwest U.S., *Echinocereus engelmannii*

This very large group of cacti from the U.S. and Mexico is mostly clustering cacti remarkable for both their serious spines and often very impressive, sometimes large, and long-lasting flowers. The name "echino" means "spiny," as applies to starfish and hedgehogs, so many are called "hedgehog cacti." Some are extremely spiny, others have combed-down, body-hugging spines that allow you to actually pick up the plant itself bare-handed. Many of the flowers are absolutely gorgeous. Track down a book of the same name by Duke Benadom if you're looking for more images and information. The "echino" ("spiny") prefix causes this genus to sometimes be confused with the genus *Echinocactus*, and once again, either pronunciation—hard "i" or soft "i"—is acceptable. There are several cold hardy species endemic to places such as Colorado and Oklahoma.

Left: A nicely staged colony of *Echinocereus* at the Orange County Cactus Club monthly meeting. Your local cactus/succulent club is a great place to learn more and talk to fellow enthusiasts who seem to be happy all the time. It's good to have a hobby, especially one that involves the natural world, with its unending variety and new areas to explore.

Top: *Echinocereus pentalophus*, shown in two different flower colors above left and right, is a scrambling and sort of messy and unremarkable plant when not in flower. But if you have patience, you are rewarded (a few days a year) with some remarkable iridescent flowers. There are several subspecies, the primary of which I believe is the thinner-stemmed *ssp. procumbens*, the aforementioned scrambler that can be presented as a hanging plant as well. An occasionally used common name is "Lady-finger cactus." Not sure what kind of lady has fingers like these. Maybe a witch.

Left: These fuzzy little "Cousin Its" are *Echinocereus longisetus* (*delaetii*). It has a remarkable resemblance to the hairy *Cephalocereus senilis*, but it is a small clumper with fuchsia purple flowers very similar to those of *E. pentalophus* in the images above.

Below left: One of the favorites among *Echinocereus* fans is the classic Claret Cup, *Echinocereus triglochidiatus*.

Below right: *Echinocereus maritimus* growing in rocky habitat on Isla Cedros, Baja California, Mexico.

Echinocereus rigidissimus
Echinocereus pectinatus

I have to take the expert's assertion that *Echioncereus rigidissimus* is a different plant than *E. pectinatus*, but my cactus sense isn't fine-tuned enough to tell the difference. Both have identical, glorious flowers. The spines are combed down so tight that you can grasp the plant itself without consequence. Both are excellent container show plants. *E. rigidissimus* has a *v. rubispina* (red-spined) form, the most desirable variety, shown here. Often called the "Rainbow Cactus," or the "Red-headed Irishman" (??), the body/spine color can be even deeper in the cold of winter, as seen at left growing in-ground through a Sacramento winter.

Photo: EW&C

Photo: Nick Basinski

Above: An old specimen echinopsis puts on a spectacular spring blooming event every year. The few days the buds grow to full size are the opening act (above left), then you get a day (maybe two if it is overcast) of the explosion above. Then you wait until next year (there may be a few "onesie-twosie" blooms over the summer and fall).

Below left: *Trichocereus* 'Flying Saucer' is one of the finest hybrids. When you see the size and color of the flower on a plant like this, it just stops you in your tracks and pulls you in like a helpless zombie drawn to beauty instead of brains. Below right is more of a light pink cultivar. When I see one of these flowers, I can't help but take a photo, even though I don't really need another one. But we're digital now and it's free, so why not?

Flower Power:
Echinopsis, Lobivia, Trichocereus

As happens often in botany, a genus or two may get subsumed into a larger group (then sometimes purged right back out), which has happened with the plants on the next few pages. Many of the medium-large, green, golden-spined clumping and beautiful flowering cacti we see in cultivation are, or were, from the genus *Trichocereus*. Many were crossed over the years with plants of the genus *Lobivia* (an anagram for Bolivia), creating what some folks used to call tricho-lobivias. Lobivias are now considered to be of the genus *Echinopsis*, and the current thinking is that all of these plants, including *Trichocereus*, are now *Echinopsis* (although some now want to extricate lobivias again—I give up). However, despite the issue being muddied by hybridization, in general many of us consider the larger and more columnar forms to still be *Trichocereus*, with the *Echinopsis* types being more globose with smaller spines, more pronounced ribs, and relatively very large, trumpet-shaped flowers.

What they all have in common are stunning flowers, many having been engineered over the years to surpass anything found in nature. And I'm sure they also don't really care what we call them.

Probably the king of all the trichocereus crosses is seen above left (there *is* a cactus under all those flowers), known as the "Flying Saucer" for the huge size of its iridescent fuschia blooms. Above right is an example of a white-flowered form that has been allowed to grow for quite a while. The grower's colony below may be "Flying Saucer" or any of a number of similar yet distinct crosses. One in particular, called "California," has slightly smaller but no less stunning flowers and looks quite like this. There typically is a huge, multi-flowered first spring awakening/blooming event—I'm quite sure that is the case in all of the images here—followed by a series of less numerous blooms throughout the summer and into early fall.

Echinopsis candicans (×2)

As mentioned earlier, although technically now called *Echinopsis*, the larger, longer, showy flowered hybrids on these pages have mostly been labeled as *Trichocereus* over the years, and I'm reluctant to let that go. As stunning as the flowers are, the plants can have a wonderful form on their own, sans flower, as seen above at the Desert Botanical Garden in Phoenix. That is important, as the flowering season can be brief. I counsel customers to like the plant independent of the flower, as that is what you'll be looking at most of the year. But boy are these blooms worth the wait.

Photos by Bob & Brent Wigand

Left: If we're still going to distinguish between the old echinopsis and trichocereus forms, which I am, then the plant at left is more of your classic echinopsis. The body is more globose, has much more pronounced ribs, and generally appears less spiny. In particular, the echinopsis flowers can be crazy big in proportion to the plant and extremely cone-shaped, almost to the point of seeming to defy physics based on size/weight to base ratio. The long-tubed flowers have evolved symbiotically with a long-tongued moth.

Right: Fuchsia blooms of a trichocereus hybrid. The flowers can look remarkably similar to those of the epiphyllum/orchid cactus groups.

Below: More beauties.

All of the stunning floral displays you see on this page are hybrids of the echinopsis/trichocereus/lobivia complex. This is just a small sample of some of the flowers being developed. For a truly mind-blowing show of time-lapse cacti flowering, check out the website "http://echinopsisfreak.com/". Words don't do it justice. Just check it out. All of the images on this page courtesy Brent Wigand, unless otherwise credited.

The deep-ribbed, globoid, and minimally spined clumping plant above is the prototypical echinopsis form. It usually has exaggeratedly large flowers with long, fluted bases. Most in cultivation likely are hybrids of true species, and identification is difficult. If you can remember to call it an echinopsis, you've passed the test.

We usually prefer to use Latin binomial nomenclature to identify plants, but in this case, it might be best to just default to the common name of "Peanut Cactus" for this little mat-forming and vigorous bloomer. Formerly known as *Chamaecereus silvestrii* but now folded into echinopsis to become *Echinopsis chamaecereus (silvestrii)*, or sometimes known as *Chamalobivia sylvestris....* let's just call it the Peanut Cactus. The most common form is the red-flowered plant above, but it has been extensively hybridized for flower color and size. There are cascading forms that work as hanging plants. In addition, the size and thickness of the plant body can vary.

The blooming beauty at left was identified by Altman's Specialty Plants as one of a series called "Rainbow Bursts," which they say are echinolobivia hybrids. This means that one parent was an echinopsis and the other a lobivia, but technically speaking these are now part of the same genus. I guess this is treating these plants based on their previously split genera. So.... Whatever it is and whatever they crossed, it's awesome, and I'm all for it.

Parodia / Notocactus

From what I've been able to ascertain, the genus *Notocactus* has now been subsumed into the genus *Parodia*, but most people I know still identify these awesome halo-style bloomers as notocacti. Here I must insert a quote from Daiv Freeman from *cactiguide.com* about this issue: *For some reason, the treatment of this particular genus is a highly emotional issue to many growers. It seems they would rather die than to ever refer to a Notocactus by the name of Parodia.*

Just consider the genus names interchangeable for now. They are South American globoids, many with that generic "spiny ball" configuration that makes them hard to identify. Most of the parodias/notocacti in cultivation are true species, as compared to the many hybrids of the trichcereus/echinopsis group. The rare subspecies, above middle, shown at a grower's off-limits greenhouse doesn't even need to flower as far as I'm concerned—what a wonderful piece of patterned geometry. There are a few nice fuzzy clumpers as well, such as *Notocactus scopa v. murielii* below.

A few pages back I did the "If you only have one cactus" thing, referring to the Golden Barrel. Okay, if you only have two cacti, this might be the next one I'd recommend. Formerly under the genus *Notocatus* and earlier *Eriocactus* (which I believe is now an invalid name), all you need to remember is the apt "magnifica" part as this can grow into a truly magnificent plant. It's already impressive as a young single plant with papery "spines" that you can pet, but as it matures it forms a cluster of various size globes. In benign climates it will continue to grow until you almost can't see the pot anymore. In addition, it's an enthusiastic bloomer with yellow flowers. Because it's from a relatively high elevation in South America, it is quite cold tolerant but too much heat/sun can be an issue in desert conditions. I'm quite sure this plant is a model for many of the artificial cacti you'll see.

Photo: Debra Lee Baldwin

Parodia leninghausii

Sometimes called the "Golden Tower," *P. leninghausii* has soft and relatively harmless spines that resemble shiny golden hair. It is an enthusiastic clumper, with papery yellow flowers. Below right is an example of an individual that sustained some growing tip damage, and over time it grew a plethora of new heads, similar to the plant on page 22. Through adversity a plant can become something more appealing than it would have otherwise.

Photo: Ron Regehr

Please pardon my dead horse flogging—in fact, please pardon that rather vulgar yet apt metaphor—but as mentioned elsewhere and often in this book, there are many more species, cultivars, and hybrids than I can possibly show you here. Indeed, there are many that I never even knew about until I started this book. As an example, Ron Regehr sent me the image at left of a nice specimen *Parodia schumanniana v. claviceps*. Looks familiar, but I had never heard of it. So I went to a couple of my cactus books and to *cactiguide.com*, which has multiple images of all 66 species of *Parodia*, along with habitat and taxonomical history for the genus, and there it was. I hope you'll take a few bounces on this little springboard I'm offering and dive deep if your curiosity is piqued. Nature is fascinating and limitless.

Trichocereus brevispinulosus

With apt common names like "Indian Corn Cob" or "Green Corn Cob" cactus, this South American clustering columnar stands apart from its brethren due to its distinct geometric body plan. It can be cold sensitive and therefore difficult in certain inland or desert locations. Flowers are large and white.

Many of the trichocereus and other columnar cacti are from regions that don't experience freezing conditions, so prudent growers take precautions during cold spells where temperatures might dip that low. In the case above, B&B Cactus Farm in Tucson, Arizona, has placed styrofoam cups over the growing tips to protect the most delicate new growth. Don't leave them on too long.

Above is *Trichocereus huascha*, best known as the "Red Torch," but the plant here blooms more orange, and if you look at online images for this plant, you'll see a variety of flower colors.

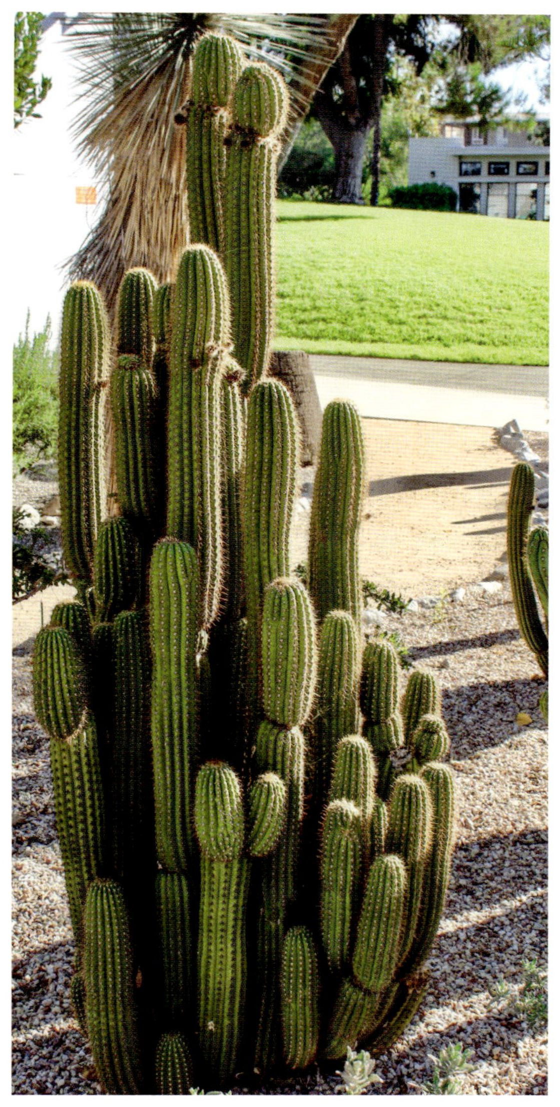

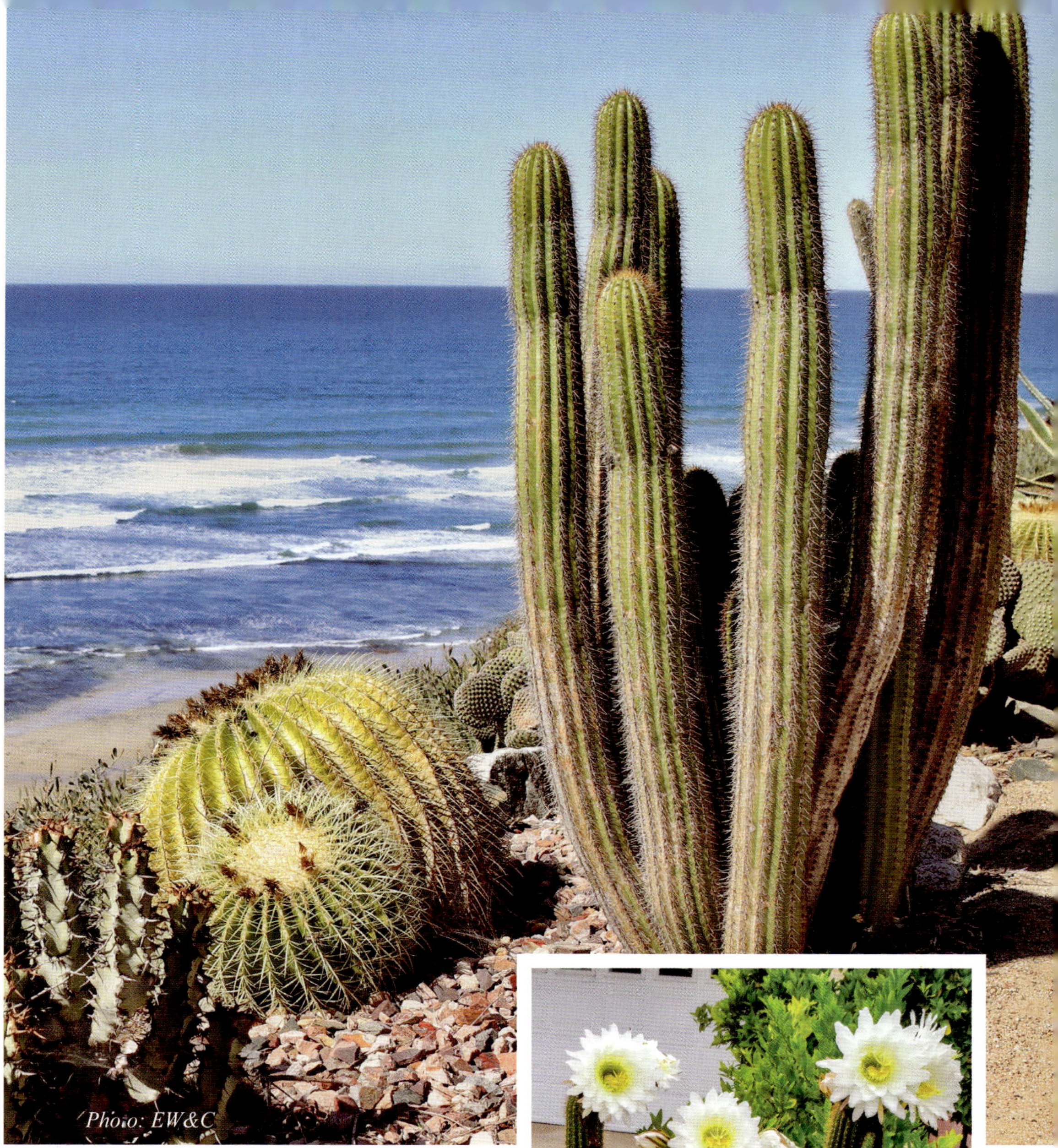

Photo: EW&C

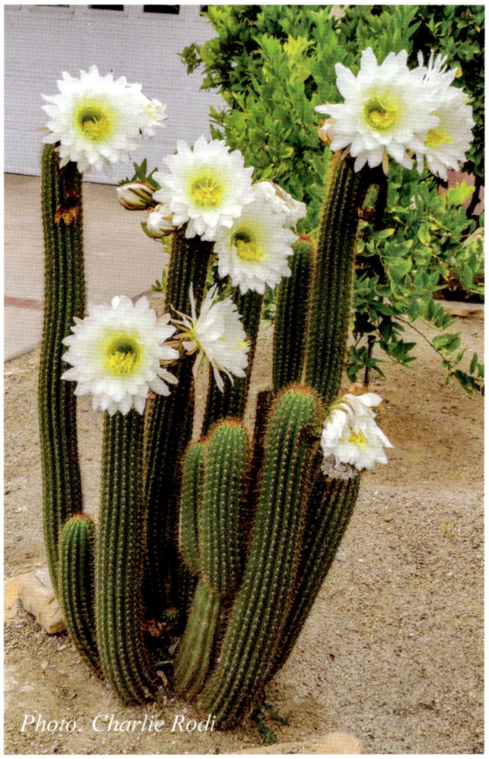

Photo: Charlie Rodi

Trichocereus (Echinopsis) spachianus

This is the classic flowering columnar cactus of many southwest U.S. landscapes. It is popular as both a container and in-ground plant, and has been in cultivation for many years. It likely is of South American origin, but original populations are uncertain. It has a reputation as a very durable plant—tolerant of extreme heat as well as freezing conditions, which no doubt contributes to its popularity and ubiquity. It offers huge white flowers from spring through late fall and can reach five to six feet in height, usually forming a substantial clump. It is a green cactus, but when backlit, the spines sometimes give it a red/brown profile. You may encounter old stands of this cactus growing among weeds along old fences in rural areas, obviously having gone native and living independently from any introduced irrigation. This plant is a survivor. It also is frequently used as grafting stock.

I was having a tough time figuring out the genus of the wonderful bowling-ball sized cacti you see at top left and on the facing page. I'd show images to a few folks, and it was always something to the effect of, "Oh yeah, that looks familiar, but ... maybe an echinopsis?" I was told by the experts at Poot's Cactus Nursery in Ripon, California, where the image at middle left was taken, that it was a Soehrensia—a pretty obscure name to me. In addition, I wasn't sure if the plants near left and on the facing page were of the same genus. So I sent an image to Brian Kemble—he'd know. He gave me a pretty thorough answer, so I thought I'd reprint it in full, just to give you a window into this whole nomenclature issue we deal with in the plant world. Here is his response:

You are right - the plants in the photos are what was originally named Soehrensia bruchii. Soehrensias are an interesting group, and there was much debate as to whether they should be seen as giant Lobivias or as stubby Trichocerei with colored flowers. This was moot when all of Lobivia and Trichocereus were lumped into echinopsis - but now they have been pulled back out again, and the taxonomists have decided that the soehrensias belong with the lobivias rather than in Trichocereus. So, the current name for this plant would be Lobivia bruchii (as Joel Lode calls it in <u>Taxonomy of the Cactaceae</u> *or else Lobivia formosa ssp. bruchii as David Hunt calls it in* <u>The New Cactus Lexicon</u>*). I think David Hunt goes too far in the direction of lumping, so I would favor just calling it Lobivia bruchii. I will attach a photo of it in flower.*

Later in the editing process, I sent the image to Mark Fryer, another expert, and he thinks it might be *Notocactus multicostatus* but notes that it is really hard to tell without flowers. So, don't feel bad if you're not sure what your cactus is.

Right: *Sorhrensia (Lobivia) formosa.*

Left: This is the same *Notocactus concinnus v. yerbalitoensis* you saw a few pages back. I put it here again as it looks like it belongs visually.

There must be a logical adaptive evolutionary explanation for a body plan like this—what looks like a spiraling assembly line of fleshy green bubbles borne in a radiating cottony apex—but I'd rather not think about the why and the how, and just enjoy the "What the ???"

Middle image: *Mammillaria magnimamma*
Top left: *M. mystax*
Top middle: *M. orcuttii*
Top right: *M. formossa ssp. pseudocrucigera*
Middle left: *M. hernandezii*
Middle right: *M. hahniana*
Bottom left: *M. huitzilopochtli*
Bottom right: *M. lloydii*

If there is a section in this book I needed help with, it is this part on the mammillarias. So many are just little collections of spiny (or not that spiny) balls, with either straight or hooked needles, and typically bloom with a halo of small flowers from pink to red to yellow. There also are so many species—it is one of the largest and most widespread genera of cactus. As with the other groups, there are a handful that are pretty easy to identify, and then a whole bunch that are not. Collectors can tell at a glance which is which—even when not in flower—but most of us are lucky if we just accurately identify it as a mammillaria. And like most of the cacti in this book, I have become much more of a fan of the genus after digging into it deeper. I actually have a little mammillaria collection now and love it.

With the "mams," there are a whole bunch of similar "generic" forms, and then some pretty cool exceptions. But after a while your eye evolves a bit, and that generic pile starts to get smaller as you shift some plants over into the cool category. Pretty soon, almost all of them are cool. A pile shift occurred for me as I put this book together. That happened as I researched opuntias as well—another category that I used to consider somewhat bland and generic (with exceptions). Now I love 'em all. Can't help it.

Mammillaria spinosissima is my personal favorite among the "mamms," And the variety known as "Un Pico" (one spine), seen above and at right, is the best of the best. Rather than the typical cluster of spines around the areole, a single white spine emerges. This cultivar has a soft and almost hairy appearance with a halo of fuchsia flowers several times a year, and reliably in early winter. It is also prone to cresting, as seen at right.

The more typical form below is *M. spinosissima v. pilcayensis*. It also is quite attractive, with a brownish-red cast and halos of lavender flowers. Below right may be the same, or just the more typical species form.

Mammillaria geminispina

Mammillaria geminispina (above) is probably the most ornamental of the clustering mamms. It has a frosted white look and will cluster in mounds. Mounding mammillarias, such as the species on this page, would easily take at least ten or more years in ideal conditions to reach the size of these specimens, assuming you start with a single head, seed-started little starter plant. Sometimes it will take on cristate forms, above right. Flowers are small and magenta, usually followed by a halo of little red "chili pepper" seed pods similar to those of *M. parkinsonii*, below middle.

You will notice that the botanic garden tag for the image above right is for the mammillaria on the facing page. However, I must point out that I frequently see either wrong or likely misplaced tags at botanic gardens. I'm quite sure that the plant here is *M. geminispina* or *M. parkinsonii*.

Mammillaria parkinsonii, below, has a similar look, but the heads tend to bifurcate into multiples, as seen below left, sometimes resembling owl's eyes or a monkey face, both common names that sometimes are applied.

Mammillaria parkinsonii

Above left: A collection of mostly white and fuzzy mammillarias. Most of these are happiest in hot and dry desert conditions. In California, some prefer to be protected from too much winter rain. I have found that to be particularly true of the "feather cactus," *Mammillaria plumosa*, shown above middle (bottom plant) and below middle. I personally have rotted a few of these little beauties, but it's hard to know they're dead right away. After several months of wondering, I just picked up the plant—you can handle these without gloves—and it was totally hollow inside. On the outside, it still looked its feathery self, but in reality it was just a dead shell. Not a happy surprise, but still a bit amusing. There are several white hairy mammillarias, one of the nicest of which is *Mammillaria hahniana*, which comes in several forms. The most attractive is the hairiest form, *v. supurba* (see the plant at the top of the upper middle image). Above right: A chubby little doughboy of a cactus, *Mammillaria rhodantha*.

Above left: Our humble little San Diego/Southern California native, *Mammillaria dioica* (seen here making a stand in a corrupted native habitat) isn't particularly remarkable but does have nice flowers with deep red stripes.
Above middle: *Mammillaria plumosa*, the "Feather Cactus."
Right: *Mammillariua formosa*

Mammillaria carmenae

Mammillaria erythra

Mammillaria perezdelarosae

Mammillaria gracilis v. fragilis (monstrose form)

Mammillaria theresae

Mammillaria bombycina

Mammillaria krameri

Mammillaria lenta

Mammillaria mercadensis

Above: *Mammillaria glassii*, offering the perfect balance of dainty pastel flowers and dense, nasty spines.

Left: One of the freakier aberrations in the cacti realm is the runaway mutant growth that can happen in *Mammillaria bocasana*, referred to as cv. 'Fred,' apparently named after the enthusiast who found the first mutation. As you can see in the top part of the image at left, the normal form is a white, fuzzy, more typical mammillaria. But the monstrose growth comes out in a proliferation of greenish, sometimes burgundy-tinged, little hairless and rubbery knobs, sort of like a runaway tumor (which might not be too far of a stretch). This hairless form can also produce a wonderful crest, as seen on page 128.

Right: *Mammillaria candida*.

Above left: A delightfully twisted example of *Mammillaria zuccariniana*.
Above middle: A crested form of *Mammillaria plumosa*.
Above right: A mature specimen of *Mammillaria matudae*. I choose to see an aardvark here, but you see what you want to see. Most times you'll see this plant as a short column, similar to the 'ears' portion of the plant here. Over time, the main body will elongate either along the ground or will cascade if given the opportunity.

Left: Brains!—Let's hope there never will be such a thing as cactus zombies (imagine a hoard of walking zombie saguaros), but if there were, I suppose these would be the brains they would prefer to dine on. These are actually the crested form of *Mammillaria elongata*. More examples of crested or cristate growth are shown in the introductions to both the euphorbia and cactus chapters of this book, but this particular plant tends to crenulate itself into the most "brain-like" of all the cristate plants. Unfortunately, it is also one of the more difficult to keep in cultivation, preferring to live in a greenhouse, at least compared to typical outdoor California conditions. I've had quite a few rot on me. They still looked perfectly fine, and I didn't know they were dead until I picked them up and realized they were hollow. Still, worth the risk if you like crests.

Below left: A naturally occurring habitat crest of *Epithelantha micromeris*—not a mammillaria! Looks like one though. This creature doesn't even look like it has roots attaching it to the ground and might just roll around on the rocks.
Below right: *Mammillaria elongata* crest in the left-hand portion of the pot, with a different mammillaria crest cozying up on the right. They are so tight in the pot that it is hard to get water in, which may be why these difficult growers are doing so well outside in the elements.

These delightful little oddities are very popular among enthusiasts for their undulating, fin-like ribs. They are quite numerous and have a wavy pattern that is suggestive of some type of undersea creature. *Echinofossulocactus* can be heavily or lightly spined, and some have quite attractive flowers, usually white to pinkish with darker mid-stripes. They can be solitary for a long time, but some will cluster in maturity. There are at least ten species, but I find them very difficult to tell apart. The most common in cultivation are *E. crispatus* or *E. multicostatus*, but there are others available. In general, there is quite a bit of subtle variation among these plants, even within the same species.

There have been some nomenclature battles with this genus, and most experts now recognize the genus as *Stenocactus*. I learned it as *Echinofossulocactus*, which has always been one of my favorite plant names—eight syllables of nerdy fun to pronounce. Below left are extra wavy iterations of *S. crispatus*, which reflects species variability as opposed monstrose growth. Below right is one that sees the need for extra defensive armament.

Melocactus azureus

Melocactus matanzanus

While there are a handful of cacti that have hairy growth in their cephalium—the area where flowers are produced—the king of cephaliums are the melocacti. In juvenile forms and without their cephaliums, I would be hard pressed to even guess the genus of these otherwise generic-looking globose cacti. But in maturity, they begin to sport what at first looks like a furry beret and—if I may continue the top-hat metaphor—growing over time into a fez and eventually a stovepipe shape. The flowers that emerge through the bristly hair generally are small and unremarkable, but they often are followed by fruit that look like tiny chili peppers. Melocacti are from subtropical regions of Central and South America, and many Caribbean islands, and thus are very sensitive to extended cold or wet conditions. This makes them a bit iffy as in-ground plants, although with good drainage I have seen them in the California landscape. They are best treated as container specimens so you can move them inside or at least out of the rain in cold/wet winters.

The handful of other cacti that form cephaliums sometimes do so laterally down the stem, as seen on page 174.

Left: *Melocactus broadwayi* exhibits a large cephalium but not as seasoned as the pancake stack at near right.

Right: *Melocactus caesius.*

Far right: An in-ground plant that was damaged by frost or trauma at some point. The plant persisted and formed multiple heads, which now means multiple cephaliums that give it the look of a radar dish array.

Above: This perfect little *Ariocarpus kotschoubeyanus* is a happy rock dweller, like most of the genus.

Left: A collector's cold frame of show plant ariocarpus beginning to bloom. Most are more likely to flower in early fall than in spring. The fuchsia-flowering plant is *A. fissuratus*.

Below: A blue ribbon award winner at the San Diego Cactus and Succulent Society's show is a very rare cultivar of *A. fissuratus* called "Godzilla," presented by Kal Kaminer.

Ariocarpus are pretty much the high-end class of collectible cacti. They are very slow growing, and old specimens are so prized that they are not generally used as landscape plants but are more in the province of containerized show specimens. Native to southern Texas and northern Mexico, they are sometimes called the "living rocks" of cacti as they tend to grow low to the ground and are hard-bodied and spineless. Sometimes they disappear into the soil as evidenced by the habitat plant surviving in a dry mud field in Mexico on page 138. The six species are *A. agavoides*, *A. bravoanus*, *A. fissuratus*, *A. kotschoubeyanus*, *A. retusus*, and *A. scaphirostris*. Like all cacti, there are unique cultivars, subspecies, and crosses, and in particular some amazing crested forms (turn the page and you'll see what I mean). I have found that these cacti don't appreciate a wet California winter, so it is best to keep them containerized and out of the cold weather rain. Move them out into full sun in the dry times

Left: A blue-green form of *Ariocarpus retusus*.
Below: *Ariocarpus trigonus* with a full head of hair.

Like some of the desert dwellers on the following pages, they prefer to be dry in the wet winter months, which places them in the greenhouse or cold-frame plant category. Ariocarpus are not commonly available at most nurseries, with the exception of some of the Arizona cactus specialty nurseries. You will see some fantastic specimens at plant shows (like the plant at left) but they do belong in the expert grower category. You need to work your way up to properly keeping these cacti.

Ariocarpus

Note: Some consider *Ariocarpus trigonus* to be a subspecies of *A. retusus*, so if you prefer the "retusus ssp." between the "Ariocarpus" and "trigonus," just visualize it being there.

Don't think for a moment you'll ever grow or acquire anything like this hypnotic hallucination of an *Ariocarpus retusus*—a true Picasso of cristate botanical architecture, grown for many years by an expert. It doesn't leave his greenhouse even for plant shows. It wouldn't be fair to other show plants. Don't ask me how or where I got this photo, —he had me look at this pen-like "flashy thing," and I remember nothing, just an image on my photo card

Astrophytum ornatum cultivar

Astrophytum myriostigma hybrid

Astrophytum myriostigma v. nudum monstrose

Astrophytum myriostigma cultivar

Astrophytum ornatum

Astrophytum asterias cultivar

Astrophytum asterias cultivar

Astrophytum myriostigma cultivar

Astrophytum myriostigma 'ooibkabuto'

Astrophytums

Translating from Latin as "Star Plant," astrophytums are some of the most prized of the smaller cacti from the southwestern U.S. and Mexico. Like the ariocarpus, they are sometimes referred to as "living rocks," a name that, in my opinion, applies better to the lithops and a few other African succulents. The most common in cultivation are *A. asterias*, *A. myriostigma*, and *A. ornatum*, all of which come in myriad forms and cultivars. One of my favorites is *A. myriostigma*, seen above in the common frosted white form, as well as a "nudum" green form. It generally, but not always, is spineless and round, and will elongate over time. There are varieties with more ornate white markings, but not quite as many as the wonderful and almost fake-looking permutations of *Astrophytum asterias*, the most famous being the Japanese cultivar "Super Kabuto," which looks like some of the whiter plants at left. Hybridizers are taking them so far that you need to be an expert to differentiate most of them. Most astrophytums have nice pale yellow flowers with red/orange interiors, but with these plants, flowers are definitely subordinate to the plant itself. They are excellent as container plants, but some of the larger types are landscape-compatible, such as the large *A. ornatum* seen at center on the facing page. There are myriad examples of crested, variegated, and just plain remarkable derivations of this genus. For space reasons, I can't show you even a fraction of them here, so I'll refer you to some of the better books on the genus (many in Japanese) or, of course, the internet. As I was finishing this book, I became aware of Coron Cactus of Japan via their Instagram page. The fantastic freaks they have developed or culled are absolutely mind-blowing.

The taller and older specimen of *A. coahuilense* above is a Mexican habitat image by Jeff Chemnick. This species looks remarkably similar to *Astrophytum myriostigma* but is a different species. At right is a beautiful example of an older *Astrophytum ornatum*—ornate indeed. Below left is a blue ribbon winner of "Super Kabuto," displayed by Miles To Go at the San Diego Cactus and Succulent Society Show. Below middle is a trio of astrophytums the way most of us keep them at home, happy in their little pots on our little porches. Below right are some more little succulent "rocks" waiting for their pots. Photos and collection of Paul Lawler.

There is a riotous diversity of astrophytum cultivars, with new varieties being isolated or developed. You've seen a few here, but go online and you will be amazed at the wonderful patterns, body shapes, monstrose forms, variegation, and strange and beautiful design within this genus. Quite a few have been developed in Asia, and have names such as "Super Kabuto" (which has many sub varieties), "Hanazano," or "Ruri Kabuto." Not to be outdone, we have some with English names like "Super Big" or "Lizard Skin."

Right: *Astrophytum caput-medusæ*, which looks nothing like the rest of the globular genus. I was put on the spot at a cactus club meeting to identify the plant shortly after its discovery and was humbled not to even be able to guess the genus. This medusoid octopus of an astrophytum must have had an evolutionary reason to develop this way, or maybe a programing glitch, but sure enough, it flowers just like its relatives. Maybe it was born from the radioactive fallout that spawned Godzilla.

The following spread on the genus *Copiapoa* features an unusually high number (for this book) of habitat images due to their availability to me and the jaw-dropping beauty of mature specimens photographed by Ron Regehr and Kelly Griffin. We do have some outstanding cultivated specimens in captivity as well, shown on this page. Copiapoas are slow-growing, like most cacti, and usually need some protection from excessive California winter rains (when we get them). The plants here primarily are greenhouse grown but are fine as outdoor container plants most of the year. You will rarely encounter large in-ground specimens outside of habitat due to occasional heavy rains as mentioned above.

A show quality copiapoa on display at the L.A. Intercity C&S Show. Collection of Gene Joseph. *Photo by Michael Souza, Plants for the Southwest.*

Copiapoas

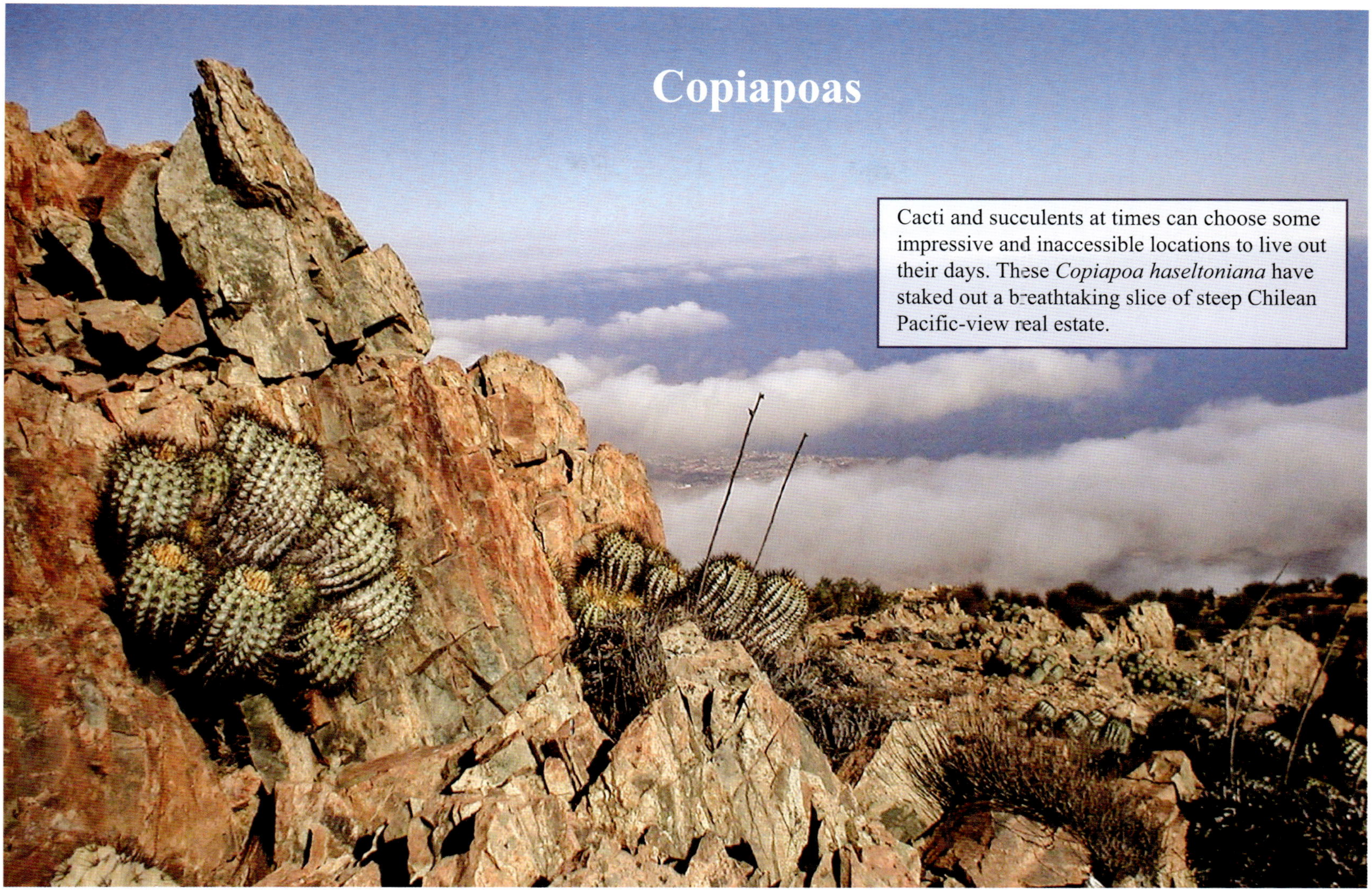

Cacti and succulents at times can choose some impressive and inaccessible locations to live out their days. These *Copiapoa haseltoniana* have staked out a breathtaking slice of steep Chilean Pacific-view real estate.

Copiapoas are among the most coveted of cacti. You will see some exceptional plants in private collections—a few included in this section—but to see the real deal, you'll need to book a trip to the Atacama Desert in Chile. Ron Regehr did just that a while back and provided the images on this page. The Atacama is a fog desert that ranges from sea level to several thousand feet in elevation and is home to copiapoas and a number of other fantastic cacti. The plants survive primarily on moisture from fog, as actual rain is rare—there often is a period of many years before it gets to what they call a "rain event" (as of this writing, that also is beginning to accurately describe Southern California, only with less fog). As California has a similar latitude and climate, we should, and can, grow these cacti, but because of our winter rains, you should keep them as container plants so you can move and protect them from particular wet winters.

Flowers are nice but not spectacular within this genus, as the beauty is much more in the form. Large clumps like the one at right resemble large clumping Old World euphorbias.

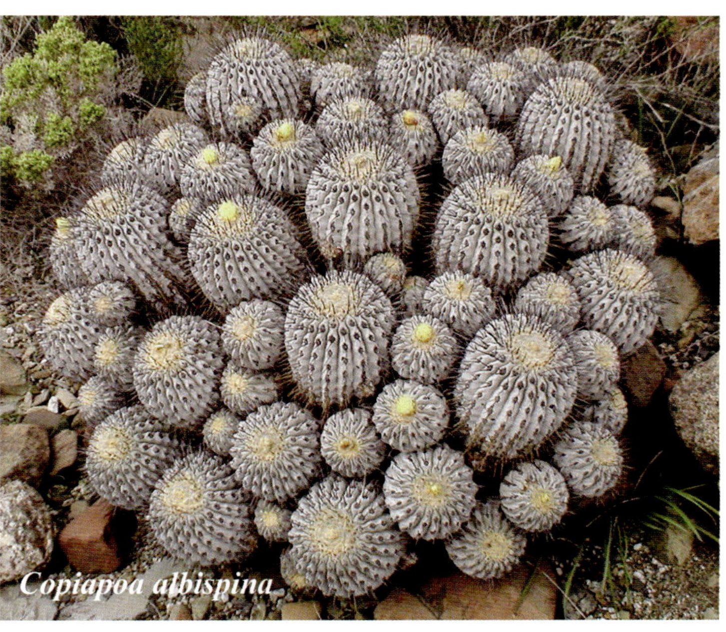

Copiapoa albispina

Spread: A slice of a grower's extensive copiapoa collection, all greenhouse grown in Central California. Inset above is the dark, almost black beauty *Copiapoa tenuissima*, exhibited at the Los Angeles Inter-City Cactus and Succulent Show. Copiapoas are not famous for their flowers, but some are nice, inset left.

At left are *C. tenuissima* exhibiting some nice mutations. The vigorous clumpers at far left would be considered monstrose growth examples, and the plants near left are crested (and grafted). You can see that the crests have been grafted by necessity onto another cactus stock. The reason for this is that once you have made the bold decision to cut up a crest (to make more), they will grow much more readily on vigorous stock than if you attempt to get them to generate their own roots.

One of the finest plant books ever published is *Copiapoa 2006* (a follow up to a similar book from 1996) by Rudolf Schulz. It has much more detail and images than I can show you here. Find it and buy it.

All of the habitat images on this page are by Ron Regehr (except upper right, *Copiapoa cinerea*, by Jeff Chemnick), from a 2004 trip to the Atacama Desert of Chile, along with Rudolf Schulz, who has written the definitive book on the genus (see facing page). Upper middle is an old cluster of *Copiapoa dealbata*, exhibiting many crested sections. Top left is *Copiapoa echinoides*, center left is *C. serpentisulata*, and below left and below right are *C. albispina*.

I don't know about you, but I haven't personally been able to visit too many of my favorite succulents in habitat, with the exception of northern Baja California, which is at least close by. I have developed a succulent habitat bucket list, and the two primary places I need to visit are the copiapoa and puya habitats of Chile, and Lesotho in Africa to see *Aloe polyphylla*. Half the fun might be getting there, but actually seeing plants like these in the place they evolved would border on a religious experience for a succulentophile.

Left: *Copiapoa haseltoniana*, a very orange form from south of Paposo.

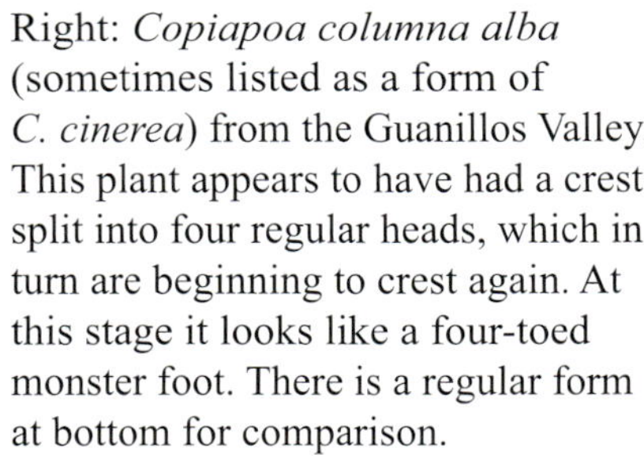

Right: *Copiapoa columna alba* (sometimes listed as a form of *C. cinerea*) from the Guanillos Valley. This plant appears to have had a crest split into four regular heads, which in turn are beginning to crest again. At this stage it looks like a four-toed monster foot. There is a regular form at bottom for comparison.

Left: *Copiapoa krainsiana* from the mountain region above Taltal resemble a cluster of snowballs from a distance.

Right: *Copiapoa rupestris* near Cifuncho—one of the best of the genus if you like nasty cactus spines.

All photos this page by Kelly Griffin.

All of the images on this page are from intrepid plant explorer Kelly Griffin and were a late addition to the book, forcing me to once again bloat my page count. But I had to add it if only for the gorgeous beach beauty reclining at left.

I was going to try to paraphrase Kelly's comments about the plants, but I'll just quote him directly here:

Copiapoas are among the most beautiful of all cacti. They occur in close proximity to the ocean and they also tend to inhabit really unique and sometimes fantastic geological features. They are well adapted to arid environments but do rely on the moisture that is present from the frequent fog off the ocean. Fewer species (very few) occur inland where it is drier and often without any appreciable rain for years. I have been often asked which is my favorite to which the answer comes: all of them! Nice plants of krainziana and solaris require some effort to see but most species are relatively easy to see in Chile. The roads go by most of the species and through their habitats—that is if you go to where they grow. C. krainsiana is a hike and Mt Perales is a trip for only 4x4 but most of the other plants are a quite easy venture from the car.

Above: This clump of *Copiapoa longistaminea* looks like it should have a cold Corona beer next to it, maybe some little sunglasses and a beach towel, too. Lucky cactus.
Below middle: *Copiapoa solaris* from the Botija Valley is another highly spined variety.
Below right: You'll oftentimes see lichen inhabiting fissures or folds in older habitat cacti, usually on the older non-photosynthetic tissue.

"Monotypic genus" is a cool term to throw around if you're trying to impress your friends with your botanical nomenclatural acuity (and so it was with those last three high-falutin' words I just laid down). All that means is that there are some plants that are so genetically unique that they are the only member of their genus. And so it is with the plant above left. *Obregonia denegrii* is the lone member of its genus—a wonderful little ball of a cactus with a spiral growth form. *Aztekium ritteri*, above middle, was also the only member of its genus, discovered and described in 1929. A relative, *Aztekium hintonii* (above right), was found nearby in 1992. A third member, *Aztekium valdesii* (see habitat image on page 136) was later discovered and published in 2013. All are highly prized collector plants.

Right: A crested (and grafted) example of a pelecyphora. At least I think it is. There is a euphorbia— *Euphorbia piscidermis*—that looks very much like this, especially in the cristate form. It looks like it is grafted onto a cactus, so it is likely the pelecyphora. Or maybe a turbinocarpus?

Below: Ah, good old *Lophophora williamsi*i, a.k.a. peyote. I'd like to think that some of the psychedelic crainionauts that are seeking this plant out for enlightenment would just admire how wonderful it is without having to eat it. How could you possibly want to ruin these cute little creatures which took a long time to reach even these small sizes? Maybe it's just because, at my age, I'm trying to hang on to my few remaining brain cells. Illegal to sell, probably not to own (all this depends on where you live, and the current state of drug laws). If you have one, hang onto it. Don't eat it. Please.

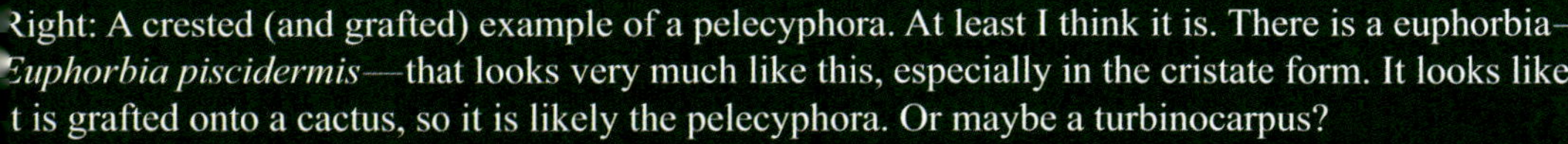

The small, obscure, monotypic, or other....

These last few pages of the cactus chapter are a catch-all section, okay, a catch-some section, of some of the primarily small and sometimes obscure and almost always collectable cacti.

Pelecyphora aselliformis (often confused with *Turbinicarpus pseudopectinata*, see the discussion on page 19) is rare in both habitat and cultivation as it has proven to be a fussy grower. But the reward is in the weirdness of its modified spines or tubercules, which look a bit like fish scale patterns, or perhaps ornate Victorian roof shingles, or like a tightly organized race of flattened mealy worms, or woodlice trying to reach a reward at the top. I have seen images of mature habitat plants that have lost most of the characteristic tubercules, but I believe this would take many years to develop in cultivation. It also has iridescent fuchsia-purple flowers with gold anthers. If you can find one, it would be worth the effort to grow this little gem. The only other known member of this genus is *P. strobiliformis*.

Coryphantha

This variable group of small, globular cacti is from an area that stretches from northern Mexico into the southwest United States. Some people confuse them with mammillarias or escobarias, but to me quite a few look more like gymnocalyciums. The bodies are defined more by grooved tubercles than ribs, and a few of them have recurved spine clusters, as in *C. elephantidens* at left. At right is *C. radians*. *Photos by Brian Kemble.*

Thelocactus

Thelocactus is yet another genus of solid-bodied, round to cylindrical spiny cacti. My favorites are similar to *Thelocactus rinconensis* with wavy tuberculate ribbing, near right. Others, such as *T. lausseri*, far right, have more conventional spiny bodies but exceptionally fine flowers (photo by Ben Grillo).

Eriosyce

This is a group of rugged South American globular cacti. Many, or perhaps all, of the plants formerly included in the genera *Neoporteria*, *Pyrrhocactus*, and *Neochilenia* are now included in *Eriosyce*, or are considered subgroups within that genus based on physical characteristics. I'm not capable of identifying many of them on sight as they fit the "spiny little ball" description of so many cacti. At left is *Eriosyce sandillon* (photo by Elton Roberts). The little beauty in the middle left image is one of the best, *Eriosyce occulta*. At middle right is *E. multicolor*, and at far right is *E. senilis* (both images by Brian Kemble). Some plants in this genus can eventually get quite large, but most seen in collection are tinier little plants as seen here.

Leuchtenbergia principis is the only species in this monotypic genus from northern Mexico. In cultivation, older specimens can develop a "foot," as seen at right, and occasionally will bifurcate (branch) into multiple heads. The papery spines tend to grow into a brambly look. Flowers are a shiny and papery yellow, followed by large seed pods, as seen here. Despite the somewhat ratty look, it is a highly desired plant by enthusiasts.

Frailea

Fraileas are a small and rather obscure group of South American cacti, usually only encountered in cultivation within a small collector community (i.e., rarely available at commercial nurseries). Flowers generally are yellow and sometimes produce fruit and seed despite barely opening at all. They may self-fertilize while still inside the plant, a process known as cleistogamy. Thanks to Daiv Freeman and his online Cactiguide for helping me learn a new word of the day.

Left: *Frailea castanea*.
   Photo: Brooke Parkin

Epithelantha is a genus comprised of either two or seven species, depending on who you talk to. They rarely exceed two inches in height, with small white flowers. *E. micromeris*, the most common, is shown here. See also page 217.

Epithelantha

Turbinicarpus is a larger genus (24 species) of slightly larger, but still small container cacti. Many are prized by collectors, and most are eager to bloom with often stunning little flowers. Shown here:
Top left: *Turpinicarpus rioverdensis*.
Top right: *T. lophophoroides*.
Middle left and middle right: *T. panarotti*.
Below left: *T. jauernigii*.
Below right: *T. pseudopectinatus*, which looks much like *Pelycyphora aselliformis v. pectinata* on page 235.

Both of these genera come from overlapping parts of the Chihuahuan desert of northwestern Mexico.

Epithelantha images by Paul Lawler.
Turbinicarpus images by Elton Roberts.

Turbinicarpus

Leuchtenbergia principis

At left is one of my favorite forms of gymnocalyciums, *G. ochoterenae ssp. vatteri*. Sometimes it develops a symmetrical "armor" with bumpy ridges that are suggestive of horseshoe crab. Similar plants are shown on the facing page (large image).

Immediately below is the classic flower form that is common to most gymnocalyciums, particularly visible in the early stage of bud. It looks like overlapping scales that ultimately fan out into occasionally colorful flowers as seen in the two plants below. However, most gymnos have more of a dirty white flower that can hardly be described as notable or particularly attractive.

The bottom row are examples of the most common gymno in cultivation: *G. mihanovichii*. The larger clump at bottom left is growing on its own roots, and bottom right is exhibiting some of the chlorotic variegation that makes it so desirable. If grafted onto a stock, as seen below middle, the entire plant can assume the extreme coloration, usually referred to as "hot-heads" or "moon cactus." These de-chlorophylled mutants can be yellow, orange, purple, or red. Unfortunately, the grafting stock is always more vigorous and wins out in the end, so you will be lucky to keep one in this state for a few years. It is a novelty gimmick, but still fun.

"Gymnos" are smaller, mostly globose and solitary container cacti, some with remarkable architecture. After you've been around cacti for a while, there are a handful that have a common look that defines the group, including *G. ochoterenae ssp. vatteri* above. The Latin name translates as "naked bud" as the flowers lack any spines, wool, or bristles (see facing page). Flowers generally are creamy white; a few others are pink or fuchsia.

Above left: *Gymnocalycium multiflorum*.
Middle left: *Gymnocalycium cardenasianum* (or *G. marsoneri*?). This plant looks to me like it has wrapped itself into its own barbed wire containment shell.
Left: *Gymnocalycium pflanzii*.
Bottom left: Not a gymno. This is another example of convergent evolution. What looks like a spineless gymnocalycium is actually *Euphorbia gymnocalycioides* from Africa. It sure looks like it belongs.
Below middle left and right: *Gymnocalycium triacanthum*. This species exhibits quite a bit of variability, with some individuals bestowed with splendidly flat and wiggly spines.
Below right: An exceptionally long-spined form of *G. cardenasianum*.

Sulcorebutia pulchra

Sulcorebutia pygmaea 'Pallida'

Sulcorebutia clizensis

Sulcorebutia rauschii violacidermis

Sulcorebutia bicolor

Sulcorebutia glanduliflora

Sulcorebutia pulchra HS 78a

Rebutia krainziana

Sulcorebutia albissima

Rebutias and Sulcorebutias

After over thirty years in the succulent business, I've yet to figure out the difference between rebutias and sulcorebutias. Some websites just default the latter into the former. The Latin "sulco" means "furrowed," so the assumption would be that the sulcorebutias have more furrowed or ridged body parts. I can't really see that in the examples here. According to the 2006 decision of the International Cactaceae Systematics Group (yes, that's a thing), sulcorebutias (former genus *Weingartia*; at least some of them were in there) have been subsumed into the genus *Rebutia*, but at this point I'm going to break out the non-scientific "whatever" and just show you a handful of examples of these smallish, sometimes perfect-looking and usually beautifully flowered little South American treasures. There are forty-one recognized species and many cultivars and hybrids. These are best kept as container plants owing to their smallish nature. If you attend a local cactus and succulent club show in spring or summer and see these in bloom, they might become your favorites.

The facing page shows just a small sampling of some of Elton Roberts' images of these tiny titans. I don't think I need to offer any superlatives here to convince you that rebutias and sulcorebutias are highly coveted by the cactus cognoscenti. Upon reflection, I will curate my cactus collection in this direction.

A collection of rebutias/sulcorebutias at a cactus show.

Eulychnia spiralis, crested form

Eulychnia spiralis

There are quite a few collector cacti that you probably will see only at a cactus and succulent show, or on the web, or if you are lucky enough to visit a collector's house. Plants like those you see on this spread are offered for sale at specialty nurseries or by online vendors, but rarely as mature as the plants here. You pretty much have to buy them young—for example, a single head as opposed to multi-head clusters—and grow old with your plant. If you belong to one of the clubs, you may have an opportunity to purchase a mature show plant when a collector decides to thin their collection, or moves (or sadly moves on). Soon after opening my nursery, I was contacted by a lady whose father had passed away recently, and she wanted to liquidate his cactus collection before the plants died, too. Not being as much of a cactus enthusiast at the time, I somewhat reluctantly filled up my truck with a bunch of spiny critters that only cost me a few dollars each. Not realizing what I had and soon sold for a slight markup, I'm hoping that the savvy collector who bought all those multiheaded copiapoas for $10 each appreciated his bargain. They were worth hundreds each. Live and learn.

Right and above is *Eulychnia castanaea f. spiralis,* one of the rare and highly collectible prizes, for obvious reasons. It looks like it was just twisted into shape. Top left shows some of the unstable growth iterations of this plant—spiral form, randomly spined and fuzzy, and a fuzzy crest. Middle above is the rare crested version of the plant. If someone comes up with a crested and variegated specimen, they will be the official King of Kaktus. I bet it will happen. *Eulychnia* is actually a genus of five rather large-growing and very spiny cacti from coastal Peru and Chile, but they are rarely encountered in cultivation at this time. I hope we'll start seeing some soon, as they are quite attractive—if you like cactus. Below left is *Blossfeldia liliputana*, the only member of its genus and perhaps the smallest of all cacti, hence the reference to being "lilliputian." It is a high-altitude South American plant that inhabits rocks and cracks with a unique ability in habitat to almost completely dry out and rehydrate like a moss or lichen. Below middle is a rare variegated specimen of *Coryphantha macromeris ssp. runyonii* (?).

Matucana aurantiaca ssp. currundayensis

Uebelmannia pectinifera

Parodia werneri

Mammillaria carnea

Trichocereus bridgesii monstrose

Mammillaria luethyi

Weingartia neocumingii f. brevispina

"Snowball Cactus," Parodia scopa

Rebutia sp.

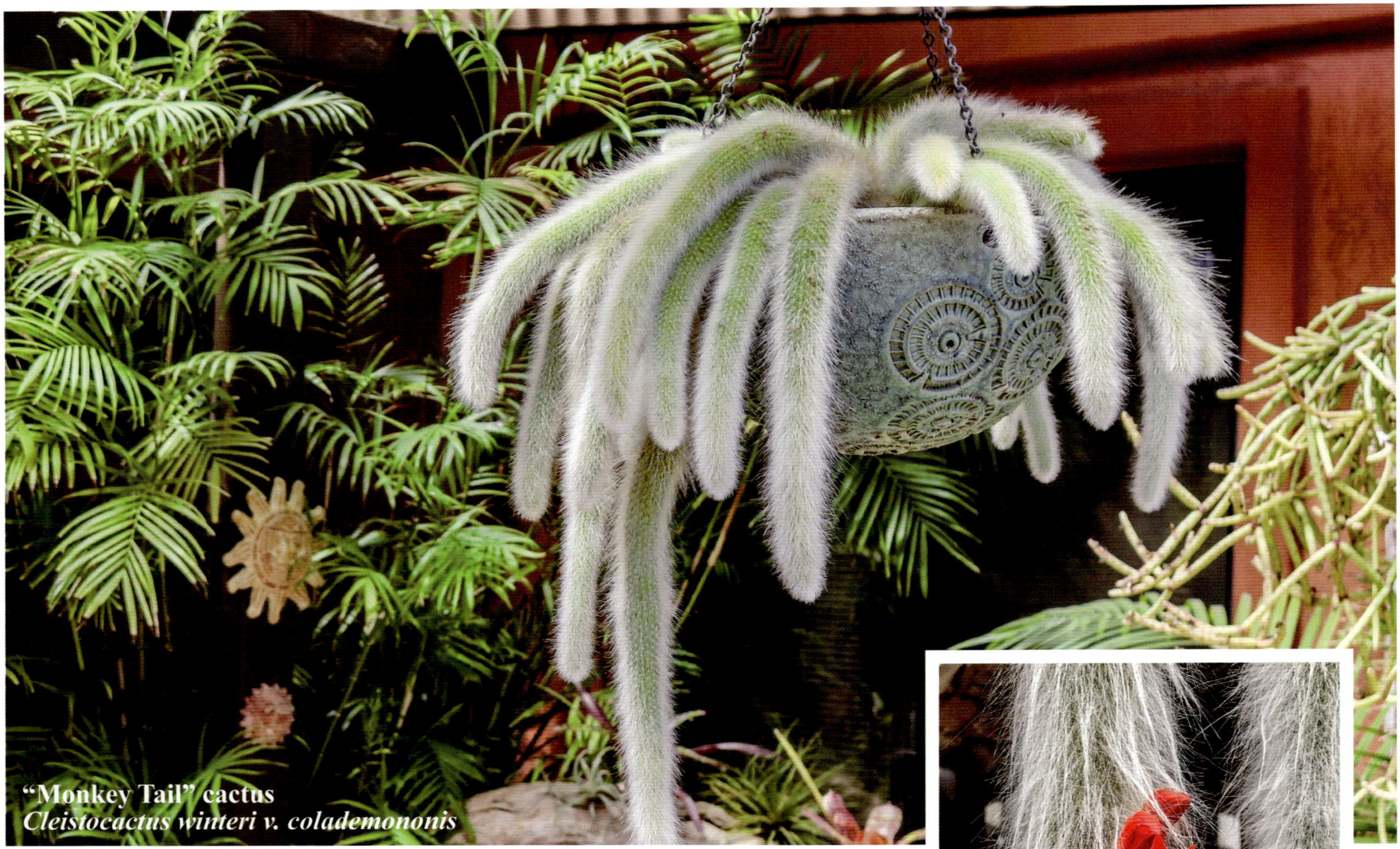

"Monkey Tail" cactus
Cleistocactus winteri v. colademononis

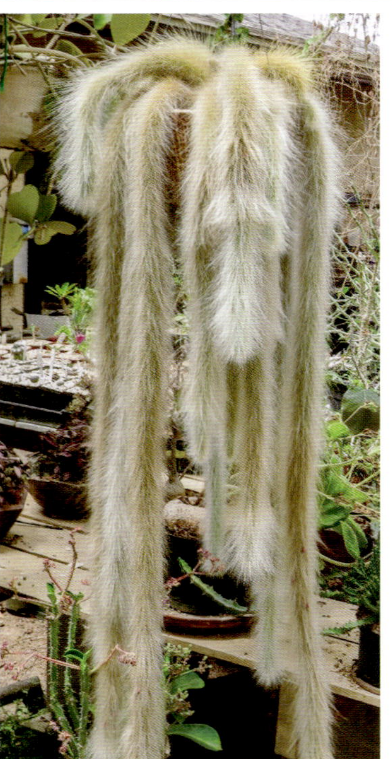

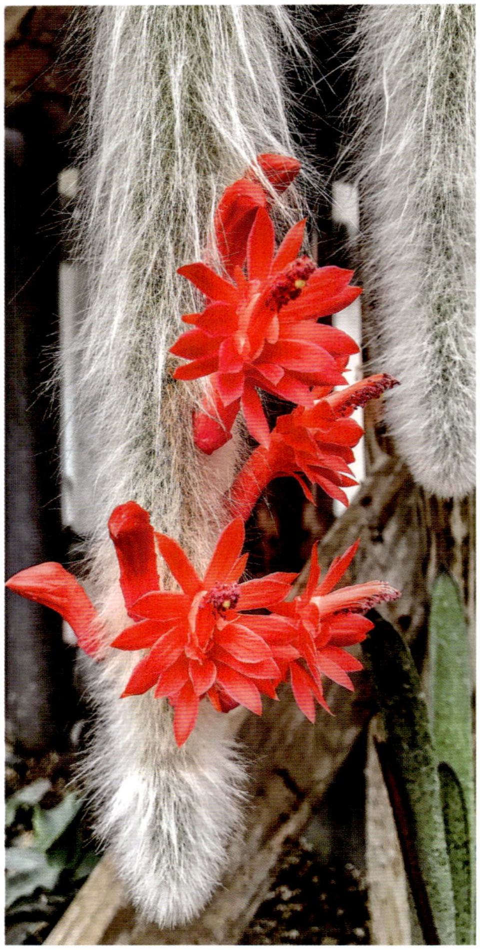

The fuzzy white monkey tail cactus, *Cleistocactus winteri ssp. colademononis,* is a fairly new hanging cactus that still is difficult to find for sale. It has excellent red flowers, and like the other cascading cacti on this spread, will fare better in partial shade or broken sun (and will do especially well in greenhouse conditions). Let's hope growers will make the effort to get more of these into cultivation soon.

"Tail" cactus

There are a few genera of subtropical vining cacti that grow in a naturally cascading or sprawling form. Many have stunning flowers, and spines that are more hairy than stiff and sharp. Most do best in less than full sun conditions as they're used to the dappled light of the jungle canopy.

Left: *Selenicereus* (a.k.a. *Strophocactus*) is a genus of mostly epiphytic, vine-like climbing plants from Central America. This is *S. testudo*, also known as the "Dog Tail" or "Tortoise" cactus (not sure where the tortoise reference comes from). Most plants in the genus have very large and usually nocturnal flowers.

"Dog Tail" cactus, *Selenicereus testudo*

Photo: Shawn Parkin

Above: A long-time favorite is the "Rat Tail" cactus, *Aporocactus flagelliformis*. It has gorgeous fuchsia flowers cascading down the relatively soft "tails" in spring. It is somewhat sun shy and prefers a greenhouse, lath, or garden window situation.

Left: The "Rick-Rack" or "Fishbone Cactus" is *Selenicereus anthonyanus* (also sometimes referred to by the genus name *Cryptocereus*). It has a unique zig-zag leaf pattern and enjoys similar conditions as the other orchid cacti: partial shade or greenhouse conditions, ample water, and room to roam, preferably in a hanging basket. Flowers are typically white but can be pink or reddish.

Known for its distinctive "dragon fruit," the several species of *Hylocereus* can be tremendous climbing cacti. I have seen one climb at least forty feet up a tree. The plant at right has worked its way almost that high on a fan palm trunk. They are distinguished from most of the other orchid cacti by their three-ribbed design and much more robust growth habit. Flowers are large and white, usually blooming at night, and holding on through cloudy days. Some plants are more prone to producing fruit than others. I know of several very old and sprawling individuals that flower profusely but never have offered fruit—they may be sterile. Said fruit when produced, in my opinion, looks better than it tastes, although that inset middle photo does look tasty, and the pink/magenta fruit is reputed to be tastier. *Hylocereus* are native to Central America and the Caribbean. They are frost sensitive, but grow well in California.

Inset photos by Hisako Leggett

Rhipsalis and *Hatiora*

I've always lumped these two genera together as they both are primarily small, non-spiny, bushy little pseudo-cacti. Both are part of the tribe Rhipsalideae—which are subtropical, bushy or pendant, often segmented plants, some with very nice flowers. They can be difficult to identify unless you spend a lot of time with them. Among the most common in cultivation is *Hatiora salicornoides* (upper left), also known as the "Drunkard's Dream," and the "Easter Cactus," *Hatiora gaertneri*, upper right. Also in this tribe is the genus *Schlumbergera*, of which several varieties claim the title "Christmas Cactus" (see facing page). Both common names are predicated upon their approximate blooming seasons. There are some rhipsalis that look like epiphyllums, such as *R. oblonga* (lower right), except the flowers are much smaller, and another visually similar genus from South America called *Lepismium*. The only member of the cactus family to have escaped the New World prior to human intervention is *Rhipsalis baccifera* (left, *ssp. horrida*) which made it to Madagascar and Africa on its own (with a little help from birds most likely).

"Christmas Cactus,"
Schlumbergera cultivar

Orchid Cacti

There are a number of tribes or genera of subtropical to tropical cacti that have evolved away from the typical fat-bodied and spiny desert forms. Most have only nominal spines, usually thin and benign. Quite a few are semi-epiphytic tree-climbers, although most will still be rooted into the ground below. They primarily are green, flat-stemmed, cascading plants, often with beautiful (albeit short-lived) flowers. Some of the primary genera are *Epiphylum*, *Rhipsalis*, and *Schlumbergera*.

These "jungle" cacti usually prefer filtered or broken sun similar to the under-tree canopy of their native habitat, primarily Mexico and Central America. A number will adapt to full sun in less than desert conditions. Being somewhat tropical, most orchid cacti will appreciate a bit extra water, primarily during warm parts of the year, along with occasional feeding. The most common orchid cacti are the ephiphyllums, highly sought after for their glorious flowers, along with the seasonal Christmas Cactus (*Schlumbergera*) and Easter Cactus (*Rhipsalidopsis* or *Hatiora*).

The good old prickly pear or pad/paddle cactus (genus *Opuntia*) have gone on quite a run since humans got involved. This New World native exists in many natural forms and species, but has also experienced a good deal of hybridization for commercial purposes (read up on Luther Burbank). It has gone around the world to be an invasive nuisance in many places including Africa, Australia, and many tropical parts of the world. Opuntias are not generally among the most desirable of ornamental succulents, but there are some sought after varieties, such as the wavy spined *Opuntia sulphurea* (below right), the purple *O. santa-rita*, and several crested varieties. The larger forms can make excellent background frames or even become cactus fences. Most do have nice papery flowers, and some are valuable for their edible pads and fruits, called "nopales" and "tuna."

Approaching this book, my enthusiasm for opuntias was lukewarm at best, excepting a few varieties such as *O. santa-rita*. However, the further I went photographing and researching the genus, the more I became a fan. They are old staples in the southwestern landscape with the classic silhouettes of Disney cartoons or old westerns. They line dirt driveways in rural areas of the backcountry. There still are patches of native opuntias in undisturbed slices of the suburban landscape. One example I always notice on my travels is at the base of the Conejo Grade in Ventura County. At least, I think they're native. That patch burned in a recent wildfire but is making a comeback.

Opuntias

Opuntia santa-rita
Photo: EW&C

This is as good a place as any to plug the *Cactus and Succulent Journal*, published quarterly by the Cactus and Succulent Society of America (CSSA). If you're committed to the hobby, you need to be a member if for no other reason than to receive the journal, full of informative articles and images of the plants we love, written by experts and focusing on cultivation as well as habitat. In addition, you can join CSSA with your subscription. The CSSA hosts a biannual convention at various locales, with internationally recognized speakers and tours to local sights of botanical interest. It is a fun way to stay engaged in the hobby and meet fellow enthusiasts.

One of my favorite covers was from a 1996 issue (above left) with an article inside about the opuntias of the Galapagos Islands. This tree of a prickly pear above is *Opuntia echios v. barringtonensis*. The photograph of the late Texan Richard O. Albert was taken in 1996 by legendary cactophile Edward F. Anderson. There is some debate whether this island gigantism was a defensive response to grazing by long-necked Galapagos tortoises or simply a propensity to become arborescent to compete for sunlight with the surrounding floristic canopy. To my knowledge, this plant is not seen often in cultivation, and if there are any, certainly none that have reached this size.

Left: A dwarf and nearly spineless light green hybrid, post-flower.

Left: The delightfully fuzzy *Opuntia pailana*.

Left: A splendidly cristate form of *Opuntia linguiformis* at the Boyce Thompson Arboretum in Superior, Arizona. The rest of the opuntias on this page? Beats me. Let's call them *Opuntia ficus-indica* or hybrids thereof (except the round blue ones below that look like *Opuntia robusta*, a.k.a "The Silver Dollar Opuntia"). *O. ficus-indica* is one of the most prominent opuntia species in cultivation around the world and has taken many hybrid forms. Some are nearly spineless, like middle above, but there probably still are some small glochids to be wary of. Many have exceptional flowers, as seen inset below right (not necessarily the flower to those particular opuntias in the larger image). Above right is an opuntia that has shed its flowers and is now ornamented with flower bases that may soon grow into fruit.

Opuntia littoralis

Opuntia linguiformis

A Luther Burbank hybrid

Opuntia aciculata

Opuntia cv. 'Sunburst'

Opuntia polyacantha v. erinacea

Opuntia zebrina fma. reticulata

Opuntia acaulis (???)

Opuntia leucotricha

Opuntia sulphurea

Assuming you like spines, *Opuntia sulphurea* is one of the coolest in the genus. It offers thick, often wavy, and very long needles, unlike any other opuntias. It formerly was very rare in cultivation, but since it has proven to be easy to propagate, it is becoming much more available, thanks in large part to Hans Britsch of Western Cactus.

Opuntia macrocentra can blush purple a bit like the more popular *O. santa-rita* seen on the facing page. This plant is less popular due to its more dramatic spines, often black in mature plants and more whitish when younger. It is reputed to be very tolerant of weather extremes and is easy to grow in most conditions.

Opuntia rufida is a minimally spined ornamental species from Mexico and into Southern Texas. It has bright yellow to orange flowers and is an excellent ornamental prickly pear.

Inset left: *Opuntia rufida minima* (also monstrose) "Desert Gem" is a delightful miniature if you are looking for a bonsai cactus (shown here with *Mammillaria fragilis* monstrose). The plant here is about three inches high. It looks green here but, in general, has a cinnamon brown cast, and a large plant might be a foot high. It is covered in glochids, so handle with care.

The variable *Opuntia basilaris* often is referred to as the beavertail cactus. Native to the Mojave and Colorado deserts, it usually has smaller pads, smaller spines, and generally is a smaller opuntia but an excellent candidate for native (or almost native) California gardens. It typically has stunning pinkish flowers. A dwarf form is *Opuntia basilaris v. brachyclada*. Some opuntias, particularly some of the *basilaris* forms shown below, occasionally will develop heart-shaped pads, just to remind you that all plants need some love—or maybe it's a sarcastic "I love you" after they leave you with a handful of glochid spines.

You can make a pretty strong case that if you are only going to have one opuntia, this is the one. The coloration is stunning, although somewhat seasonal in its intensity. This Sonoran Desert native, sometimes referred to as *Opuntia violacea*, has yellow flowers, and spines can vary in size depending on subspecies. It does have some nasty glochid spines but is worth the occasional unpleasant encounter. There is a dwarf form called "Baby Rita."

Top left is an unidentified opuntia in spring bloom. Above left shows two different clones or hybrids of what may be old Burbank hybrids, differing in both pad color and flowers/fruit. Above middle and right is *Opuntia monacantha* cv. 'Maverick' (sometimes called "Joseph's Coat"), a prolific, twisting cultivar with delightful patterned variegation.

Top: A properly spiny *Opuntia littoralis* (I think) shows off its deep magenta, post-bloom fruit. Plant these big hedges towards the back of your succulent garden.

Left: There is a South American genus, *Tacinga*, that basically is a southern hemisphere version of *Opuntia*. The only species I know of that is commercially available is the plant seen here, *Tacinga inamoena*. It has delightful flowers that morph from magenta buds into little orange flowers, giving it a two-tone effect. It is a tropical cactus and usually suffers over time as a landscape plant in California climates. It might be best kept as a container plant that can be moved if needed to protect it from the elements.

Below: A psychedelic pattern likely caused by a relatively benign virus. Can you find the cartoon characters? It might take some peyote (see page 237) to open your doors of perception, but I think there's some Grateful Dead imagery going on here.

Above: The regular form of the gold-toned *Opuntia microdasys* at left, and a close-up of the coral-shaped crested form at right.

Below left: A burgundy-red spined iteration of *Opuntia rufida*. I had to go back and check my original image to see whether I messed with the color saturation here, and I didn't. This plant isn't usually quite this red, and it might have been in a bright new growth phase.

Below right: The white and gold forms of *Opuntia microdasys*.

The Glochidians

Opuntia microdasys and other
microspined devils

Above: A landscape specimen plant of *Opuntia microdasys* offers a classic cactus profile, if somewhat in miniature.

Left and below: A white form of *O. microdasys*.

The cacti on this page look soft and fuzzy to the touch—and they are, but don't do it. They all carry fine, hairlike spines called glochids, found only in *Opuntias*. They are tiny but barbed, and if touched, are more irritating than painful, but they can be *very* irritating. I often wish I had one big nasty spine to dig out rather than a cluster of little devils that are difficult to even see, let alone dislodge. You can try tweezers with a magnifying glass, duct tape, or even apply some Elmer's glue and let it harden before peeling it off. Sometimes just scraping your skin with a credit card will remove some. Some opuntias have a combination of large spines surrounded by glochids, but the plants on this page are of the glochid-only variety. Despite all of negativity I just laid on you, the glochids can make for a beautiful fuzzy and sometimes colorful plant. Flowers are typical of the genus.

There are a number of arborescent opuntias, many of which are more subtropical in nature. The tree-forming plant above likely is of the related genus *Consolea*, native to the Caribbean and Florida. This variety can develop a spiny and thick trunk, reaching up to twenty feet high. Flowers are small but a very pretty orange or yellow. It has larger spines on the trunk and a lot of nasty little glochids on the leaves. Handle with care. The plant below left has a very green and tropical look and responds well to water, as a subtropical would. *Consolea falcata*, above left, has an attractive, if spiny, profile, highlighted by the blue wall.

Right: A well-staged show plant that appears to be in the process of becoming crested or monstrose.

Sometimes called "Eve's Needle" or "Eve's Pin," the proper genus name of this common cactus—*Austrocylindropuntia*—is a seven-syllable mouthful, and most of us refer to it as *Opuntia subulata*. It is from South America (the "austro" part), and it is cylindrical rather than flat padded, so I'm going to try to start calling it by its proper name. You will see a few more members of the genus in a few pages.

Having just said it out loud a few times, I'm still going to call it an opuntia. Some Latin names just sound like you're trying too hard to show off, and this is one, in my opinion. Getting that out of the way, this longtime staple of the California landscape is as durable as most of the other opuntias, is easily grown from cuttings, and can make an impressive fence. It usually is spiny, but there are spineless, or minimally spined forms. One feature of *A. subulata* in its various forms are the flesh green "leaves" or protospines that cluster around the growing tips, sometimes blushing red. Don't feel bad if you mistake the spineless form for a euphorbia.

Even more intriguing are the crested and monstrose forms. The spineless crest at left is one of the finest. Several other cultivar forms are shown above. Top right is the crested version of the closely related *Austrocylindropuntia vestita*, and the plant below it is a cross of *A. vestita* with *A. subulata*.

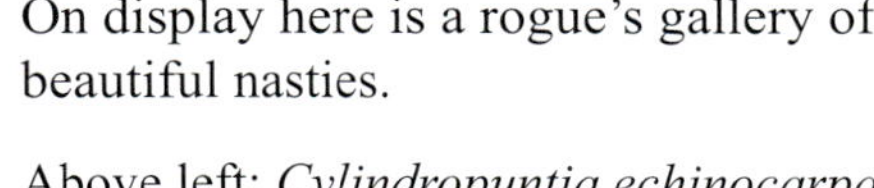

On display here is a rogue's gallery of beautiful nasties.

Above left: *Cylindropuntia echinocarpa*
Above middle: *Cylindopuntia prolifera*
Above right: *Cylindropuntia bigelovii*
Left: *Cylindropuntia spinosior*
Right: *Cylindropuntia echinocarpa*
Below left: *Cylindropuntia echinocarpa*
Below middle: *Cylindropuntia davisii*
Below right: *Austrocylindropuntia malyana.*
    Okay, this one isn't a beautiful nasty.
    It's more of a cute but not quite cuddly.

Chollas
(Cylindropuntias)

Plants referred to as "chollas" are those of the genus *Cylindropuntia*. They are characterized by their cylindrical stems, as opposed to flat stems seen in most opuntias, and are particularly known for their extremely nasty spines. I admire these plants from afar and won't let them in my nursery. If you just touch a spine, it will stick in your finger, the entire section will break off when you recoil, and you'll be sporting a new appendage until you can figure out how to get it off. Do not use your other hand or you will then have a new worthless appendage stuck to the old worthless appendage. I speak from experience. Having said that, they are beautiful desert sentinels in their own right, and their spines are stunning when backlit against a setting sun. They even have nice flowers. Still, this cactus is one that gives the rest a bad name.

Austrocylindropuntias are South American close cousins of the North American opuntias. As the name implies, they essentially are cylindrical opuntias from the south, in this case the Southern hemisphere.

Above left: *Cylindropuntia imbricata* is a bushy plant with purple flowers, which give way to yellow ripening fruit as you see here.
Middle image: An unidentified cholla, perhaps *Cylindropuntia echinocarpa*, makes a statement in a desert garden. That statement might be "stay back."
Above right: *Cylindropuntia ramosissima* is a many-branched, thin form. Perhaps a little weedy in appearance, but it backlights beautifully.

Cylindropuntias will break off in segments, as seen at left. Often they will fall off on their own, waiting to attach to an unfortunate animal or human that brushes up against them, with the goal of eventually detaching farther away and vegetatively re-establishing themselves to form a new colony. This admirable self-preservation strategy is what makes them so dangerous to work with. A case in point is Debra Baldwin's example of an encounter, below left. She still had one hand for the camera.

When I first opened my nursery, I bought a few small chollas, but after talking with another enthusiast, I decided that this would be one group I would no longer attempt to carry or sell. This was based on a story he told me about a young lady who was admiring a cholla and made the poor decision to try to gently touch a spine with her index finger. The slightest touch is all this plant needs to strike. They sometimes are called the "jumping cholla" or "jumping cactus" because the barbed tip will hook into your skin before you even realize you've touched it, like it jumped onto you. She instinctively pulled back when she realized the little segment had detached and "jumped" onto her finger, and the other end lodged into the tip of her nose. Then she just reacted and tried to pull it off with her other hand, and now she had both hands appearing to be stuck to her nose, all connected by one little 4-inch piece of cholla. I can't recall how he said she got out of this predicament, but I'm sure scissors and tweezers and some blood were involved.

So while I don't allow chollas into the nursery, I still admire them from afar at botanical gardens and in their desert habitat. I have done a few special orders for folks who wanted to build an effective wall against predators, but I left it up to them to do the actual planting. I know how they can jump.

Above: The "Boxing Glove Cactus" is one of the few crested forms of cholla in the trade. The crested/monstrose form of *Cylindropuntia fulgida v. mamillata* can contort into what looks like a series of clenched fists or boxing gloves. The example above has very recessed spines that make it more user friendly.

Late afternoon sun at the Desert Botanical Garden in Phoenix lights up chollas in a wonderful mixed display of desert beauties, here framed by the gorgeous blue *Yucca rigida*.

Right: This geometric cluster of *Cylindropuntia echinocarpa* in Piedmont, California, looks like some type of interlocking jacks from hell.

Tephrocactus articulatus v. papyracanthus, above middle and right, is referred to aptly as the "paper spine" cactus. Others, such as the form of *T. articulatus* above left, resemble pine or spruce cones. The segments of these plants easily detach if touched or moved.

Sometimes it seems nature has a sense of humor. I swear that the plant below left is real and not somebody's art project involving painted foam balls and toothpicks. It is *Tephrocactus geometricus* (sometimes referred to as *Opuntia geometricus*, and also associated with the species name *alexanderi*, shown below right and so identified at the Desert Botanical Garden in Scottsdale, Arizona.). It is a bit variable, and conditions can change its appearance. The show plants at below left and middle are just about spineless. Some specimens have small spines (see below right) and/or more of a purple tone. It is very slow growing and best kept as a container plant as it is not sturdy enough for most landscapes.

These relatives of the opuntias are primarily from Argentina. They are characterized by their rounder or globoid "pads" or segments, as opposed to the flatter pads of most opuntias. The most famous members have paper-like spines, as seen above.

Puna (Maihueniopsis) bonnieae

This little South American opuntioid has been lumped in, and split out of, a few different genera. Over the years, it has been lumped into *Austrocylindropuntia*, *Opuntia*, *Tephrocactus*, and the even more obscure but perhaps now proper *Maihueniopsis*. I like the nice simple name Puna; it sounds kind of cool and funny, so I'm going with it. There are only a couple of other species that belong in whatever genus *P. bonnieae* currently resides in. The small but mature plant at left is one of the few examples I've seen, which won a ribbon at a cactus show. It will take some work to track one down. I love the monochromatic color scheme of the various tightly packed heads, and it does offer pretty pink opuntia style flowers. From what I've learned, it grows best as a graft on *Austrocylindropuntia subulata*. Habitat images show it growing sucked almost flat into the ground, similar to lithops in habitat.

Puna (Maihueniopsis) clavarioides

This confused little freakazoid seems to grow in both a natural conical form as well as a monstrose or mutated form as a matter of course on the same plant. The genus name *Ausrtrocylindropuntia* or *Maihueniopsis* also is attached to this plant sometimes. It occasionally is called "Dead Man's Fingers," which is a fun and decadent term. Being a very tiny and clustering plant, keep it containerized.

Bottom two photos by Elton Roberts

Pereskias

Of the three subfamilies of Cactaceae (Opuntioideae and Cactoideae being the other two), the Pereskioideae stand apart both visually and genetically. It is believed that the ancestral forms of the entire cactus family likely resembled present-day pereskias, which are generally thin-stemmed and leafy, most with some form of spines, and a few are not really very succulent at all. Endemic to a large area stretching from Mexico all the way to Brazil, most pereskias are tropical to subtropical in nature, but those in cultivation generally qualify as easy to grow xerophytes.

Some pereskias have a resemblance to roses, at least at a distance, and more so in body structure than flowers. At left is *Pereskia grandifolia v. violaceae*, one of the most ornamental of the group. In warm weather with plentiful irrigation, it is a full green bush, at times covered in lavender and white flowers. It tends to defoliate in cool winter conditions, which is true for most pereskias.

Below left is one of my favorites for its warm, orange/red leaves: *Pereskia aculeata*. The only form I am familiar with is this colorful variety, but in my research, I have found this Caribbean plant to be a scrambling vine and an invasive species in the tropics—and most of the images are of a much greener plant. Perhaps the form in cultivation is the cultivar "Godseffiana"; it certainly isn't a runaway grower in dry California. The plant below is an unidentified pereskia I have owned for years. It has adopted a natural bonsai form, going leafless in the winter, leafing out in summer with occasional papery white-pink flowers.

Kingdom: *Plantae*
　Phylum: *Magnoliophyta*
　　Order: *Gentianales*
　　　Family: *Apocynaceae*
　　　　Genus: *Pachypodium*
　　　　　Species: *namaquanum*

Pachypodiums are members of the Apocynaceae ("periwinkle") familiy. They are relatives of the plumerias, whose kinship is quite obvious if you look at the flowers and leaves. It is most apparent in *P. lamerei*, seen above, which is pretty much a fat and spiny plumeria. The flowers can be long-lasting, if not as fragrant. There are a handful of pachypodiums that are relatively easy growers, such as *P. lamerei*, *P. geayi*, and *P. lealii ssp. saundersii*. The more difficult growers are many of the caudiciform, yellow-flowering varieties that look so awesome in habitat photos. Unfortunately, most are greenhouse plants in cultivation as our winters usually are just a bit too wet and cold for them as compared to their native Madagascar where many are denizens of the famous "spiny forest." There are a few from Africa as well, which are a bit more California friendly. All typically are winter deciduous.

The flora of Madagascar has had a long time to evolve some unique body plans. That's particularly true with the fat, water-storing caudiciforms, writ large with the magnificent baobab trees. This page features a small slice of the pachypodium wing of its botanical wonders, all images courtesy of plant-stalker Jeremy Spath. Above left and right are *Pachypodium rosulatum*, one with a guardian boa. One of the most unique of the pachys is *P. brevicaule*, below left and middle. This "living boulder" seems to straddle some strange kingdom between plant and animal, and maybe mineral. There are a handful of extreme pachycaul (fat) pachypodiums, but this one truly grows in a boulder form, with barely any branches or arms at all, along with minimal leaves most of the time. *P. brevicaule* is one of the most difficult to grow in cultivation, with some growers having better success grafting it onto one of the more vigorous pachypodium bodies, such as *P. lamerei* or *P. geayi*. The red-flowered *Pachypodium baronii v. windsori* is a highly desired plant but is also a finicky grower outside of habitat.

Below right: A large stand of *Pachypodium geayi*, still magnificent in a nearly leafless state.

These comical and likely very old *Pachypodium brevicaule* examples remind me of a cluster of tardigrades, the microscopic creatures known as water bears or moss piglets. We can see some crazy parallels with living things. Many other succulents resemble coral reef plants and animals.

Pachypodiums in Habitat

Pachypodiums (translation: fat foot) are almost always plump character plants that are prized among succulent enthusiasts. While we have some impressive specimens in cultivation, the real deal are the habitat plants, as you can see on this spread. Most of the species are from Madagascar, although there are a few important members from the African continent.

At left and below are *Pachypodium lealii*, which hails from Mozambique, Swaziland, and South Africa. The more squat form below is representative of a regional strain from a lower altitude in central Namibia.

Photos: Mike Hackett

The unique crested *P. lamerei,* above left, lives in the greenhouse of the UC Berkeley Botanical Garden. It's rather famous for its pose—it appears to be flexing its arms in the classic body builder crouch with some crazy "muscles" on its bulging biceps. The plant was donated to the garden in an earlier stage of cresting. The story I heard is that the owner says a cat jumped onto it and broke the growing tip of the then uncrested, single-stem plant. He says it responded by growing into a crest. This is a nice story, but it defies the axiom that nobody knows how to actually cause a plant to crest. All kinds of techniques and chemicals have been tried over the years to stimulate fasciation (cresting), but as far as I know, there has never been a reliable or universal agent to cause it to happen. It is just a mutation that will occasionally pop up of its own accord. However, if there is a cresting trait in the genetic makeup of a particular plant, it may hold true, and even non-crested parts (or reverted to normal parts) may one day crest. The only sure way to make more crests is to cut one into more crests. Having said all that, if you're not happy with your cat, you might want to give it a go. I'm kidding. It won't work.

Below left: Once a pachypodium has reached maturity and flowered, you will occasionally find seed pods developing post-bloom. They usually develop in pairs and can resemble green bananas. At some point, the pods will begin to split open, as seen in the lower middle image, and wind-born seeds will begin to float out and disperse, so catch them before they do, and try to germinate and grow your own plants. (Disclaimer: The opening seed pod image might actually be from a *Fockea edulis*, but pachypodium pods look and behave similarly). Below right is the larger and thicker-leaved form known as *v. ramossum*, in full leaf in late January. This three-foot plant might be five years old or more at this point, likely yet to flower in its life, but it is landscape hardened to the point that it might only briefly drop its leaves just prior to growing a new flush in spring.

Pachypodium lamerei

One of the more endearing of the spiny succulents is the "Madagascar Palm," *Pachypodium lamerei*. It is the most common pachypodium in cultivation, with its common name moniker a nod to its palm-shaped profile. It is, of course, not a palm; as mentioned earlier, it's part of the Apocynaceae (periwinkle) family, closely related to the plumerias. Typically a single straight-trunked plant, it will branch upon flowering with age (usually by around ten years old and a few feet high). Old specimens can develop fat, bottle-shaped trunks with a branching canopy and long-lasting, late summer flowering events. It typically is deciduous in the winter months but is one of the least prone of the genus to winter rot from rain. Just stop watering when the leaves begin to turn yellow. It can, at times, produce crests, as seen at left and on the facing page. Like most in this genus, it doesn't deal well with freezing or near freezing and winter wet conditions, so provide good drainage.

Pachypodium geayi

Pachypodium geayi probably is the second most frequently cultivated pachypodium behind *P. lamerei*. It is distinguishable by its thin, gray-green leaves with pronounced and usually pinkish mid-leaf stem, as well as fine, silver, fuzzy hairs around the new leaves and spines. It can grow to well over six feet in captivity, with smaller white flowers, and it's considered to be an easy grower. It will branch with age, usually after flowering, but not as enthusiastically as *P. lamerei*. I have seen hybrids with this and *P. lamerei*.

I have talked to several growers who have told me that *P. geayi* seems to be more cold tolerant than *P. lamerei* in inland conditions where occasional winter freezing conditions are more common.

An observation about growing pachypodiums in California and, perhaps, anywhere outside of its native habitat and latitude:

Many growers have found older pachypodiums to eventually show bleached or burned trunks, almost always on the southern exposure side of the trunk, as seen in a rather minor example on the pachypodium trunk, near left. It doesn't seem to be anything harmful, but it tarnishes the look of the plant. A guess about what causes this would be exposure from a lower angle and more intense sun than a plant would evolve with in a lower latitude and more tropical environment. I have noticed these trunk burns after fall heat waves, when the sun can be quite harsh and is hitting the plant more "sideways" than the more overhead and possibly diffused sun and heat of Madagascar. California's Santa Ana conditions can be brutal for plants (and people) that aren't accustomed to it and aren't genetically predisposed to dealing with that intense sun and dry heat.

I have seen southern exposure trunk burns on some cacti and euphorbias as well, which can be compounded when a plant is freshly relocated from a lower light or more protected location, or perhaps has been placed at a different orientation that it was before. Some people will mark a plant's directional sides prior to moving, and plant accordingly in its new location for that reason.

Photo: Russ Hunsaker

Pachypodium namaquanum

Also known as "half-men" due to their profile in Namaqualand, a 170,000 square mile arid region in southern Africa, this character plant has remarkable frilly leaves and develops a fat trunk with age. It is tenuous as an in-ground plant in California—I've seen some successes and failures. Plant it high, among rocks and with good drainage. If you can keep one going long enough for it to flower, they are quite stunning. While most deciduous leafy succulents, including most pachypodiums, will generate new leaves in spring, this species tends to stay dormant until mid-summer, but then it usually holds leaves deep into winter, long after the other species have shed theirs.

Left: *Pachypodium rutenbergianum* is a thin-leaved, vigorous brancher. Most young plants have very skinny long stems topped by a flush of leaves, but it will develop a stout, branched trunk with age.

At right is an aberrant form of *Pachypodium lamerei* with more rounded and slightly crenulated leaves—just an outlier that popped up in a seed batch. We're always on the lookout for such wonderful weirdlings.

The literature is a little bit vague on *Pachypodium sofiense*. What to my eyes looks like an especially nice form of *P. lamerei* is sometimes referred to as a subspecies of *Pachypodium rutenbergianum*, which it doesn't really look like. The internet wasn't much help in figuring this out, but it's a nice pachy with pretty green, glossy leaves and white flowers. It's reputed to be a fast grower, so let's hope we get more into cultivation. The owner of the plants here considers it his favorite and the most durable of the genus.

When is it safe to plant?

If you live in a Mediterranean climate such as coastal California, most succulents can be transplanted—either in pots or ground—any time of the year. However, if the plant in question hails from a more temperate or subtropical region that doesn't have a winter wet/cold cycle, it might be prudent to suspend transplanting activities during the winter months.

There always is a bit of a transplant shock any time you mess with a plant's roots, but generally, in warm weather, most succulents show no ill effects from the process. Some of the thinner and leafier euphorbias might begin to weep and shed some leaves after transplanting but respond shortly after being watered and exposed to sun.

To be on the safe side, succulents that tend towards winter dormancy and leaf dropping, such as most pachypodiums, should not be transplanted from roughly October through March (unless you have a greenhouse) as they are preparing to "go to sleep" for the winter. This would apply to any other cacti or succulents that you know are from similar subtropical climates. Winters in the Southwest U.S. can be colder and wetter than parts of South and Central America or subtropical Africa, so avoid that undue stress.

Pachypodium lealii-saundersii is one of the easier pachyodiums to grow and, over time, can become a nice fat caudiciform, as seen above. It can be presented as bonsai, and older specimens will display white to white/pink flowers, reminiscent of a spiny *Adenium obesum*. The subspecies *saundersii* shown here is the most available and encountered in the trade, but there is a straight *P. lealii* that differs slightly in having less shiny to almost fuzzy leaves, and may grow a bit thinner and less branchy—see the examples on page 273. I personally cannot tell the difference, at least in small plants. There is an excellent introduction to this and the other pachypodiums by Geoff Stein on the Dave's Garden website. If you can find it, the out-of-print book *Pachypodium and Adenium* by Gordon Rowley is another wonderful resource with images of plants in habitat and cultivation.

After thirty years of goofing around with succulents, I still can't immediately distinguish between *Pachypodium succulentum* and *P. bispinosum*. They just blend into the same plant in my head. Having said that, they are two distinct species, and the primary difference is in the flowers. *P. bispinosum* has more bell- or funnel-shaped, pink/white, tiny flowers, and those of *P. succulentum* are more open and divided. I believe *P. bispinosum* is a bit more prone, as well, to forming a fat base with advance age, as seen at right, and *P. succulentum* will form more of an arborescent/tree shape, as seen below. There is a hybrid between the two (as well as the "Arid Lands" variety of *Pachypodim succulentum x. Pachypodium namaquanum*). Both are a bit easier to grow than some of the yellow flowered forms on the facing page.

Below left is *Pachypodium succulentum*, with the typical flower shown inset. The middle image flowers are the more bell-shaped type found on *P. bispinosum*. Note the yellow aphids that have eagerly colonized these new buds. You do want to try to get rid of them by whatever means necessary. From my experience, they don't present a big hazard to the plant itself, but they are prone to the occasional infestation by mealies or spider mites, so keep an eye out. Far right image is unidentified, but my guess would be *P. succulentum*.

There is a subspecies of *P. succulentum*, known as *ssp. griquense*, that has smaller, primarily white flowers.

Pachypodium bispinosum

Pachypodium succulentum

The fat, mostly yellow-flowering, very difficult to grow pachypodiums

The pachypodiums on the preceding pages are somewhat sensitive to winter wet and cold but are generally growable in cultivation without too much extra work. The rest of the genus is another story. The specimens on this page have spent most or all of their lives in greenhouses, at least in the cooler months. The collection below middle was bought by another collector, who in turn wants to sell them as soon as he can because these plants make him understandably nervous. In his eloquent words, it sucks when they croak.

I hesitate to recommend a site like Pinterest to do further research, as the information can be scant or wrong or nonexistent, but if you want to see some crazy images of pachypodiums, go check it out. There are some examples of huge, in-ground plants thriving in more tropical locales, as well as expertly staged show plants.

Left: Unidentified, likely *Pachypodium rosulatum*.

There are a handful of caudiciform pachypodiums, mostly yellow-flowering. The main species are *P. gracilis*, *P. baronii* (red flowers), *P. rosulatum*, and *P. brevicaule*. There are many more. I tend to dump them all into one category: really cool plants that always die on me. If you have a greenhouse for the winter months, then you've got a chance, but I've found all of these to be difficult growers, particularly during the cool and wet winter months. For that reason, they are not recommended as landscape plants, but if you like a challenge and fancy yourself to be a good grower with a greenhouse, you can produce wonderful, fat and flowering show plants like those seen here.

Kingdom: *Plantae*
Phylum: *Tracheophyta*
Order: *Caryophyllales*
Family: *Didiereaceae*
Genus: *Alluaudia*
Species: *montagnacii*

Alluaudias
(Didiereaceae)

This group of Madagascan succulent curiosities is properly known as the *Didiereaceae*, subfamily *Didiereoideae*, but nobody outside of academia refers to this group by either of those names. The handful we encounter in cultivation are mainly from the genus *Alluaudia*, with really just two members of the genus *Didieria* only occasionally encountered (*D. trollii* and *D. madagascariensis*). *Alluaudia procera*, seen here and on the next page, is far and away the most prominent member in cultivation due to its superior form, as well as ease of cultivation and propagation.

These all are Madagascan plants that do well in California's Mediterranean climate and will even grow in the Southwest desert regions. However, they don't like to freeze, and they are best kept as container plants in the desert so they can more easily be sheltered from frost. All typically are deciduous, shedding leaves in the fall and starting up again in spring. Their spines are similar to euphorbias—sharp, but not quite cactus sharp, and not as easily detached into your skin if gently handled.

Crested examples of *Didiereaceae* do exist, but from what I have observed, all of them eventually will revert to normal growth—the one I owned did. Based on general design and spines, some alluaudias look superficially like certain euphorbias, especially their fellow Madagascan euphorbias. One euphorbia in particular, *E. didiereoides* (rare in cultivation), looks quite a bit like some type of alluaudia or didierea. Hence the species name, a nod to convergent evolution.

The subfamily *Portulacarioideae*, which includes the popular soft succulent *Portulacaria afra* or "Elephant Bush," recently has been folded into *Didiereaceae* but is not included here.

By far the most commonly encountered member of the Didiereaceae in cultivation is the "Madagascar Ocotillo," *Alluaudia procera*. It has, at first blush, a very similar profile to the classic ocotillo, *Fouquieria splendens* (page 295). It also sometimes is called the "False Ocotillo," which I don't like as it seems to imply that it is a lowly impostor. The ocotillo might as well be the 'False Alluaudia'. They both are fantastic plants that offer an excellent example of convergent evolution.

This Madagascan plant generally is thicker and more fully leaved than the fouquierias and is an easier plant for coastal California. The leaves emerge in early spring and remain until yellowing and falling off in late fall or winter. Flowers are not as showy as the red ocotillo flowers—they are large, cream-colored balls at the stem tips, as seen at right. *Alluaudia procera* usually forms a multi-stemmed tall clump of spires and can reach a height of 30 feet or more. Older specimens often display a thicket of lateral stems "octopussing" around the base, similar to *Didierea trollii*. It grows easily from cuttings.

Above: Variegation is rare, but not unheard of, in this genus. I even took home a crested *Alluaudia procera* once, but it slowly worked its way out of the fan crest and into multiple arms, as plants sometimes do.

Alluaudia ascendens

Alluaudia ascendens might be the most dramatic large alluaudia, but it's rarely seen in cultivation. At first, it appears very similar to *A. procera,* but it is slower to branch. It usually is a large, single trunk for many years before branching, as seen in the mature specimen shown at left at Grigsby Cactus Gardens in Vista, California. I suspect the plant is rarer simply because there are fewer cuttings to be had. By the time an old specimen finally branches, most owners don't want to cut on them.

Alluaudia ascendens has several characteristics that differentiate it from *A. procera,* primarily its heart-shaped leaves (inset image), and also a different flowering mechanism. Where *A. procera* has large, creamy, round flower spheres at the growing tips, *A. ascendens* has less remarkable flowers that are short and hug the upper portion of the stems, making them difficult to see from a distance.

The only treatment of the family to my knowledge is this thin book/pamphlet by Gordon Rowley from the early '90s. It is a habitat-oriented look at the Didiereaceae, with some nice images of what old habitat plants can look like. It is complete, including some of the more obscure relatives.

Alluaudia montagnacii

Quite rare in cultivation, *Alluaudia montagnacii* is unique due to the beautiful density and symmetry of its pronounced white-silver spines. It has dark green and round leathery leaves that almost look black from a distance. Although images from habitat in Madagascar show large plants typical for the genus, very few in captivity have reached such size. The three-foot tall plant at near right actually is quite old and large compared to most you will see. I believe it is a better container plant, as it is a very slow grower. The handful of relatively large specimens I've seen have been in botanical gardens, and even those pale in comparison to the larger alluaudias. It is not a particularly difficult grower, just hard to find.

Alluaudia dumosa

This always leafless and almost spineless plant has a reputation for looking like it is permanently deciduous, or even dead, but that is just the way it grows. It is the kind of plant only a mother would love, but it is on the radar among enthusiasts of Madagascan or just rare or unusual succulents. It is not particularly difficult to grow, and it is somewhat cold tolerant considering where it is from.

Deciduousness

Most leafy succulents will, at some point, shed leaves, particularly if they are living in a place that experiences colder/wetter winters than they would in their native habitat. This applies to many pachypodiums, alluaudias, and euphorbias in U.S. cultivation. Don't panic if you see leaves yellow and fall in the autumn months. They should fill out again when the weather warms in the spring. Very young container specimens need more protection in the winter. More mature and established plants will often hold their leaves year round, or just drop them briefly in the spring as new leaves replace them. As I write this, we are experiencing a relatively cold and wet California winter, yet there are several large alluaudias and pachypodiums in the area still in full leaf in late February.

Some of the Canary Island endemic euphorbias, such as *Euphorbia lambii*, experience a similar winter wet/summer dry lifestyle, so they tend to lose leaves in the summer instead, needing little irrigation until leafing out again in the fall/winter. Those plants essentially live like natives, as do most fouquierias (following section), which are more opportunistic about leafing out after rain events.

Alluaudia humbertii

One of my earliest "collector" acquisitions was an old specimen of *Alluaudia humbertii*. It had a natural bonsai look with a fat central trunk and radiating arms (I still have it 25 years later, still contained and stunted.) The plant at left is a different example of another semi-bonsai with naturally horizontal radiating arms. When planted in-ground, it can become a large and graceful plant, as seen at right at The Huntington Botanical Gardens. It grows easily from cuttings.

Alluaudia comosa

Similar to *Alluaudia dumosa*, *Alluaudia comosa* might not be among the most ornamental in the genus and, hence, usually is encountered only in botanic gardens or collections of serious Madagascan plant fans. I have rarely, if ever, seen it in full glorious leaf; it seems to prefer existing in a semi-deciduous state, as seen here, with more of a brambly and tumbleweed look. If you look closely at the large image, it actually is in full leaf. At near left is a mature *A. comosa,* in habitat, photographed by Brian Kemble. To my knowledge, we don't have any plants in cultivation close to this size.

Didierea trollii

Of the two members of the genus *Didierea*, *D. trollii* is the most available and easiest grower. The "Octopus Plant" grows in a prostrate tangle of limbs close to the ground for many years but eventually develops vertical columns over ten feet tall. It can create quite a striking specimen with age, as witnessed in the mature specimen at left at the San Diego Zoo Safari Park. Flowers are infrequent in cultivation and are small and close to the leaves and spines. It usually is leafless in winter, but older specimens will hold leaves most of the year.

Didierea madagascariensis

Neither of the two species of the genus *Didierea* is common in cultivation, with *Didierea madagascariensis* being the rarest. It is a very slow grower, and the three-foot high plant at left is one of the larger I've seen. Images from Madagascar show arborescent specimens with profiles similar to the larger alluaudias.

Decarya madagascariensis

Of the four genera of the subfamily Didiereoideae, even less encountered than the Didierea are Alluaudiopsis and Decarya, the latter shown above and below middle and right. *Decarya madagascariensis* is a shrubby plant with distinctive zigzag branching. It has a bit more charm if kept contained and somewhat pruned to highlight its shape, seen in the show plants below, as opposed to the more bushy and tumbleweed-like plant grown in-ground above.

The two-volume Succulent and Xerophytic Plants of Madagascar by Werner Rauh (Strawberry Press) is a must-have for die-hard succulentophiles. Published in the nineties, it is an image-heavy tour through a botanical wonderland and goes into great detail on the pachypodiums, alluaudias, euphorbias, and uncarinas that I'm showing you in this book, along with many other beauties (baobabs!). Seeing actual habitat giants will put Madagascar on your travel bucket list as it has for me. These books are out of print, but still available as of this writing.

Kingdom: *Plantae*
Phylum: *Magnoliophyta*
Order: *Ericales*
Family: *Fouquieriaceae*
Genus: *Fouquieria*
Species: *purpusii*

Fouquierias are endemic to the American Southwest and much of Mexico. They range from airy tree shapes to stout columnar character plants. The best known is *Fouquieria splendens*, the famous ocotillo, an easily recognized desert sentinel. The king of the genus has to be the boojum, *F. columnaris* (right).

Fouquierias tend to leaf out during wet periods and will drop their leaves during dry or cold times. Because most are desert dwellers, they will reliably leaf out after summer monsoons or any winter rainfall they receive, and probably hold their leaves longer with irrigation in warm weather. There will always be periods of dormancy.

In Mediterranean/coastal climates, most seem to spend quite a bit of time in the leafless state. They certainly respond to rainwater better than hose irrigation, meaning they will wake up and leaf out after the first fall or early winter rains. They usually keep their leaves until late spring and tend to defoliate in the summer. Sometimes, summer watering brings the leaves back, sometimes not. I try not to push it and let the plants do what they want to do.

The ocotillo, *F. splendens*, does better inland but will live at the coast, even flowering on occasion. *F. diguetii*, being from a more similar climate in Baja California, tends to leaf and flower better along the coast but has more of a bushy or horizontal profile than the more upright *F. splendens*. We tend to substitute the "Madagascar Ocotillo," *Alluaudia procera*, if we're looking for a similar profile to the true ocotillo as it grows better for us and is arguably a more impressive plant (except for the flowers).

This is sort of a funky genus name to pronounce. Most say "foo-kee-AIR-ee-ya" or "foo-CARE-ee-ya," but others pronounce it "Foo-QUEER-ee-ya," which sounds kind of queer to me (I mean "queer" as in "strange or different").

Below: You can keep fouquierias long-term as container plants. I acquired this fat little boojum over twenty-five years ago, have repotted it once, and it seems fine being dwarfed. Maybe I should liberate it one of these days.

Fouquieria columnaris

I became succulent-aware in my mid-twenties, but my first ventures into Baja California as a teenager in the seventies made a lasting impression about the cool weirdness of nature. Like the other surfers in the van, I was eager to get to the surf spots near Cabo San Lucas, but we had to pass through some 700 miles of desert first. When you first turn inland after El Rosario, the Cataviña desert tells you pretty quickly that you've entered a different biome. I still have some old Super 8 movies taken out the van window of crazy boulder fields with these even crazier, giant, upsidedown trees that looked like leafy carrots, along with huge cactus and some kind of fat trees and red cactus. I learned later that these were the boojums, the càrdons, elephant trees, and ferocacti.

On a few subsequent Baja surf trips after I became a plant guy, I always wanted to stop the car and do a bit of photo-botanizing. Being the only plant guy in the group, I was told they could drop me off and pick me up on the way back, or I could stay in the truck and finish the surf trip which, of course, I did. Since then, I've finally taken a few Baja California trips with fellow succulent enthusiasts and had the opportunity to experience this fantastic world just a day's drive south of home. I highly recommend it.

Fouquieria columnaris is a very slow grower, and as it can only be propagated by seed, larger specimens will be very expensive. To see some amazing examples, legally imported from Baja California many years ago, check out the Baja Hill at the San Diego Zoo Safari Park— the best Baja garden not in Baja. Huge specimens can be seen at The Huntington Botanical Gardens, as well. There are also a handful of private residences that boast some old and very large "cirio" (which means "large fat candle"—smaller, constrained plants in bloom can look like a lit candle) that were imported from Mexico in the fifties and sixties before the Mexican government wisely began protecting its native flora. The old genus name was *Idria*, and some of us old timers still use it.

Fouquieria columnaris

Above: Fall color for many fouquierias occurs in late spring as they approach summer dormancy. This shedding boojum is the same plant from the previous spread, page 291.

Above: A forty-foot plus, branching *F. columnaris* at The Huntington Botanical Gardens. I tell new succulent enthusiasts that the HBG is a mecca for us plant geeks—they planted some hundred-year-old plants there almost a hundred years ago. That may be a bit of an exaggeration, but not by much. I'm sure the boojum above was an old imported specimen from Baja California (back when that could legally be done), and it and a few others have been growing there for at least sixty years. It is seen here in late spring flower.

Right: Photo of *F. columnaris* taken by Viggo Gram near the town of Cataviña in the central Baja California Desert. This telephone pole of a plant is easily fifty feet tall. I'd love to see how they handle severe wind storms, but they obviously do. The specimen on the facing page shows how they prefer to grow among rocks (this is called "saxicolous"). Rock crevices are perfect protected incubators for seeds, allowing water to accumulate and provide radiant heat for seed germination and young plants, as well as protection from predators.

Fouquieria splendens prefers life in the desert but will live reluctantly at the coast. The farther inland you live, the better most in this genus will do. As mentioned previously, *Alluaudia procera* (page 283) is a better alternative for coastal Mediterranean climates. Most fouquierias are opportunistic about leafing out when they receive rain water (like a few plants, including most weeds, they seem to be able to tell the difference between rain water and hose water). They typically are leafy from fall through spring and prefer to go dormant over the dry summer months. In their desert southwest habitat, they do experience monsoon summer rains, which will induce at least temporary leaves that time of year. Flowering seems to be most prolific after spring rains, even holding or forming flowers after leaves have dropped. As you can see in the image below, they look cool even when dormant.

If you are worried that your plant is not waking up, try bending the stems near the tips. If they are flexible, it is still waiting to wake up. If it feels dry and wants to snap, you might have a problem. I have seen a number of large *Fouquieria splendens* dug up from desert nurseries and transported bare root to coastal California, with mixed results. I think big plants prefer to live where they grew up. If you live near the coast, try starting with a 1- or 5-gallon, seed-started plant and let it acclimate.

Fouquierias all have a defining characteristic with respect to their leaves and spines. The first leaves appear to have hard bases that become the spines after the rest of the leaf falls. The leaves that subsequently appear when the plant leafs out after a rainfall sprout at the base of these new spines and don't have a petiole (the stalk that joins a leaf to a stem). If you look at the plant at left, you'll notice that the leaves do, indeed, seem to attach directly to the stem without a stalk.

Above middle: Although we all like the green fullness of a plant in full leaf, there can be a beauty in one in a dormant state such as the unidentified fouquieria—likely *F. splendens*—seen here in temporary dormancy. Having said that, it is always a relief to see the new leaves or flowers emerge. If a plant like this had died, it might be some time before you figured it out.

Above right: Hybrids do exist in this genera, but there are not many that I know of. One delight created by Joe Stead around 2010 is a cross of *Fouquieria purpusii* and *F. diguetii*, named *Fouquieria* 'Pink Instead,' a play off his last name and because the resulting flowers are pink, a happy result of the white flowers of the former and the red flowers of the latter. It doesn't always work that way when you are trying to combine species for an intermediate feature.

The ocotillo is one of the classic desert statement plants, whether you see it in habitat or in the landscape. Fouquieria splendens is the primary and most upright among several species, offering a profusion of vertical leafy stems with seasonal fire red torches of flowers at the tips. Flowers will persist or even form when the plant is in a leafless state.

Fouquieria macdougalii/diguetii

I always have had difficulty distinguishing *F. diguetii* from *F. macdougalii*. Both are nicely shaped shrubby forms, perhaps a bit more treelike and full than some of the other more airy varieties. They will develop thick trunks with age, but they are larger plants that are more suited to the landscape than containers. *F. diguetii* is native to Baja California Sur, *F. macdougalii* to mainland Mexico at the same parallel, directly across the Sea of Cortez. This makes me think they once were the same species that may have diverged a bit upon separation by the creation of the Gulf of California. In addition, there also is a small population of *F. columnaris* on the Mexican mainland that also is directly opposite from their Baja California counterparts.

I've found that most fouquierias perform a bit better—i.e., stay in leaf—in the warmer climates at least five or more miles inland from the California coast. The cooler and damper marine layer conditions that are favored by some succulents, such as aeoniums, don't play as well with these true desert dwellers.

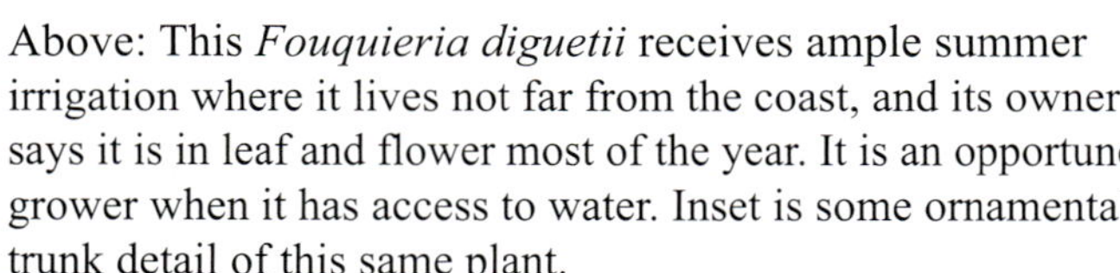

Above: This *Fouquieria diguetii* receives ample summer irrigation where it lives not far from the coast, and its owner says it is in leaf and flower most of the year. It is an opportune grower when it has access to water. Inset is some ornamental trunk detail of this same plant.

Growers have been creating some hybrids between these two species and a few others, and the plant at left may, indeed, be a nice newbie.

Above: December flowers of *Fouquieria diguetii* give this fully leaved and bushy plant (due to early winter rainfall) the feel of a decorated desert Christmas tree.

Fouquieria fasciculata

This plant and *F. purpusii* on the following pages are two of the most prized members of the genus. Both are caudiciform plants that will grow a swollen trunk and are suitable as bonsai-style specimens. *F. fasciculata* has fine, soft reddish spines and white flowers, and is a very slow grower. Indigenous to a very limited region of central Mexico, it will reluctantly grow from cuttings but is best started from seed, which is scantily available. Shedding leaves will sometimes persist in a vibrant red color.

Other than a few magazine articles, *The Genus Fouquieria,* by Robert Scott, is the only book/pamphlet I know of dedicated exclusively to the genus. It covers all eleven species in sixty pages, with excellent photos and keys to identification by flower and leaf. It could have had some more thorough proofing, but who am I to talk?

As mentioned previously, by far the most common in cultivation is the ocotillo, *F. splendens.* The other plants seen on these pages are available occasionally, and there are a handful that are rarely encountered, including *F. burragei, F. formosa, F. leonilae, F. ochoterenae,* and *F. shrevei.* All of these more obscure species have a similar look to the rest of the genus and might best be described as leafy, upright sticks. Some are sparse and others more shrub-like, with occasional showy flowers and periods of leafless dormancy.

Occasionally available at some of the desert nurseries, *Fouquieria shrevei* is one of the more attractive of the genus, with an orange trunk developing in maturity. It has the classic airy tree shape of many other fouquierias, with white flowers, as seen below. It is native to a small region of the Cuatro Ciénegas Biosphere Reserve, about thirty miles west of Monclova, Cahuilla, Mexico, where Brian Kemble captured these images.

Fouquieria shrevei

"

Fouquieria purpusii always has been one of the most prized specimen succulents among collectors. It looks a bit like a dwarf form of the larger relative, *F. columnaris*, but with more vigorous and fine leaves, and a greener trunk. They develop a stout trunk, or caudex, with age, and make fantastic bonsai specimens in containers, or dramatic attention grabbers in the landscape. The three plants on this page all are cultivated specimens. They are a challenge to start from cuttings so most are grown from seed. *F. purpusii* is rare and expensive, but always has been one of my favorites. If you see one for sale, buy it!

Fouquieria purpusii

Fouquieria purpusii is close to being a perfect succulent. It has the appealing stout character profile as both a large or smaller container plant, nice bright and tiny leaves, and develops a colorful green to yellow-green fissured trunk as it grows. The only downside is that it is not frequently available as it usually is a seed-started and slow-growing plant.

Above: Succulent afficionados Jeremy Spath, Braden De Jong, and Zarac Lompart have triumphantly reached *Fouquieria purpusii* habitat deep in the mountains of Oaxaca, Mexico. It takes quite a bit of dedication and willingness to hike in some extreme temperatures and difficult terrain to see your favorite plants in habitat, but I'm pretty sure these guys think it was worth the effort. If you look closely, you can see some orange/red flowers or, perhaps, seed pods on the tips.

Left: A small part of Ben Grillo's collection sits for a portrait. *Fouquieria purpusii* holds the center stage, with *F. fasciculata* at left, and what appears to be a similarly shaped euphorbia at right to show a visual kinship in an African plant.

Kingdom: *Plantae*
  Phylum: *Angiosperms*
    Class: *Eudicots*
      Order: *Vitales*
        Family: *Vitaceae*
          Genus: *Cyphostemma*
            Species: *juttae*

Cyphostemmas

This wonderful group of fatties doesn't have a single member in the spiny club and wasn't initially on my radar for inclusion in this book, but they certainly make a sculptural statement similar to many of the other plants herein. Just pretend they have spines if it bothers you. Cyphostemmas (formerly of the genus *Cissus*) are succulent members of the grape family. As you can see in several of the images here, they do form attractive red berries—essentially grapes—but be advised that they are toxic and should be avoided. I'm not sure about the extent of the toxicity, but I have heard tales of extremely swollen tongues and rashes, so don't even think about it. If you are worried about kids or animals eating them, clip them off when they begin to color up. Most cyphostemmas are deciduous in Mediterranean climates, dropping their leaves around December and leafing back out in early spring. They are not quite as tropical as some of the other succulent caudiciforms, such as adeniums, and most can withstand the winter rainy season in California even while dormant, so they are suitable as landscape plants, as evidenced above. They do appreciate some summer watering.

By far the most common is *C. juttae*, featured prominently here. It is popular as a container specimen but also grows well in-ground in California. The more rare species, including *C. uter*, *C. currorii*, *C. seitzianum*, and a few others, usually are seen as containerized specimens, but you occasionally may find landscape examples at botanic gardens or collectors' backyards.

At right and below are a couple of fatties photographed by Mike Hackett in their native Africa. At right is *Cyphostemma uter*, happily ensconced in a pile of rock rubble, which is always a nice seed-starter situation for succulents and other plants.

Below is just an awesome and perfect specimen of *Cyphostemma currorrii* located in a parking area at Sheilam Cactus Garden and Nursery in South Africa. Notice the New World cacti growing along the left side of the image. Mike said the owners were very much into cacti, and like those of us in the Southwest U.S., their similar climate lets them indulge in plants from across the pond. I'm sure they don't take the *C. uter* for granted, but it might not garner quite the excitement a plant like that would get over here. Their nursery has been operating since 1954, and I do hope to visit it when I make my bucket list Africa trip someday.

Above is a sample of Mike's collection of cyphostemmas, among many other wonderful succulents. Notice the emphasis on pots and presentation. The light leaves are *C. seitzianum*, the crinkle-leafed plant at right is *C. uter*, and the plant front and center is his own hybrid between them. These too are hybridize-able plants.

Once or twice elsewhere in this book I've offered a bit of insight into my bookmaking process. My initial hope was to keep it to 300 pages. Now, as I near completion, due to the breadth of the subject and availability of so many images from friends old and new, I think it may end up closer to 350 pages, and you might have paid an extra $5 for a very heavy book. But if you're looking for content, I hope you're happy. I was happy when I stumbled onto some of Mike Hackett's fantastic succulent images on Instagram, and he agreed to let me use a few. I have a lot of images from the cultivated world, but Mike has been to Africa with a great camera and a great eye. The habitat cyphostemmas in this section are very old descendants of ancestors that evolved where they live (or at least close by). I know of a few fifty-year-old specimens of *Cyphostemma uter* in California that come close to the plant above, but I like seeing it here growing in its homeland. And that African sky!

Cyphostemmas make excellent bonsai candidates provided you are willing to expand your definition of bonsai to include imaginary outer space plants. They present well in shallow dishes, which allows you to really show off their stout, caudiciform bodies. The collector plant above left is *C. seitzianum*. Above middle is the even rarer *C. uter*. Above right is a *Cyphostemma seitzianum* in the care of Jim and Roberta Hannah. Note that there are a quite a few more members of this genus that are scarce or as yet unavailable in cultivation.

At right is a large landscape specimen of *Cyphostemma juttae*, in winter dormancy in Fallbrook, California. Once they reach this size (about three-foot square in this case) by at least twenty or more years of age, they look just as impressive in the leafless state.

Left is *C. cirrhosa* with an exceptional head of new spring foliage. This is one of several varieties that can form long, vining growth.

Right: An old specimen of *Cyphostemma juttae* has spent a lifetime in a plastic pot, finally reaching the edge of the rim as it awaits a permanent planting. In all likelihood, the roots have made their way out of the drainage holes, allowing it to start growing in earnest. The owner here would be wise to simply cut away the pot, build up the soil around it, and let it grow away. C'mon, Gary.

Left: New cyphostemma leaves usually start out a deep burgundy red, will shift to green over the summer—often getting quite large and heavy—then dry and drop in early winter.

Above: *Cyphostemma juttae* is the easiest and most available of the genus in cultivation. The plant above is part of the wonderful succulent landscape of Pitzer College in Claremont, California.

Above left: Please heed the warning sign—The Huntington Botanical Gardens.

The winter-naked plant at right in private collection in Vista, California, has to be ancient to have formed such a bulging beauty.

Left: One of the characteristics of cyphostemmas is the papery peeling bark it sheds as it grows. Try to leave it be.

Kingdom: *Plantae*
Phylum: *Magnoliophyta*
Class: *Lilopsida*
Order: *Poales*
Family: *Bromeliaceae*
Genus: *Aechmea*
Species: *comata*
cv. *makoyana*

This is just a small sample of the fantastic xerophytic garden known as "Aloes in Wonderland"—Jeff Chemnick's outstanding collection of otherwordly plants in Santa Barbara, California. As you can see, there is much more than just aloes. Here a "Dragon Tree" (*Dracaena draco*) presides over cycads, bromeliads, orchids, and a cyphostemma.

The term "succulent" can be a bit nebulous around the periphery. All of the plants on prior pages can safely pass most definitions of the term, including the "If you step on it, does it leave a wet spot?" test. However, having been involved in the hobby and business for many years, there are quite a few genera that are not technically succulent in nature but still pass the most important tests of us succulentophiles: They are exceptionally cool and usually architecturally appealing, sun-loving, xerophytic, mostly spiny, and neglect-tolerant plants that just look like they belong with the rest of our plants. If you own a lot of succulents, you probably also will have some, or many, of the plants in the following section.

When I visit a succulent or cactus collector's house, it inevitably also showcases a number of terrestrial/xerophytic bromeliads, tillandsias, a few of the easier orchids, or perhaps cycads, plumerias, and dry climate/desert trees. That includes my own collection, as well. On the following pages, we'll take a quick look at some of the major players in these non-succulent or, perhaps, semi-succulent groups. Once again, it will be just a tip-of-the-iceberg taste that hopefully will push you to learn more about all the wonderful xerophytic plants in cultivation.

The cycads on this page all are part of the extensive collection at Lotusland in Montecito, California. The Santa Barbara area has an exceptional growing climate, employed to its fullest at this magical and old established estate. All of the various gardens—cacti, palms, aloes, and more—are a sight to behold. The cycad collection is one of the best in the world. The beautiful blue beauty at right is *Encephalartos horridus*. If you only own one cycad, I'd recommend this or one of the other blues.

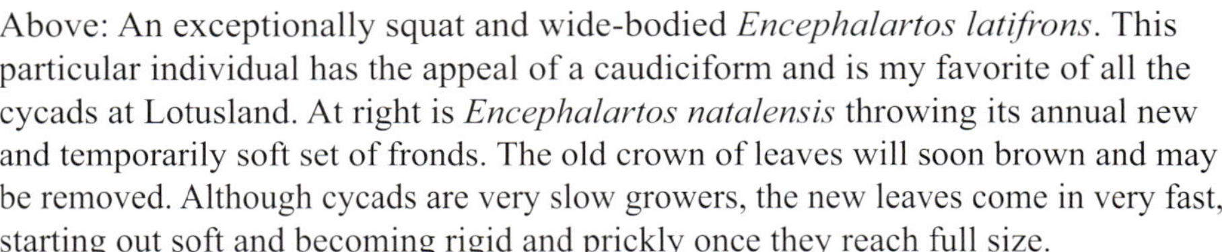

Above: An exceptionally squat and wide-bodied *Encephalartos latifrons*. This particular individual has the appeal of a caudiciform and is my favorite of all the cycads at Lotusland. At right is *Encephalartos natalensis* throwing its annual new and temporarily soft set of fronds. The old crown of leaves will soon brown and may be removed. Although cycads are very slow growers, the new leaves come in very fast, starting out soft and becoming rigid and prickly once they reach full size.

Cycads

Cycads are primitive, palm-like plants that appeal to those of us who love succulents, and thrive in the same hot and sunny conditions as most of the other plants in this book. The ubiquitous "Sago Palm" of the genus *Cycas* is one of the most popular. Other genera sought out by enthusiasts include *Encephalartos*, *Dioon*, *Macrozamia*, *Zamia*, and *Ceratozamia*. As you will read on the following pages, they are slow-growing and expensive, and many are in the realm of the well-off private collector. You can always start with some babies and grow old with them, like I'm doing.

As with every other group of plants in this book, I'm just giving you a sample here in a few pages. There are several excellent books and websites for further research.

Cycads have been around since the days of the dinosaurs and, based on fossil records, have changed little since then. Like conifers, they are gymnosperms. This means that their seeds are exposed rather than "hidden" inside a fruit. There are male and female plants which produce two different types of cones: The male cone contains the pollen and the female one the seeds. The pollen is transferred from the male cone to the female cone by insect pollinators (or humans with a paint brush). The "coning" is a slow and wonderful process to watch evolve over months, and seed starting is difficult and best left to professionals. You certainly don't get a cycad in hope of any colorful flowers, but the architecture and color of the cones is equally fascinating, and long-lived.

While not exactly matching the definition of what a succulent is, cycads do fit within the parameters of what we succulentoholics appreciate. They are sculptural, exotic looking, and xerophytic/sun-loving plants that have that "look-at-me" quality that can't be denied. They fit right into a succulent landscape, as seen in the collector's yard above (this primarily is a cycad section, which transitions into the rest of the succulent garden elsewhere). The reason you don't see a lot of these beauties in the landscape ("Sago Palms"—*Cycas revoluta*—excepted), is that they are very slow-growing; seed-started plants and mature specimens are very expensive. A single blue cycad with a bowling ball sized caudex can easily run into the four digits—that's why you don't see them in front yards. There has been quite a bit of theft of mature specimen cycads, both from private collections and botanical gardens, as well as African, Central American, and Australian habitat. Many old plants in both cultivation and *in situ* have been microchipped for that reason. Sadly, there is a bit of espionage in the cycad world. Most cycads are endangered in habitat, some critically, and a few are extinct in the wild. Fortunately, some of those have persisted in cultivation and may eventually be reintroduced into the wild.

As a nursery owner, I appreciate the enthusiasm of collectors of all types of plants. But when I encounter a cycad collector, I know I'm dealing with someone who is serious in their pursuit of rare botanic beauty. I felt myself being drawn into the cycad world just a bit early on, but the price tag was always just too prohibitive to take a deep dive, plus I had enough of the other plants drawing my attention. I decided to get a few of the small blue ones and just grow old with them. Serious cycadists likely were drawn to the blue forms first as they just stand out so much, but once you start to spread out into all the other greenies, well, it's a slippery slope. It isn't easy for a novice to differentiate between many of the other cycads, and I've intentionally kept myself somewhat ignorant of that larger realm. Can't afford it.

Encephalartos natalensis

If you want to see some impressive collections, check out Lotusland in Montecito, The Huntington Botanical Gardens, the Los Angeles County Arboretum, the UC Berkeley Botanical Garden, the San Diego Botanic Garden, and any of the other larger botanic gardens or zoos in California. There also are some outstanding private collections, but most of those prefer to remain under the radar. Colors can range from green to greenish blue to sliver- or powder-blue. Get as large as you can afford, plant it in a prominent location in your garden or large container (backyard and out of public view), and plan to put it in your will. Cycads appreciate in value, and you can look at them as your botanical mutual fund—one that grows in value—but you do have to keep them alive, which fortunately isn't hard. Monetary value aside, just enjoy the sheer beauty and coolness of the plants themselves.

By far the most common cycad in cultivation worldwide is the omnipresent "Sago Palm"—*Cycas revoluta*. Native to southern Japan and eastern China, *C. revoluta* has been a staple in both tropical and temperate landscapes for many years, and it is quite cold tolerant, handling such snowy locations as the U.S. Midwest and Eastern Seaboard. It will completely defoliate in very cold winter conditions, but in temperate locales it will hold leaves throughout the winter, only yellowing as the new flush of soft leaves is produced in the spring. Like most cycads, it is dioecious, with male and female flowering cones on separate plants. You can see the developing male cones (of course those are male) in the upper and middle left images, and a much more lovely (of course) female cone on the images below, with the developing seed pods becoming exposed in the bottom image. The cones grow fast; the male cones grew from the baseball size in the top image to full size in the middle shot in just over a month. Sadly, the cone withers soon after reaching full size. I purposely didn't throw another "of course" into that last sentence. There might be a metaphor in there someplace.

Be advised that all parts of most cycads, and particularly their seeds, are poisonous, so be careful with pets. Unlike almost all of the other cycads, you can find *Cycas revoluta* available in many sizes at relatively affordable prices at most nurseries or large box stores. If you are replacing your established garden with xerophytic plants or succulents, you can leave any sagos you might currently have in place and build the garden around them, as they blend nicely with almost all types of plants.

Above left and middle is *Zamia furfuracea*, probably the next most widely available and popular cycad after *Cycas revoluta*. Commonly known as the "Cardboard Palm" (not really sure why—I suppose some folks feel the leaf texture resembles cardboard), this Mexican native grows well in Mediterranean climates and even better in tropical locales like Hawaii, where it can be used as a hedge. It also is popular as an indoor plant, provided it receives adequate light. Above right is a new flush of leaves on a hybrid cycad—cycads can be, and often are, hybridized.

At right is a trio of *Encephalartos arenarius* at The Huntington Botanical Gardens in San Marino, California, showing new leaf flushes.

Below left looks a bit like a crime scene but is just a hybrid encephalartros cone that has ripened and is shedding fruit. I'm sure that, in its native habitat, there are creatures which likely would ingest and then broadcast these seeds, but in cultivation this is where the owner needs to begin seed collection and the somewhat laborious process of germination. Most cycads are propagated by seed, but can also be started vegetatively via offsets of those species that tend to form "pups" with age. Be careful if you try this as cycad spines can be as nasty as any cactus and must be handled with care. Below middle is a Jeff Chemnick hybrid called "Blue Meanie" (*E. trispinosus* x blue form of *E. arenarius*). It has a nice yellow edge to the leaves and stems. Both plants are located at Aloes in Wonderland. Below right is what appears to be a cluster of *Encephalartos trispinosus* but is likely one plant, which has matured to the point of forming multiple suckers or pups attached to the base.

This is the show-stopping flowering event of a South American puya. I used the term "event" on purpose because I put the more spectacular puya inflorescence right up there with an amorphophalus bloom for pure jaw-dropping spectacle (at least if you are a plant geek or nature lover). The iridescent blue flower tower at left is from *Puya berteroniana*, a large, light silver-green leaved puya from Chile. It is the larger cousin of the better known *Puya alpestris* (page 322). I planted this particular plant at left for my neighbor, telling him that it was the latter and expecting the little one-gallon starter to reach blooming age in maybe five years, and it would be worth the wait. Well, it grew about ten times the size I expected over the next ten years, without flowering, and I finally figured out it was instead *Puya berteroniana*. This was confirmed when it finally threw out this amazing eight-foot flower tower. Of course, the owner was on vacation when it finally bloomed. I saved this image for him. Then it took two years off and is finally flowering a second time as I write this, and the owners are out of town again.

A bit of a pricey collector's item, this book is one of the most beautiful plant books ever published. You think I have a lot of images in this book? *Blooming Bromeliads* has more, with a more colorful subject matter, done pre-digital, which I can't fathom. It is a little weak on terrestrials like puyas, but, nevertheless, try to find a copy if you can.

Hechtia 'Silver Tongue Devil'

Bromeliads don't quite fit into the category of a succulent plant—most don't pass the "If you step on them, do they leave a wet spot?" test (some do). While the majority of bromeliads (and all the attendant subgenera) are more tropical in nature, there are many that pass all the other succulent tests: partial to full sun tolerant, xerophytic, and, most importantly, they just have an architectural appeal that speaks to succulent enthusiasts. In their Mexican, Central America, and South American habitats, there are quite a few that live right alongside cacti in dry, desert or semi-desert conditions. While many of the more tropical bromeliads live epiphytically above the forest floor, with roots serving as holdfasts in the trees, the plants featured in the first sections are primarily considered terrestrial, with below-ground roots serving in the more traditional capacity.

The first pages of this section feature the rigid and sharp-edged, dry climate, terrestrial bromeliads— dyckias, hechtias, puyas, and deuterocohnias. The last few pages show some of the more traditional, thin-skinned, and tropical-looking plants such as aechmeas and billbergias, which in the early stages of this book were not slated for inclusion here. However, I've learned over the years that many will handle quite a bit of sun and owner indifference (at least along the coast) and are tolerant of the benign neglect that succulent folk tend to bestow upon their plants. Bromeliads can help soften and "tropicalize" a succulent garden and also provide abundant color, either via foliage or flowers, or both.

Hechtia texensis

Dyckias and Hechtias

Hechtia rosea is an exception to most hechtias, producing a long-lived, beautiful, ruby red flower.

It is difficult for most of us to tell the difference between dyckias and hechtias. In general, many dyckias have a dark skin, but there are some that have a white or lighter silver tone, similar to most hechtias. Dyckias often have more colorful flowers (typically yellow or orange) on long stems, while hechtias have a taller inflorescence but usually are not as colorful. Both genera have sharp, saw-toothed leaf edges and are nasty to work with or weed around. Even though most freely form pups around the main plant, they are suckered in hard and are much trickier to extract than, say, an aloe or agave pup is. That is why you don't see as many available. They aren't hard to grow, but they are very hard to separate to turn into more plants. That usually involves unpotting the plant, turning it upside down, and using a saw or serrated knife. Those of us who also have a collection of cacti and other spiny plants will tell you we are more wary when working with many of these bromeliads. There will be blood.

Facing page: A sampler of dyckias and hechtias. I'm convinced that most of these terrestrial bromeliads in cultivation are hybrids. Few are reliably named, and many are offspring of related species and are just going through a human-induced evolutionary experiment. To the best of my knowledge, there are no intergeneric crosses between the two genera.

The late Bill Baker was an early and enthusiastic propagator of these plants, and the plant at bottom right may be one of his called "Baker's Beauty." But the seed he collected and disseminated over the years to other growers likely has been unintentionally crossed, so even the collectors that I occasionally buy these plants from are unsure of the parentage, and usually answer my question about what it is by saying "I'm not really sure, but it sure is nice!".

As most of the plants on the facing page were acquired without names, all I can do here is offer a best guess. I'm pretty sure bottom left and middle are *Dyckia* 'Brittle Star' (or 'Arizona'); top left and middle might be two phases of *Hechtia* 'Aztec Sun'; middle center might be *H. sphaeroblasta* in a temporary banded spring color phase (it goes green for long stretches). The others? Just nice hechtias. Or dyckias. Heck, I don't know. Sure are nice.

The *Hechtia glomerata* (?) above left is in temporary full color. They can spend most of the year in a greener phase and usually enter a red phase in the spring months. Most will form clumps in time, and flowers for most hechtias are born on multiple tall stalks, usually with small white or cream-colored flowers. The attraction is much more in the foliage. Above is an *Ursulea tuitensis* growing with *Dudleya candida* in a sidewalk mailbox planter. I had never even heard of this genus prior to researching this image. There are many more related and often obscure related genera than I have room for here.

Left and below: *Hechtia lanata*, a Mexican native with nice recurved leaves. Another color shifter, this plant will oscillate from apple green to more of a frosted blue gray, as seen below. It also is a prolific clumper and bloomer, as seen at left. Hechtias are dioecious (male and female flowers). The plant at left is a male. How can I tell? The owner told me so. Female flowers are equally large and dramatic; the difference is in the details. The hechtias shown on this page are, at present, still rarely found in cultivation or for sale. I hope *H. lanata* or its hybrids become more available soon.

Above is *Hechtia glauca*, known commonly as the blue hechtia. In the summer warmth, the geometrically arranged leaves usually display the glaucous blue phase, as seen above left. In the cool of winter, it can flush into a much more apple green color, with red leaf edge blushing, as seen at right. This large plant is a favorite among collectors. It does have a reputation for being a temperamental grower.

Below left is a Mexican habitat image by Jeff Chemnick of *Hechtia sphaeroblasta* in full color.

One example of a more obscure terrestrial bromeliad is *Ochagavia litoralis*, below right, from a small Chilean genus. Ochagavia leaves are similar to those of hechtias or dyckias, but the flower is much more reminiscent of the more common *Aechmea* genus. A few other occasionally encountered bromeliad genera that at least visually align with the sharp, rigid, and xerophytic terrestrials shown here are *Bromelia*, *Encholirium*, *Fascicularia*, and *Orthophytum*.

Brian Kemble sees mandalas when he looks at hechtias and dyckias. I must concur.

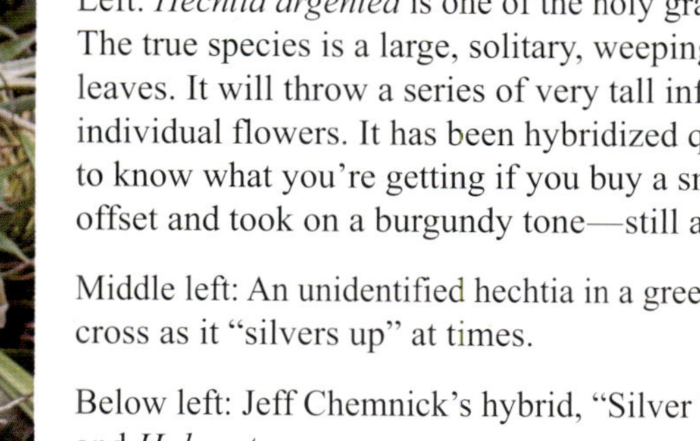

Left: *Hechtia argentea* is one of the holy grail prizes for collectors of these types of plants. The true species is a large, solitary, weeping plant with shiny silver-gray thin and serrated leaves. It will throw a series of very tall inflorescences in the spring, with small creamy individual flowers. It has been hybridized quite a bit with other hechtias, so it can be hard to know what you're getting if you buy a small one. I thought I had one until it started to offset and took on a burgundy tone—still a gorgeous plant, but not the real deal.

Middle left: An unidentified hechtia in a green phase; the owner suspects it is an *H. argentea* cross as it "silvers up" at times.

Below left: Jeff Chemnick's hybrid, "Silver Tongue Devil," is a cross of *Hechtia argentea* and *H. lanata*.

Below: A cluster of dark burgundy dyckias (possibly one of many *D. fosteriana* crosses) at the Ruth Bancroft Garden in Walnut Creek, California. Dyckias frequently have orange to red-orange flowers; hechtias usually are taller, cream colored and less showy.

Puya alpestris

The stunning flower tower of *Puya alpestris* has been described as a metallic teal color and is an event worth timing your vacation around. Like most puyas, *P. alpestris* (a.k.a. the "Sapphire Tower") forms a mound of multiple, thin, and serrated silver-gray leaves, similar but smaller and thinner than the equally impressive *Puya berteroniana* on page 325. Flower colors usually are in shades of iridescent teal to a darker turquoise-blue, as seen at left and below. I was surprised to find one bloom green, shown above. Plants often will surprise you and break from orthodoxy when you're not expecting it. Foliage is silver gray, similar to but smaller and thinner than that of *P. berteroniana* on the following spread.

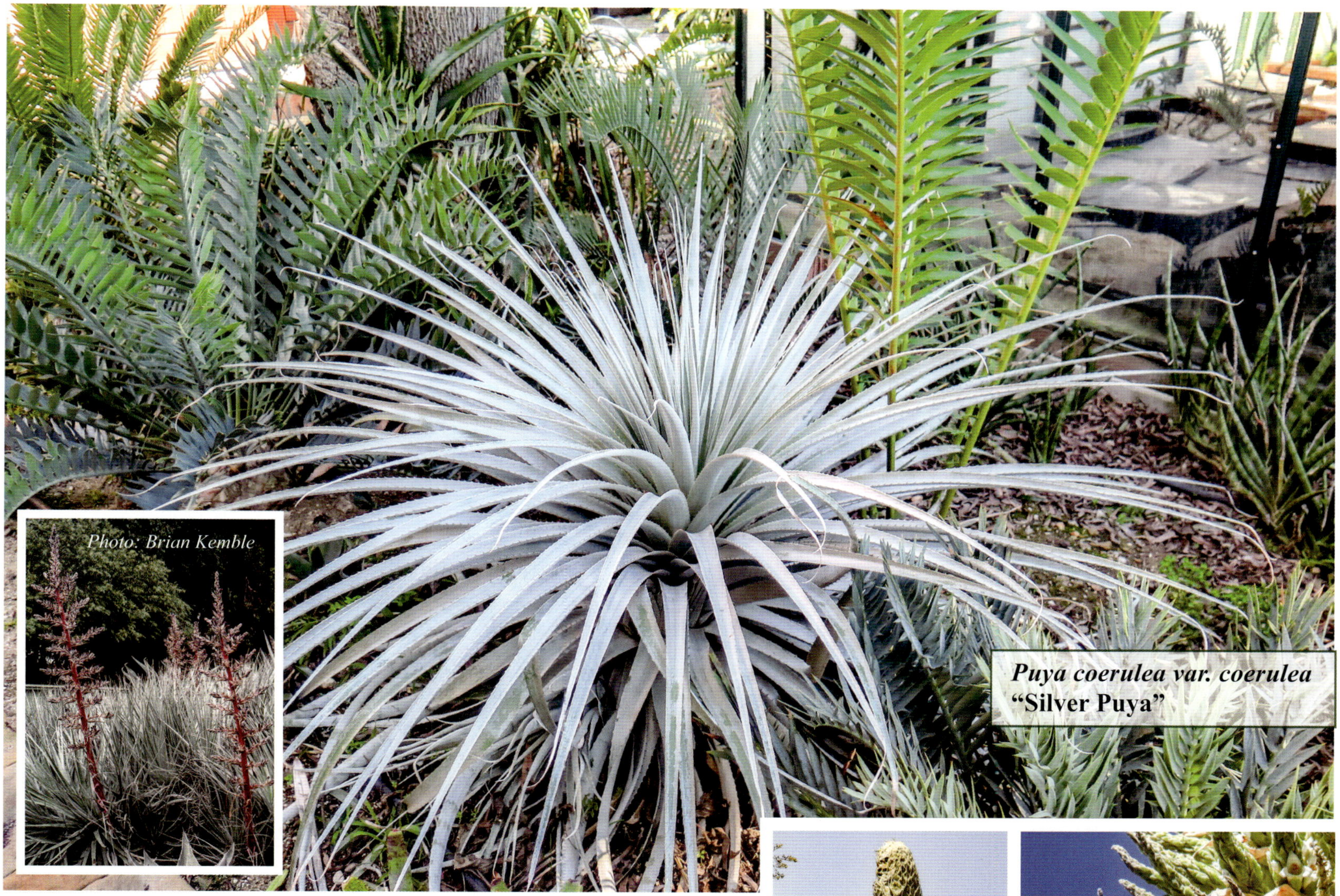

Puya coerulea var. coerulea
"Silver Puya"

Some of the most spectacular flowering bromeliads—in fact some of the most spectacular flowering plants, period—are puyas. Native to most of the Andean countries of South America, the handful in cultivation are easy, full sun growers but can take quite a while to reach maturity and bloom. The most famous is the Sapphire Tower, *Puya alpestris*, seen in bloom on the facing page. Puya rosettes often are monocarpic, meaning they will die after blooming. But since they're clumpers, with usually just one or a few rosettes blooming at a time, you don't even notice the dead post-flower portion being subsumed into the clump as new growth emerges. It will just persist and get bigger. Blooming season for most puyas, at least in California, tends to be fall through early spring.

A plant I only know from the internet is the granddaddy of all puyas, *P. raimondii*, shown at right in flower at the UC Berkeley Botanical Garden, with a ten-to-twenty-foot flower stalk that dwarfs the already quite tall plant. There have been a handful grown to blooming size at a few California botanic gardens, but it is not a frequently available plant in cultivation and not as easy to grow, perhaps due to its native high-altitude environment. I recommend that you go on line to check out some examples of that magnificent plant in habitat flower. To learn more about puyas, check out Geoff Stein's section on the Dave's Garden website—an excellent resource on the internet for photos and information on many plants in this book.

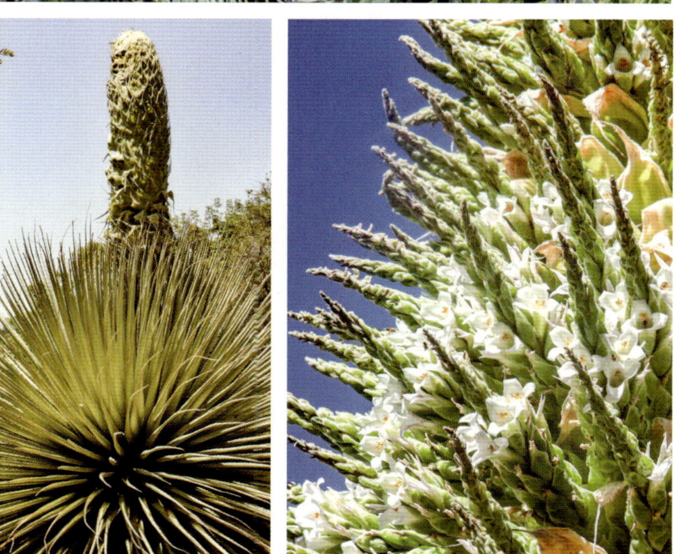

Puya raimondii

Photo above left by Brian Kemble. Above right by Paul Licht.

Before I write my little blurb about each plant for this book, I do a little internet research to back up what I already know about the plant, or to see if there is a bit more I can add to the description. The caption below I took verbatim from the Annie's Annuals' web page about this plant. I can't improve on it, and I agree with their enthusiasm. Annie's Annuals is a fantastic nursery in Richmond, California, where you can find rare and wonderful plants. It is worth visiting. Maybe you can pick up some rare puyas—or dudleyas, or aeoniums, or much more.

If you've got the room in a rock, succulent or dry garden you must devote some space to this thrilling Bromeliad! Marvelous compact and architectural, silvery-white, serrated rosettes to 40" tall (spreading to 5' across) command adoration, even if they never bloomed—but they do! Totally stunning blue-purple blooms displaying electric green stamens emerge from large red pine-cone-like clusters held high—to 3'—above the foliage on stiff, upright stems from late Winter to Summer. To-die-for! Perfect companion plant for Aloes and Agaves. Well-drained, fertile soil for perfect presentation. Can be grown in a large container. Hardy to 20°F. Deer resistant and snow proof!

The blooming beauty above at Lotusland and at right at the Cal State Fullerton Botanical Garden likely is a *P. venusta* hybrid in spring bloom.

If you want to see some mature stands of puyas in Southern California, visit The Huntington Botanical Gardens, the Los Angeles County Arboretum, or Ganna Walska Lotusland. All have some ancient monsters that occupy quite a bit of real estate. The *P. venusta* at left was photographed at the UC Berkeley Botanical Garden which, along with the Ruth Bancroft Garden in Walnut Creek, has some of the larger specimens you will find in Northern California.

The puya with perhaps the most striking blue flower of all isn't even in cultivation yet. Check out *Puya weddelliana* online—something to hope for.

Puya berteroniana

Although *Puya alpestris* seems to be the most famous of the genus, my personal favorite is the larger *Puya berteroniana*. It is a slow grower and slow to reach blooming maturity, but like other members of the genus, there is no "off" switch to tell it to stop growing. It can occupy several square yards of real estate over time. The flowers seem to be more of a day-glow metallic blue than the turquoise/teal of *P. alpestris*. Once the first flowers open, the actual blooming event lasts a week or two at most, so time your vacation accordingly. The long lateral portions of the flower are reputed to serve as a perch for bird pollinators. As with most puyas, it is rarely available, so if you see one for sale, jump on it (figuratively speaking).

The specimen of *Deuterocohnia brevifolia* at left was a plant I sold as a six-inch juvenile. The owner had to move, so twenty years later it came back to me, now larger than a basketball. Sadly, it was a temporary stay as I sell plants for a living (I try not to get too attached, but it's hard not to), and this specimen found a new home as a surprise birthday present from his wife to a succulent enthusiast in Avila Beach, California.

Below: An example of convergent evolution—at least in a visual or morphological sense—is the non-succulent high-altitude mounding plant *Azorella compacta*, also known as "Llareta." This species is from the Andes, and it mounds to conserve heat and water. Unlike the deuterochonias, the various species of azorella are soft to the touch.

The beautiful blob at right has spent many years overtaking the spot it was started in on the corner of this wooden bench. Provided they receive some water, these plants will eventually swallow the containers they are planted in, and then keep working on taking a toehold on whatever is next, albeit it at a glacial pace. This specimen staked its claim at a grower's lath-house in Vista, California. I'm quite certain there is a black plastic flat inside it. If you were to dissect the mass, you would find each tiny rosette has a long stem/root that connects to the original base/pot, which I'm sure no longer has any soil, so the plant essentially lives on water alone by now.

The specimen of *Deuterocohnia brevifolia* above has become an iconic fixture at Grow Nursery in Cambria, California. Every time I see this image, I'm reminded of a moon or planet undergoing a meteor bombardment with miniature impact explosions—or maybe volcanic eruptions. I see things.

The tightly mounding masses of sharp and rigid rosettes shown here are deuterocohnias, formerly of the genus *Abromeitiella*. There are other deuterocohnias that more closely resemble dyckias or puyas, but the mounding types shown here are the most prominent. They basically are succulent in nature, enjoying full sun and needing very little water. Older containerized specimens, as seen here, or the habitat-like mounds at the UC Berkeley Botanic Garden, above right, take many years to reach such magnificence. There are two primary varieties available in cultivation. The most desirable form is *D. brevifolia*, with hundreds to thousands of tight, incredibly compacted, small, green rosettes. *D. lorentziana* (left) looks similar but has larger rosettes and comes in both a green and silver-gray form. Small, green, tubular flowers emerge at times but are unremarkable (facing page).

These plants will mound over and engulf any shallow pot you start them in. You can even get creative and turn them into a self-contained hanging orb, as Peter Walkowiak has done above.

Above: *Vriesea hieroglyphica* is one of the most ornamental of the bromeliads but, unfortunately, is not quite as sun and neglect tolerant as the aechmeas and neoregelias on the following pages. That is true of the *Vriesea* genus in general (various cultivars seen above left)—at least in non-tropical or Mediterranean situations. They grow well in dappled shade with just a bit of extra irrigation, which is best applied topically as spray as opposed to soaking the soil. The flowers of this and many other bromeliads are quite striking, as well, but be advised that, like agaves, most bromeliads are monocarpic, meaning the plant slowly dies upon flowering. Usually the flowering event also triggers offsets that will take over for the bloomed-out and withered original plant.

Left: A tropical-themed mound of bromeliads and succulents at Waterwise Botanicals in Bonsall, California. Various aechmeas and billbergias crown the mound in bright yellow-green and orange hues, with mangaves and pachyphytums transitioning to more of a cool color scheme at bottom. These plants are thriving in a full sun and relatively harsh inland California climate (I can sense you desert dwellers rolling your eyes). Generous summer water helps.

If you're wondering what these tropicals are doing in a cactus book, well, I see where you're coming from. When I started working on this book, I didn't anticipate including bromeliads or orchids. My main groups were to be primarily (but not exclusively) the spiny plants. But many, if not most, succulent enthusiasts also collect some of the hardier bromeliads, in particular the more sharp, rigid, and xerophytic terrestrial varieties like you've seen on the prior handful of pages. Some of those are as sun and drought tolerant (and spiny) as any succulent. The more traditional bromeliads you see here generally are softer and much more tropical in appearance, although many do have some benign leaf serrations that are at least suggestive of a defensive strategy. In habitat, most are epiphytic, but they will also grow in-ground. You might be surprised how easy and forgiving many of these plants are, particularly in coastal areas where they can take part-day to even all-day sun. They can really color up a succulent landscape.

Just as it is difficult for a novice (or even an expert) to differentiate, at first glance, between some of the various globular/spiny cactus genera, so it is for most of us with many bromeliads. The basic shapes of many aechmeas, billbergias, neoregelias, and close relatives can be very similar. The visual difference usually lies with the flowers.

Soft Bromeliads and Orchids

Left: The comically curly leaves of an unidentified bromeliad, likely *Quesnelia marmorata* 'Tim Plowman.' The darker plant in back appears to be a form of *Billbergia* 'Hallelujah.'

Left and right: Two colorful iterations of *Aechmea blanchetiana*, growing in full sun in coastal California. Both of these are from the collection of Pam Koide-Hyatt of Bird Rock Tropicals in Encinitas.

Inset left: The "tank" bromeliads hold tiny aquatic ecosystems, including flowers, in the reservoir.

Above left: *Billbergia* 'Teng Ee.' That's its real color and its real name, and the image actually is in focus—the pattern just melts into a watercolor blur in places. Photo by Ben Grillo.
Above middle: One of my favorites, *Billbergia* 'Hallelujah,' comes in several shades of spotted or patterned pinks and burgundies.
Above right: *Quesnelia quesneliana* in flower.

Certain aechmeas, neoregelias, and billbergias are resilient plants that can provide stunning color and flowers in a succulent landscape and can cohabitate nicely with desert plants, as you can see below left in a succulent landscape in Point Loma by Michael Buckner (a.k.a. the Plant Man). I've been tucking these types of plants into my own landscape for a while now. They provide a pop of color and tropical softness that contrasts well with desert plants—if that is a look you're going for.
Right: A nice mix of succulents and tropicals.
Bottom right: A winning billbergia at a bromeliad show.

At left is *Tillandsia fasciculata*, an epiphytic plant in its Mexican habitat. However, it pretty much will grow where you put it—ideally in filtered sun, as seen here in glorious bloom, tucked in next to a rock. Tillandsias and most bromeliads are monocarpic. This means the blooming rosette dies after flowering, but this always triggers more offsets to grow below the bloomed-out portion, and over time you end up with more plants. This also would apply to the flowering variegated *Aechmea recurvata*, above middle, which will blush deep red upon flowering. *A. recurvata,* in both the green and variegated form, is a very sun-tolerant, bullet-proof plant. Above right is an agave impersonator identified at a prominent botanical garden as *Orthophytum glabrum*, but it does look quite different from online images I've seen. *Orthophytum* is just one of many genera in the very large bromeliad family.

Below left is a collector's vertical tillandsia display. This is an excellent way to showcase these epiphytes, ideally in dappled sun or partial shade. They do appreciate more frequent watering in the warm part of the year. Below middle is the orange flower of *Aechmea mulfordii*. Below right is *Aechmea* 'Blue Tango,' which has a stunning, long-lasting, and almost fake-looking inflorescence.

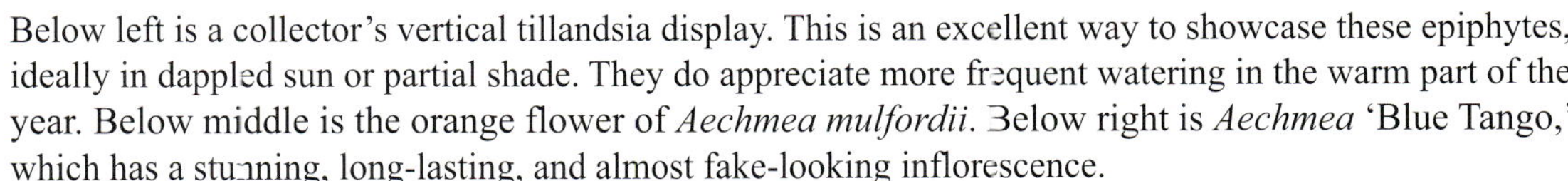

Above: *Eulophia petersii* is known as the "Desert Orchid," and likely is the most drought tolerant of all orchids. It prefers summer water, which it stores in its pseudobulbs. It has small green/pink flowers on very tall stalks which rise above the cover of shrubs and weeds that it grows under in habitat. You should provide at least some afternoon shade if you live in a hotter inland climate. There are other members of the genus but, at present, very few are available in cultivation. It reproduces prolifically, as you can see above.

Above right: Succulent growers usually have a few token orchids, myself included. Most orchids take more work than the once-a-week water and benign neglect requirement we have for our plants. Called "terrestrial," "reed-stem," or "poor man's" orchids, *Epidendrum radicans* (like ephiphyllums, these often are called just "epis") come in many flower colors and fit the low maintenance profile. Flowers are long lasting, and the foliage can get rangy or weedy over time. But these plants are very sun tolerant (partial sun inland) and although they like water, they can survive without it for a while. Although not a favorite among the true orchid snobs, it is beloved by the rest of us.

Left: The long-lived summer bloom of *Portea petropolitana*, a very durable and prolific bromeliad. Also a fun Latin name to drop.

Right: We're getting pretty far afield here, but cymbidiums also are some of the easier orchids to grow outdoors. I hesitate to call them succulent in nature, and this slope is getting slippery, so let's move on....

Xerophytic Subtropicals and Trees

Plumeria

The lush San Diego garden above is a mix of succulents, bromeliads, and a few succulent trees, highlighted here by a plumeria that is approaching tree height. Plumerias are subtropical and xerophytic Central American natives (sorry, Hawaii) that should be considered succulent in nature. They do appreciate a bit more water in the warm season and tend to do best in slightly warmer inland Southern California climates, as most love the extra sun and heat. If you drive through some of the inland Orange County suburbs, you will see twenty-foot high plumerias covered in leaves and flowers poking over walls and fences, the result of a plumeria boom dating back to the tiki days of the fifties. Most flower colors of the most vigorous growers are shades of white with a yellow center, but there are a number of colors in cultivation. I've found that some plumerias will thrive if they find the perfect spot, while others tend to be sparse and leafless/flowerless most of the time. They can be finicky. This is one genus where a species name is seldom used as most are old cultivars. They're just plumerias, identified either by flower color or cultivar name, such as "Samoan Fluff" or "Aztec Gold" or "Vera Cruz Orange," ad infinitum.

The famous "Monkey Puzzle" tree is not remotely a succulent, but it sure can pass the visual and tactile tests (the entire tree is so sharp, not even a monkey could figure out how to climb it. But I bet a lemur could). I'm including it in this book as an author's prerogative—I just love them, although it is a difficult grower where I live. It actually is a South American high-altitude member of the araucaria family, primitive pine-like trees, of which the Norfolk Island Pine is the most famous. The Monkey Puzzle will live in Southern California but seems to do much better in the cooler climate farther north, all the way up into coastal Canada. It's not easy to find, but if you do, I'd recommend giving it a try, locating smaller specimens in a slightly shadier, cooler part of your garden. The individual shown here is growing happily in full sun in San Luis Obispo, California. If you want to make a prehistoric garden from the days before flowering plants, try this plant with cycads and tree ferns.

There are other "How is this not a succulent?" xerophytic plants. Check out the dangerously sharp Anchor Plant, *Colletia paradoxa*, shown at right, which can grow into a large shrub. Photo by Randy Baldwin at The Huntington Botanical Gardens.

Araucaria araucana

Araucaria araucana

Colletia paradoxa

Uncarina grandidieri

Uncarina grandidieri

Uncarina grandidieri is a wonderful, small caudiciform tree from Madagascar. It will develop a stout, water-storing trunk with age and is suitable as either a container specimen, as seen at left, or in-ground in Mediterranean or tropical climates. Leaves are soft and fuzzy, and in the warm months, the plant usually is covered in vibrant yellow flowers with deep purple throats. If it ever develops seed pods, be wary. They are cute and fuzzy but have barbs that will grab you like a cholla. I believe they attach to lemurs as a mode of transportation in habitat. *U. grandidieri* is the most common form, but *U. roeoesliana* and *U. decaryi* also are available and grow similarly.

Brachytriton rupestris

The "Australian Bottle Tree" does fit the bill as a succulent tree—it is from a dry climate and has a trunk that swells over the years into a water-storing caudiciform shape. Young trees begin slender, but they can grow quite rapidly into something like the fat juvenile below—perhaps a ten-year-old specimen at Aloes in Wonderland in Santa Barbara, California. Ancient specimens, like the one at left in Balboa Park near the San Diego Zoo, almost resemble baobab trees, and trunks occasionally can begin to split. I've seen enough scary movies to advise against going in there.

There are a few other brachychitons that are planted in conjunction with xerophytic gardens, including *B. acerifolius* (beautiful red flowers) or *B. discolor*, but none quite match the bloated majesty of *B. rupestris*.

If you've owned, or at least seen, the bonsai versions of the elephant trees in cultivation (see facing page), I recommend a trip to northern Baja California to see them in person. You begin to notice these leafy boulders in the Cataviña desert area, and they populate most of the central and southern parts of the peninsula, including both the Gulf and Pacific islands. This is where I photographed the old beauties at left and below. They are quick to leaf out after precipitation, and also quick to drop leaves shortly afterwards. In late spring, you may see creamy white to pink flowers covering otherwise leafless plants.

Character old-timers like these are quite common in Baja California, usually growing artistically among rock outcroppings. You will find some nice examples of *Pachycormus discolor* in California and Arizona botanic gardens but nothing quite like the habitat specimens such as these. Give it another fifty years and maybe we'll catch up.

If you're a succulent fanatic visiting an area where *Pachycormus discolor* grows, all you need to do is pull off the highway and you'll find a stunning display of abundant flora. Many parts of Baja California rival Africa or Madagascar for succulent diversity and density.

Left: An award-winning show plant specimen of *Pachycormus discolor* at the Intercity Cactus and Succulent Show and Sale at the Los Angeles County Arboretum. This plant is in post-leaf summer bloom.

Bursera fagaroides

Elephant Trees
Pachycormus, burseras, commiphoras, etc.

Pachycormus discolor

Straddling a line between a succulent and a woody tree are the fat, water storing, desert dwelling "Elephant Trees." This general term would apply to the New World genus *Bursera* as well as the Old World genus *Commiphora*, and perhaps most famously to *Pachycormus discolor*, a monotypic genus from Baja California, where it coexists with the other famous elephant tree, *Bursera microphylla*. The commiphoras are part of the larger Burseraceae family. They also are fat-trunked, small-leaved trees that lend themselves to bonsai treatment, but they are not as common in cultivation. Myrrh is a resin derived from *Commiphora*; frankincense comes from the related genus *Boswellia*. I suppose I should finish the list of immaculate conception gift origin stories so, as I'm sure you already know, gold comes from pots at the end of the rainbow. You may groan now.

Bursera microphylla

In cultivation, most of these are grown as bonsai/container plants due to their thick profiles, but they will grow fine (and relatively faster) in-ground. Landscape plants can become bushier and lose some of their structural appeal unless they are thinned out occasionally. They can be opportunistic at leafing out although most will tend to drop leaves in the winter months.

It takes many years to develop the thick trunks you see on the plants on this page, some or all of which were likely field-collected specimens from the long-ago days when that practice wasn't frowned upon. Seed-grown plants tend to be skinnier when grown in pampered conditions. *Bursera fagaroides* seems to be the easiest, fastest growing, and most available species in cultivation.

Bursera microphylla

Pseudo**Bombax ellipticum**

In the title above, I put the "pseudo" in smaller font because, although that technically is the proper genus name, most people don't bother with the "pseudo" part. In fact, as I write this, I've learned that we finally may get to drop the prefix. I've never encountered a "true," i.e., non-pseudo, bombax in cultivation. This is a wonderful "fat plant" that will develop a fissured green and brown caudex with age. It is an excellent plant for container culture but also grows well in-ground. Native to southern Mexico and Central America, it is deciduous in the winter months. New leaves emerge a bright burgundy-red, as seen at left, but will turn green over time. Older plants have a flower that emerges as a long, banana-shaped bud and then peels back to reveal long, white, hanging stamens, giving it the common name "shaving brush plant." There is a rarely encountered pink-flowered form as well, seen lower right.

Rock Figs

There are hundreds of species of ficus. Some are xerophytic, and the two primary (and closely related) types in cultivation are the Baja California rock figs, _Ficus palmeri_, seen here, and _Ficus petiolaris_. Both are true desert dwellers and are often seen in habitat clinging to rocks and cliffs with roots exposed, similar to the root-over-rock plant at right, or the habitat example below left. Although both form a fat caudex, _F. palmeri_ makes a better bonsai with smaller and more compact leaves. _F. petiolaris_ does have more ornamental red-veined leaves, but the leaves tend to be larger. Both plants will grow in-ground in California where they can get to be very large and grow more like a typical tree.

Operculicarya decaryi/pachypus

These are another variety of what may be considered "elephant trees" from Madagascar. Although there are eight species, the only one known in cultivation for many years had been *Operculicarya decaryi*, seen here. In recent years, the similar *O. pachypus*, shown below, has made a push among collectors. The main difference is that *O. pachypus* has a more attractive zigzag stem arrangement and grows in more of a natural prostrate bonsai form, as seen in the dormant specimens below. It is slower to "wake up" into leaf and also later to shed leaves in winter. *O. decaryi* has a much more vertical growth habit unless pruned. Both types have individual strains that can form wonderful, gnarly, and undulating trunks, as seen in the above middle two images. They have fine miniature leaves and are tolerant of small containers (see the wonderful show plant owned by Jim Hannah, above middle right, and Julian Duvall's larger masterpiece at right). All of these characteristics make them perfect candidates for bonsai treatment, along with their malleability that allows them to be wired and trimmed into many shapes. Rudy Lime has long been a master of the craft of bonsai succulents, and *Operculicarya decaryi* has been one of his favorites. That is his sculpted pine-shaped plant above left.

Operculicaryas typically are winter deciduous but are hardy enough that they shouldn't need greenhouse overwintering in Mediterranean climates. They also can be grown in-ground, where they tend to become very bushy unless trimmed back—particularly *O. decaryi*. As with the burseras, flowers are negligible.

The last few pages have shown some of the succulent caudiciform trees that are both landscape compatible and wonderful container/bonsai specimens. Some of the other succulent trees that I don't have room for here are from the genera *Adansonia, Commiphora, Delonix,* and *Moringa*. Another natural continuation here would be to include more of the caudiciform succulents, such as *Adenium, Adenia, Fockea, Dorstenia*.... This really takes us down another rabbit hole of mostly container/collector succulents, and I'm afraid we've already gone down enough rabbit holes in this book. Plus, I'm already over my intended page count. My fifth and likely final book about the succulent hobby will focus on these types of plants (I'll revisit some of these final pages in a bit more detail), and go into show plants and cactus/succulent clubs and a bit of history of how this wonderful horticultural niche came about. I think we've reached a good stopping point, but I hope you can dig in for further research. There will not be a test.

340   *Spiny Succulents*

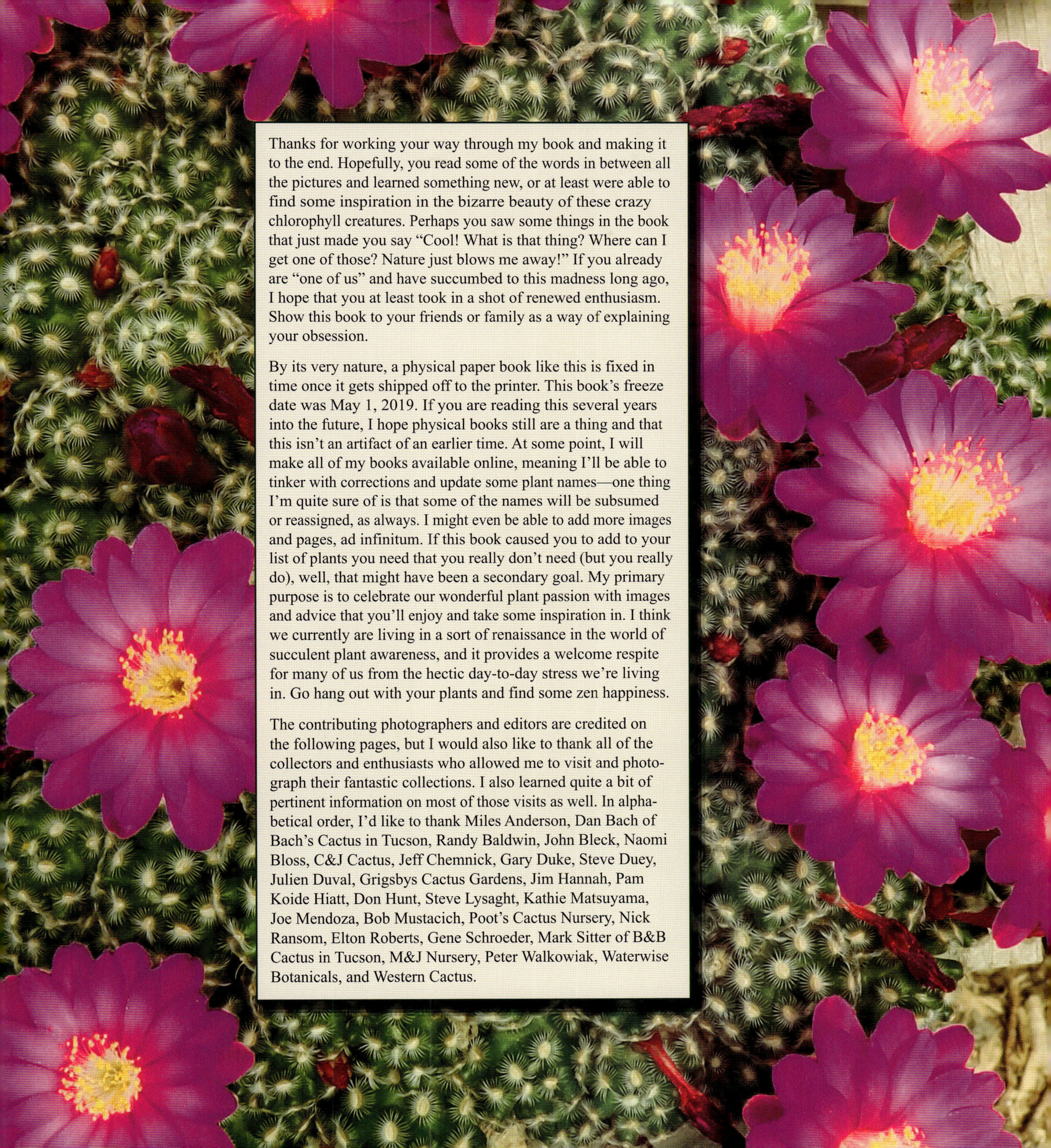

Thanks for working your way through my book and making it to the end. Hopefully, you read some of the words in between all the pictures and learned something new, or at least were able to find some inspiration in the bizarre beauty of these crazy chlorophyll creatures. Perhaps you saw some things in the book that just made you say "Cool! What is that thing? Where can I get one of those? Nature just blows me away!" If you already are "one of us" and have succumbed to this madness long ago, I hope that you at least took in a shot of renewed enthusiasm. Show this book to your friends or family as a way of explaining your obsession.

By its very nature, a physical paper book like this is fixed in time once it gets shipped off to the printer. This book's freeze date was May 1, 2019. If you are reading this several years into the future, I hope physical books still are a thing and that this isn't an artifact of an earlier time. At some point, I will make all of my books available online, meaning I'll be able to tinker with corrections and update some plant names—one thing I'm quite sure of is that some of the names will be subsumed or reassigned, as always. I might even be able to add more images and pages, ad infinitum. If this book caused you to add to your list of plants you need that you really don't need (but you really do), well, that might have been a secondary goal. My primary purpose is to celebrate our wonderful plant passion with images and advice that you'll enjoy and take some inspiration in. I think we currently are living in a sort of renaissance in the world of succulent plant awareness, and it provides a welcome respite for many of us from the hectic day-to-day stress we're living in. Go hang out with your plants and find some zen happiness.

The contributing photographers and editors are credited on the following pages, but I would also like to thank all of the collectors and enthusiasts who allowed me to visit and photograph their fantastic collections. I also learned quite a bit of pertinent information on most of those visits as well. In alphabetical order, I'd like to thank Miles Anderson, Dan Bach of Bach's Cactus in Tucson, Randy Baldwin, John Bleck, Naomi Bloss, C&J Cactus, Jeff Chemnick, Gary Duke, Steve Duey, Julien Duval, Grigsbys Cactus Gardens, Jim Hannah, Pam Koide Hiatt, Don Hunt, Steve Lysaght, Kathie Matsuyama, Joe Mendoza, Bob Mustacich, Poot's Cactus Nursery, Nick Ransom, Elton Roberts, Gene Schroeder, Mark Sitter of B&B Cactus in Tucson, M&J Nursery, Peter Walkowiak, Waterwise Botanicals, and Western Cactus.

Nick Basinski is a California native plant enthusiast, which extends into the biomes of neighboring Baja California and the Sonoran Desert communities. He is a senior inspector for the San Diego County Department of Agriculture.

Michael Buckner (a.k.a. The Plantman) has been involved with succulents since he was a kid. He is a recognized authority on succulents and other xerophytic plants, and is also known for his unique landscape installations. Mike might spend more time outdoors and in situ than anyone I know.

Jeff Chemnick is another all-around plant guy, an expert and grower of cycads, aloes, bromeliads, and a host of other xerophytic plants. He leads expeditions to Mexico and still is discovering new species. He operates Aloes in Wonderland and is a Research Associate at Lotusland in Santa Barbara, California.

Kelly Griffin is another world traveler, seen here hanging out with the copiapoas in Chile. He is a renowned authority and speaker on all things succulent, and currently is the Succulent Plant Development Manager at Altman Specialty Plants in Vista, California.

It's not enough for Mike Hackett to have one of the finest personal collections of succulents, but he also visits them in habitat to get the big picture. He takes a big camera and truly takes big and beautiful pictures.

Brian Kemble has been an authority on succulents and a host of other plants since the seventies. He has traveled the world to visit plants in situ, and is currently the Curator of the Ruth Bancroft Garden in Walnut Creek, California; Vice President of the Institute for Aloe Studies; and a board member of the Cactus and Succulent Society of America.

Jonna and Julien Micoud are the rare husband and wife team where both are equally under the spell of succulents, cacti in particular. They and their young family spend quite a bit of vacation time visiting nurseries and botanic gardens. Apparently their kids have yet to rebel.

Woody Minnich was not involved in the creation of this book (I didn't ask him) but might beat all the other characters on this page in a game of succulent jeopardy. A book on this subject can't possibly exclude at least a mention of Woody. Kelly sent me this image of a copiapoa popping a Woody, and I had to use it somehow.

Jeremy Spath is seen here doing what he does: getting to a remote locale to find succulents in habitat, and bringing back excellent images. I was with him on this Baja California trip. To get where he is, it was a ten-hour drive, then a plane to an island, then a panga to the most isolated part of said island, then a 2500-foot, 4-hour elevation climb through cacti and boulder fields. It's fun!

Brent Wigand is an aloe guy, a cycad guy, a cactus guy, just a plant guy, and grower extraordinaire. He has an eye for plants and is good at picking winners and getting them into production. In this image it appears he's working on the elasticat.

My succulent obsession has been eclipsed somewhat by my succulent photography obsession, which accelerated when I began a bookmaking kick a few years back. I can't possibly own every succulent, but eventually I'll have a good image of most of them. I'm so glad we've gone beyond the era of film and the drugstore drop-off. I guess I miss it a little.

Most of the images in this book were taken with my Canon G15, a wonderful and reasonably small "point and shoot." But over the last few years, more and more of my images were taken with an iPhone, which might offer a few less creative options, but I really can't tell the difference in images between the two devices. The technology with both cameras and smart phones today is just astounding. All you have to do is select Auto, point, and shoot. You do need to be mindful of lighting conditions, background distractions, spider webs, etc., and, most importantly, where the plants are and when they might be blooming. It's a rewarding hobby, even if it just serves to enhance your screensaver library.

The majority of the images in this book are from cultivated plants in private collections in California and Arizona. There are some images from public botanical gardens in the same states, and even a few from the East Coast and Kew Gardens in London. Habitat images have introduced some of the sections, and almost all of those came from the photographers credited on the facing page.

About half way through putting the book together, one of my sons badgered me into joining Instagram, which I reluctantly did, only because I thought it might increase traffic to the nursery. I ended up following some wonderful succulent junkies. When I saw that some had better images of a particular plant than I had, or had images of plants I didn't have or that I needed, I messaged them, and most were happy to let me use them. My first and favorite Instagrammers who have donated images are Jonna and Julien of earthwindandcactus, brookeinthegarden, insane_succulents, and pablo_law. There are a ton of other fantastic pages dedicated to succulents of all types.

As a self-publisher, I've developed a process where I send early versions of the book to some succulent gurus I know, mostly for backup on the "plant stuff"— proper identification, spelling, information I might have wrong or hadn't considered, or perhaps they might have a few new images I need to see. I'd like to thank these "editors." I put that word in quotes as I don't want any of them to think they are culpable for any mistakes that made it through to the final print. Thanks to Debra Lee Baldwin, Jeff Chemnick, Brian Kemble, Gerhard Marx, and Ron Regehr for combing through some early versions. I now know I've been spelling "alluaudia" wrong for thirty years, and I've been missing that second "L" in "mammillaria." I'm also very lucky to know some of the most knowledgeable people in the hobby. More help in plant identification came from such succulent luminaries as John Bleck, Gary Duke, Kelly Griffin, Elton Roberts, and Gene Schroeder. Then there is the punctuation, italics/capitalization, and general spelling issue—not my strong point but designer/editor Russel Ray tried. Any mistakes that made it through are on me. I hope it didn't ruin your reading experience.

Finally, I'd like to thank Russel Ray for helping me get the deal finalized. He took my rough draft and converted it into the printer friendly form you're reading here. Russel followed my basic layout but improved it in subtle ways, and also provided welcome editorial input and background research. I'm sure we'll still end up with a few typos or punctuation issues, but there would have been a lot more were it not for Russel and my other editors. I learned after my first book that you can't proof your own work.

Index

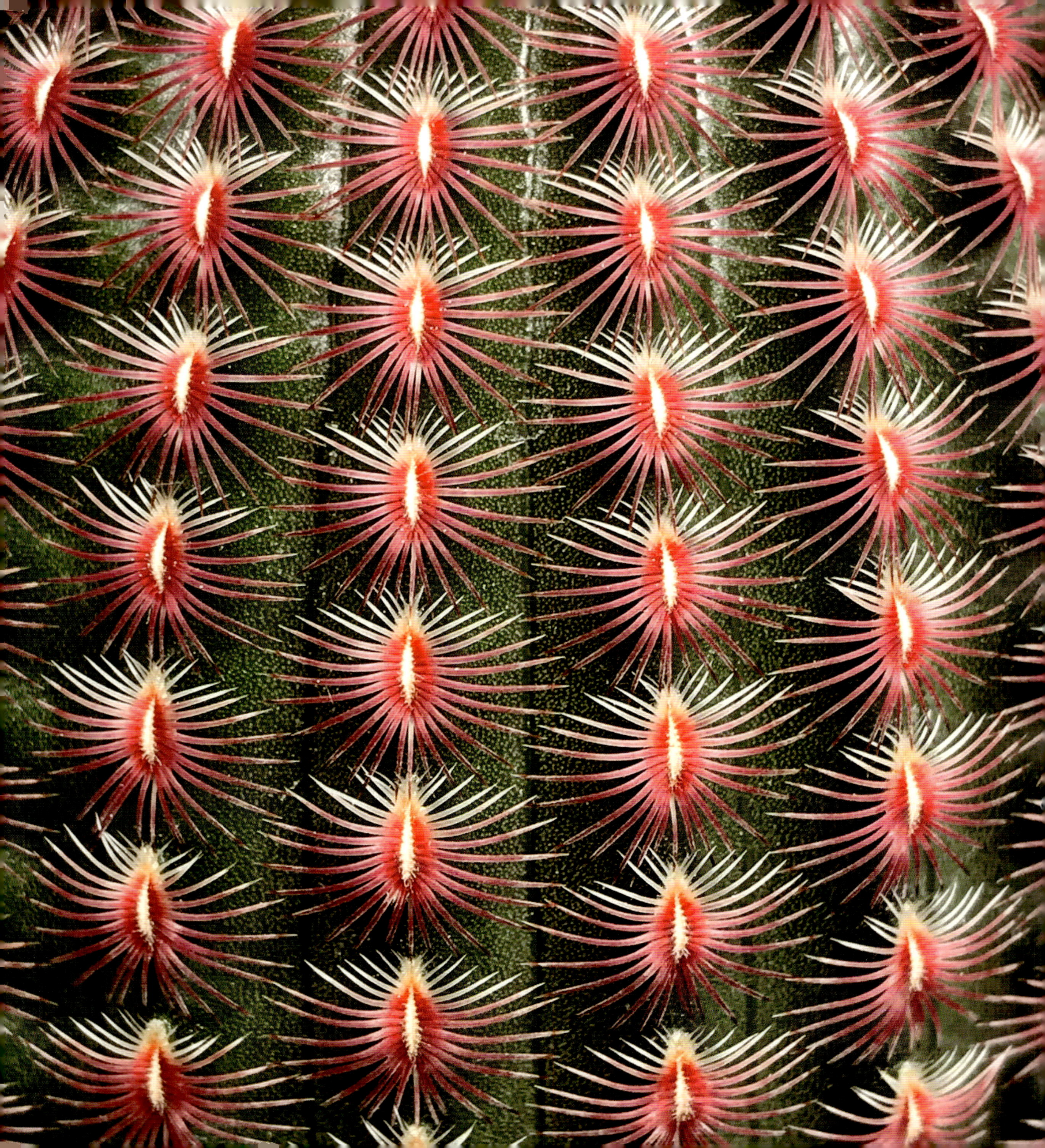